THE HAMILTON COLLECTION

The
HAMILTON
COLLECTION

———————★———————

THE WISDOM AND WRITINGS
OF THE FOUNDING FATHER

EDITED BY DAN TUCKER

BLACK DOG
& LEVENTHAL
PUBLISHERS
NEW YORK

For my parents

CONTENTS

★ ★ ★

INTRODUCTION

★ ★ ★

In 2015, Lin-Manuel Miranda, the son of Puerto Rican immigrants to New York, brilliantly turned the American founding father and unrepentant elitist Alexander Hamilton into a rapping, dancing, populist hero in the smash hit Broadway musical *Hamilton*. Miranda presents Hamilton as a scrappy immigrant who spoke truth to power and used his extraordinary intelligence to bootstrap his way into the top echelons of the American military, government, and society.

But how accurate was this depiction of him? What was Hamilton, the man, really like?

When one looks at the broad contours of Hamilton's life, it is difficult not to be moved by the extreme hardship of his youth: born out of wedlock, abandoned by an insolvent father, and orphaned with no money or prospects before he turned thirteen. Against the backdrop of these circumstances, the magnitude of his inborn gifts, his incessant drive, and his enduring achievements are all the more dazzling. In an extraordinary coincidence, or perhaps an intervention of fate, his arrival on the North American continent coincided with the moment that American colonists were in the early stages of what developed into an open and violent rebellion against the British Empire. "I wish there was a war," he had written as a fourteen-year-old already hungry for glory, in a letter to his childhood friend Edward Stevens.[1]

The rebels could not have wished for a more relentless advocate for independence, or a more ambitious and determined soldier, or a more skillful administrator than the gifted and arrogant teenager who arrived in their midst in 1772, a few years before the Boston Tea Party.

Hamilton quickly emerged as a leader of the colonial movement, distinguished himself on the battlefield, and indisputably had a hand—oftentimes, a forceful, guiding hand—in the creation of many of the American institutions that have defined and sustained the nation since its inception. As Ron Chernow, whose 2004 biography of Hamilton served as the inspiration for the musical, writes, "If [Thomas] Jefferson provided the essential poetry of American political discourse, Hamilton established the prose of American statecraft. No other founder articulated such a clear and prescient vision of America's future political, military, and economic strength or crafted such ingenious mechanisms to bind the nation together."[2]

So why has Hamilton been so frequently derided as an autocrat, an apologist for monarchy, and worse?

Hamilton was one of the most prolific correspondents, pamphleteers, and disseminators of political propaganda of the American Revolutionary era and the early years of the republic. His pen could be a devastating weapon, as anyone on the receiving end of one of his trademark attacks, notable for their bite as much as their astute reasoning, would have attested.

His political enemies returned the favor in kind. Perhaps more than anyone else, Thomas Jefferson, Hamilton's ideological and political nemesis, can be said to have engineered the decline in Hamilton's reputation. Jefferson engaged Hamilton in both political and personal battles during their time in George Washington's administration, orchestrating numerous public attacks on Hamilton that escalated through the Adams administration and into Jefferson's own presidency. After Hamilton's death, Jefferson, attempting to maintain his political ascendancy and to seal his political triumph, perpetuated those attacks.

John Adams, another antagonist of Hamilton's, had a more personal reason to loathe him: Hamilton had sabotaged his political career by undermining his presidency and ultimately helping limit it to one term. More frank and direct in his attacks than Jefferson, and more personally insulting about Hamilton's illegitimacy and background, Adams, too, continued to vilify Hamilton long after the latter's death.

Thanks to his own vanity and hubris, Hamilton had done an impressive job of damaging his own reputation before his death at forty-nine in 1804. By the time he was forty-five, he had essentially become politically irrelevant. Without his protector and alter ego, George Washington, to shield him, Hamilton became prey to the enemies he had made over the course of his political career, and to the fallout of his own rather colossal misjudgments. He was cast out of the Adams administration, for example, when Adams discovered that Hamilton had been quietly but powerfully influencing Adams's cabinet members without his knowledge or approval. Without Washington's protection, Hamilton's fears of besiegement by domestic and foreign enemies became more extreme, his judgments less reliable, his temper more volatile.

Hamilton sometimes displayed a tin ear for "retail" politics — the flesh-pressing business of influencing people in small groups and as individuals — as when he praised the British Constitution as "the only government in the world 'which unites public strength with individual security'"[3] while addressing the Constitutional Convention in 1787. How could he not have known that this idea might have raised the hackles of the very people who only a few short years before had risked their lives fighting the British government? His "confidential" letter-writing campaign to thwart the candidacy of John Adams, whom he believed incapable of effective governance, was a naïve miscalculation. How could someone with so profound a mistrust of human nature expect those letters, caustically critical of Adams, to remain secret?

One can find plentiful evidence in Hamilton's letters and published writings not just of his elitism, but of his anti-democratic beliefs as well. His opponents and critics seized on the latter charge to give credence to their depiction of Hamilton as a closet monarchist and autocrat, but Hamilton would unhesitatingly have pleaded guilty to opposing democracy. Steeped in the writings of the Scottish philosopher David Hume, he had a deep distrust of human nature ("I have an indifferent opinion of the honesty of this country,"[4] he wrote to George Washington in 1783). Human fears and frailty, in combination with the tumultuous nature of life in general, would lead inevitably to disorderly mob rule and conflict, in Hamilton's view. He saw direct democracy (as opposed to republicanism) to be a direct, slippery, and downhill road to anarchy. By the end of his life, he viewed the depredations of the French Revolution as vindication of these beliefs, referring to those, like Jefferson, who opposed a strong central government in favor of individual liberties as "Jacobins." Alluding to Jefferson's policies in a personal letter written in 1802, Hamilton lamented, "Mankind are forever destined to be the dupes of bold & cunning imposture."[5]

He also stirred up regional antipathies, though it was his express aim not to do so. He saw manufacturing and commerce, the engine of the northern states, as complementary rather than antagonistic to the agrarian economy of the south that Jefferson favored and idealized. Nevertheless, it is not difficult to trace in the arguments that Hamilton made in his "Report on the Public Credit" and his "Report on the Subject of Manufactures," as well as in the capitalist juggernaut that his policies and institutions unleashed, the fault lines that led up to the Civil War right up to Occupy Wall Street and beyond.

Given the fact that Hamilton was frequently derided for his Caribbean birth (a "Creole bastard," John Adams had called him), his nativist streak is inexplicable. Placed against the background of the violence of the Terror in France and Napoleonic expansionism throughout Europe and the Middle East, his girding against infiltration by foreign agents fomenting revolution in the United States is only somewhat more understandable. To most modern sensibilities, these fears tip over into jingoism and paranoia—though jingoism and fear mongering always seem to play well in times of upheaval and uncertainty. Perhaps, given the circumstances of his life at that time, cast out of the Adams administration, widely and routinely attacked in the press, denigrated in the halls of Congress, no longer shielded by George Washington—and having suffered the devastating loss of his eldest son, Philip, in a duel—it could be argued that Hamilton anticipated besiegement on every front in his life.

Unsurprisingly, Hamilton was a champion of contrarian causes. His representation of Loyalists after the Revolutionary War is one example of this. Another one, confounding to critics of Hamilton's "aristocratic" tendencies, was his consistent and principled opposition to slavery. Abolitionism was certainly not unprecedented at the time—Hamilton was one of thirty-one founding members of the New-York Society for Promoting the Manumission of Slaves (a group that sought to abolish slavery) in 1785, along with John Jay and Aaron Burr. But Hamilton's firsthand experiences on the Caribbean side of the slave trade gave his views added insight and understanding. Few of his contemporaries, for example, shared his conviction that blacks had intrinsic abilities equal to those of whites. Of course, his mother had owned slaves (one of whom had been assigned to him), as did his in-laws, so it must be said that Hamilton is not exempt from the criticism to which his slave-owning fellow Founders—especially Jefferson—have been justifiably subject.

As maddeningly brilliant and hubristic as Hamilton's public life was, his letters to family and friends reveal a warmth and wit that put him in his best light. One gets the sense from them, particularly those to his sister-in-law, Angelica Schuyler Church, that Hamilton was simply fun to be with, and that he was a loyal and confiding friend. His letters to his wife, Elizabeth, reveal his tender and protective side. He was, in spite of his brief affair with Maria Reynolds, a loving husband and father.

One can only read the correspondence leading up to Hamilton's duel with Burr with a queasy sense of what is to come, and wonder whether in the early days of the nineteenth century Hamilton's reasons for pursuing the duel seemed less flimsy than they do now. Hamilton undoubtedly had his reasons for provoking Burr and then passively allowing the events leading up to the duel to unfold, down to his decision to throw away his shot (whether he actually did throw his shot away or not is open to question).

But they remain elusive, even after reading and re-reading the words he so carefully wrote in the days leading up to the confrontation in Weehawken. In any case, it is a great irony that the man who took Hamilton's life on the field of honor represented, to Hamilton, the embodiment of a man without honor.

It is extremely unlikely that the United States would have emerged as a world power without Hamilton's federal system of finance, which harnessed the economic power of the individual states together to produce a single, more powerful driving force. Some of Hamilton's other contributions likewise contributed to American ascendancy over the last two-plus centuries: the Treasury with a publicly funded debt, a central bank, an independent judiciary and a strong executive, a standing army, the coast guard. Without these things individually and in combination, it is impossible to conceive of the United States' becoming the world power that it is, nor is it difficult to imagine its having devolved into a fractious continent resembling a more rustic version of Europe had Hamilton's contributions been absent.

Ultimately, Hamilton saw the fragile and nearly impossible art of governance as a balancing act between the forces of despotism and anarchy. Nearly 250 years of American history are testimony to the enduring power of his vision—his judgment that institutionally, at least, a strong, well-funded federal government was needed in order for the country to become a viable power has served it well. Yet, today's newspaper headlines show that we continue to struggle with the visions of Hamilton and Jefferson—to find the proper balance between centralized authority and individual liberty, between federal authority and states' rights.

So, what was Hamilton like as a man? It is tempting to say that he was brilliant and flawed, and to list his many extraordinary, endearing, and maddening qualities. This book is an attempt to allow him to tell his story in his own words. Hamilton's DNA runs through the American system and psyche in a way that is in abundant evidence today, and the more we can understand his character, choices, and context, the more we can understand about ourselves and our future.

EDITOR'S NOTE: All of Hamilton's letters and published writings reproduced in this book are taken from the astonishing Founders Online website (www.founders.archives.gov) operated by the National Historical Publications and Records Commission of the National Archives in cooperation with the University of Virginia Press. I have preserved Hamilton's spelling and grammar in order to retain his authentic voice and the sense of the historical period.

In some cases, Hamilton's letters were cobbled together by scholars (led by Harold C. Syrett) from multiple sources, among them signed original manuscripts retained by the recipient; manuscript copies made and retained by Hamilton himself; and copies of these letters made by family members and others after Hamilton's death. I have chosen not to distinguish between these sources, as the variations are slight and do not materially affect the understanding of Hamilton that I am seeking to create here. For those wishing for that level of nuance, I refer you to the Founders Online website mentioned above, where you can while away many a pleasurable hour in the company of America's founding fathers, and some of the mothers too.

"BASTARD BRAT OF A SCOTTISH PEDLAR"

★ ★ ★

John Adams's epithet for Hamilton, which gives this chapter its title, only begins to describe the cruel circumstances that Hamilton faced during his childhood on the Caribbean island of Nevis. He was indeed born out of wedlock—his mother, Rachel Faucette Lavien, descended from a French Huguenot family and had been previously married to Johann Lavien and was unable to obtain a divorce. Lavien was, by all accounts, an exceptionally cruel husband (even by the standard of the time) from whom Rachel had fled. Hamilton's father, James Hamilton, descended from Scottish nobility, and was in the midst of an unsuccessful run in the Caribbean sugar trade when Hamilton was born. James Hamilton deserted the family when Alexander was ten.

After his father left, Rachel moved with Alexander and his older brother, James, to the nearby island of St. Croix and opened a small store in Christiansted, the island's biggest city. Because Hamilton was born out of wedlock, he was denied membership in and schooling by the Church of England, so his mother enrolled him in a private school run by a Jewish headmistress, and arranged for private tutoring.

In February 1768, he and his mother contracted a severe fever from which Rachel never recovered. She died in the sickbed that she shared with Alexander, who was orphaned before he turned thirteen.

1

The probate court report on the disposition of the estate of Hamilton's mother reveals the family's diminished circumstances. It also, according to most historians, sets the year of Hamilton's birth as 1755 rather than 1757. Eager to appear the boy prodigy, Hamilton had perhaps intentionally obfuscated his age.

The record shows Hamilton's mother's name as Rachael Lewine. According to contemporaneous records, her surname should have been spelled "Lavien," though Hamilton himself spelled it "Lavine."

Probate court transaction no. XXIX

Which in the Probate court protocol is recorded as No. XXIV sc. the case of the deceased Rachael Lewine

James Towers, by His Royal Majesty of Denmark and Norway duly appointed administrator of estates in the Christiansted jurisdiction on the Island of St. Croix in America, and Ivar Hofman Sevel, appointed bailiff in the same jurisdiction, together with Laurence Bladwil, administrator of estates, Isaac Hartman, and Johan Henric Dietrichs, appointed town and probate court recorder in the aforesaid jurisdiction, make known that

In the year 1768 on the 19th day of February in the evening at 10 o'clock sharp the probate court met in a house here in town belonging to Thomas Dipnal [landlord to Hamilton's mother and her children, and the man who paid for her funeral], where an hour earlier a woman, Rachael Lewine, died, in order to seal up her effects for subsequent recording. Present at this transaction were the aforesaid Thomas Dipnal and Friedrich Wilhl Larsen as witnesses to the sealing up of a chamber containing her effects together with a trunk etc., thereafter were sealed an attic storage room and two storage rooms in the yard, after which there was nothing more to seal up, except some pots and other small things which remained unsealed for use in preparing the body for burial, among them being 6 chairs, 2 tables, and 2 wash-bowls. The transaction was then closed.

In witness thereof
    As Witnesses:

James Towers
Johan Henric Dietrichs
Thomas Dipnal
Friedrich Wilhm Larsen

In the year 1768 on the 22 of February the probate court administered by me, James Towers, as acting administrator of estates, and by me, Johan Henric Dietrichs, duly appointed by the King as town and probate court recorder in the Christiansted jurisdiction on the Island of St. Croix in America, met in Thomas Dipnal's house here in town, where on the 19th of this month Madam Rachael Lewine died, and whose effects were forthwith sealed up, in order now to take an inventory of them for subsequent distribution among the decedent's surviving children, who are 3 sons, namely, Peter Lewine, born in the marriage of the decedent with John Lewine who, later, is said for valid reasons to have obtained from the highest authorities a divorce from her (according to what the probate court has been able to ascertain), also 2 other sons, namely, James Hamilton and Alexander Hamilton, the one 15 and the other 13 years old, who are the same illegitimate children sc. born after the decedent's separation from the aforesaid

A view of Christiansted Harbor, St. Croix, where Rachel Faucette Lavien, Hamilton's mother, kept a store.

Lewine. The above mentioned Peter Lewine has resided and still resides in South Carolina and according to reports is about 22 years old.[1]

Several years before his death, Hamilton wrote a detailed description of his family background in a letter sent to William Jackson, a close friend and Revolutionary War comrade, in response to a personal attack on his origins made by a political enemy in 1800. Its purpose was clearly to improve his reputation, but the letter nevertheless offers a concise family history.

To William Jackson:

[New York, August 26, 1800]

I think it proper to confide to your bosom the real history of it, that among my friends you may if you please wipe off some part of the stain which is so industriously impressed.

The truth is that on the question who my parents were, I have better pretensions than most of those who in this Country plume themselves on Ancestry.

My Grandfather by the mothers side of the name of Faucette was a French Huguenot who emigrated to the West Indies in consequence of the revocation of the Edict of Nantz [or "Nantes," the 1598 edict in which King Henry IV of France had granted substantial civil rights to French Protestants, or Huguenots] and settled in the Island of Nevis and there acquired a pretty fortune. I have been assured by persons who knew him that he was a man of letters and much of a gentleman. He practiced a[s] a Physician, whether that was his original profession, or one assumed for livelihood after his emigration is not to me ascertained.

My father now dead was certainly of a respectable Scotch Fami[ly.] His father was, and the son of his Eldest brother now is Laird of Grang[e.] His mother was the sister of an ancient Baronet *Sir Robert Pollock*.

Himself being a younger son of a numerous family was bred to trade. In capacity of merchant he went to St Kitts, where from too generous and too easy a temper he failed in business, and at length fell into indigent circumstances. For some time he was supported by his friends in Scotland, and for several years before his death by me. It was his fault to have had too much pride and two large a portion of indolence—but his character was otherwise without reproach and his manners those of a Gentleman.

So far I may well challenge comparison, but the blemish remains to be unveiled.

A Dane a fortune-hunter of the name of *Lavine* came to Nevis bedizzened with gold, and paid his addresses to my mother then a handsome young woman having a *snug* fortune. In compliance with the wishes of her mother who was captivated by the glitter of the [left blank] but against her own inclination she married Lavine. The marriage was unhappy and ended in a separation by divorce. My mother afterwards went to St Kitts, became acquainted with my father and a marriage between them ensued, followed by many years cohabitation and several children.

But unluckily it turned out that the divorce was not absolute but qualified, and thence the second marriage was not lawful. Hence when my mother died the small property which she left went to my half brother Mr Lavine who lived in South Carolina and was for a time partner with Mr Kane. He is now dead.[2]

Lavien's estate was awarded in probate to Peter Lavien, Alexander's half-brother, but a family friend bought her books and returned them to Hamilton. Left with nothing but these books, Hamilton took a job at a well-known St. Croix mercantile house, Beekman and Cruger, while his older brother, James, apprenticed with a carpenter. The boys were adopted by their cousin, Peter Lytton, who committed suicide only a few months later. Alexander was then taken into the home of Thomas Stevens, who some scholars believe may have been Hamilton's biological father.

In this letter to Stevens's son, Hamilton's boyhood schoolmate and friend Edward Stevens, Hamilton expresses ambition and knowledge of the world beyond his fourteen years: he yearns for a war to prove his mettle and rise above his status as a clerk. Stevens was a student at King's College in Manhattan (later renamed Columbia University), which Hamilton was destined to attend, though at the time of this letter he could not have known it.

To Edward Stevens:

[St. Croix, November 11, 1769]

...As to what you say respecting your having soon the happiness of seeing us all, I wish, for an accomplishment of your hopes provided they are Concomitant with your welfare, otherwise not, tho doubt whether I shall be Present or not for to confess my weakness, Ned, my Ambition is prevalent that I contemn the grov'ling and condition of a Clerk or the like, to which my Fortune &c. condemns me and would willingly risk my life tho' not my Character to exalt my Station. Im confident, Ned that my Youth excludes me from any hopes of immediate Preferment nor do I desire it, but I mean to prepare the way for futurity. Im no Philosopher you see and may be jusly said to Build Castles in the Air. My Folly makes me ashamd and beg you'll Conceal it, yet Neddy we have seen such Schemes successfull when the Projector is Constant I shall Conclude saying I wish there was a War.[3]

Shortly after joining the firm of Beekman and Cruger, Hamilton's abiding interest in literature and love is on full display as he submitted the following impassioned and somewhat overwrought poem for publication by the Royal Danish American Gazette, *the St. Croix newspaper.*

To the Printer of the Royal Danish American Gazette:

[St. Croix, April 6, 1771]

I am a youth about seventeen, and consequently such an attempt as this must be presumptuous; but if, upon perusal, you think the following piece worthy of a place in your paper, by inserting it you'll much oblige Your obedient servant,

A.H.

In yonder mead my love I found
Beside a murm'ring brook reclin'd:
Her pretty lambkins dancing round
Secure in harmless bliss.
I bad the waters gently glide,
And vainly hush'd the heedless wind,
Then, softly kneeling by her side,
I stole a silent kiss—
She wak'd, and rising sweetly blush'd
By far more artless than the dove:
With eager haste I onward rush'd,
And clasp'd her in my arms;
Encircled thus in fond embrace
Our panting hearts beat mutual love—
A rosy-red o'er spread her face
And brighten'd all her charms.
Silent she stood, and sigh'd consent
To every tender kiss I gave;
I closely urg'd—to church we went,
And hymen join'd our hands.
Ye swains behold my bliss complete;
No longer then your own delay;
Believe me love is doubly sweet
In wedlocks holy bands.—
Content we tend our flocks by day,
Each rural pleasures amply taste;

And at the suns retiring ray
Prepare for new delight:
When from the field we haste away,
And send our blithsome care to rest,
We fondly sport and fondly play,
And love away the night.
Cœlia's an artful little slut;
Be fond, she'll kiss, et cetera—but
She must have all her will;
For, do but rub her 'gainst the grain
Behold a storm, blow winds and rain,
Go bid the waves be still.
So, stroking puss's velvet paws
How well the jade conceals her claws
And purs; but if at last
You hap to squeeze her somewhat hard,
She spits—her back up—prenez garde;
Good faith she has you fast.[4]

Hamilton seized on his role in the mercantile office of Beekman and Cruger to make himself indispensable and learn the essentials of international shipping and trade. In short order, he learned to manage complex, multi-currency transactions, track freight through a dizzying array of ports, negotiate prices in a cutthroat marketplace ("believe me Sir I dun as hard as is proper" he wrote in one letter), and even chart courses for ships. The following letter to Nicholas Cruger of Beekman and Cruger shows Hamilton's astuteness and attention to detail—and his assertiveness—with regard to running the family's business.

To Nicholas Cruger:

View of the Christiansted harbor square, where Hamilton's employer, the mercantile firm Beekman and Cruger, conducted its business.

[St. Croix, February 24, 1772]

...I now congratulate myself upon the pleasure of addressing you again, but am sorry I shall be [obliged] to communicate some dissatisfactory occurrencies.

Your Sloop Thunderbolt [arrived] here the 29th of the preceding Month with 41 More Skeletons. A worse parcel of Mules never was seen; she took in at first 48 & lost 7 on the passage. I sent all that were able to walk to pasture, in Number 33. The other 8 could hardly stand for 2 Minutes together & in spite of the greatest care 4 of them are now in Limbo. The Surviving 4 I think are out of Danger, and shall likewise be shortly sent to pasture. I refused two great offers made me upon their first landing to Wit 70 ps. a head for the Choice of 20, and 15 ps. a Head for the abovementioned Invalids, which may give you a proper idea of the condition they were in.... The Sloop was 27 days on her passage from the Main—not for want of swiftness, for tis now known she Sails well, but from continual Calms & the little wind she had was quite against her. Capt Newton seemd to be much concernd at his Ill luck tho I believe he had done all in his power to make the voyage Successful. But no Man can command the Winds. The Mules were pretty well chosen & had been once a good parcel. I receivd only a few lines from your Brother: no Sales nor anything else; he excusd himself being Sick. I desird him as directed to furnish the Sloop with a few Guns but she went intirely defenceless to the Main; notwithstanding several Vessells had been obligd to put back to get out of the way of the Launches with which the Coast swarms. When Capt Newton urgd him to hire a few Guns for the Sloop He replied to this effect—that I only had mentiond the matter to him but that you had never said a word about it. This last time I mentiond it again & begd the Captain to hire 4 Guns himself if your Brother did not which he has promisd to do...

...The Lumber you contracted for is arrivd & I am a good deal puzzled to fulfill your engagements; it is rather early you know to receivd & Cash is scarce. Mr Beekman would Ship on freight which would ease the matter but he can receive none yet. However I must manage some how or other. It would be a pity to pay dead freight.[5]

On the last day of August in 1772, a violent hurricane tore through the Caribbean, devastating parts of St. Croix, including Christiansted, Hamilton's home. His account of the hurricane, in a letter to his father, who lived at the time on St. Kitts, came into the possession of the town's Presbyterian minister, Hugh Knox (already an admirer of Hamilton's), who thought it remarkable and submitted it for publication to the Royal Danish American Gazette. *The dramatic account displays Hamilton's reverence for steadfastness in the face of adversity and his belief in the importance of Christian obedience.*

To the Printer of the Royal Danish American Gazette:

[St. Croix, September 6, 1772]

Honoured Sir,

I take up my pen just to give you an imperfect account of one of the most dreadful Hurricanes that memory or any records whatever can trace, which happened here on the 31st ultimo at night.

It began about dusk, at North, and raged very violently till ten o'clock. Then ensued a sudden and unexpected interval, which lasted about an hour. Meanwhile the wind was shifting round to the South West point, from whence it returned with redoubled fury and continued so 'till near three o'clock in the morning. Good God! what horror and destruction. It's impossible for me to describe or you to form any idea of it. It seemed as if a total dissolution of nature was taking place. The roaring of the sea and wind, fiery meteors flying about it in the air, the prodigious glare of almost perpetual lightning, the crash of the falling houses, and the ear-piercing shrieks of the distressed, were sufficient to strike astonishment into Angels. A great part of the buildings throughout the Island are levelled to the ground, almost all the rest very much shattered; several persons killed and numbers utterly ruined; whole families running about the streets, unknowing where to find a place of shelter; the sick exposed to the keeness of water and air without a bed to lie upon, or a dry covering to their bodies; and our harbours entirely bare. In a word, misery, in all its most hideous shapes, spread over the whole face of the country. A strong smell of gunpowder added somewhat to the terrors of the night; and it was observed that the rain was surprizingly salt. Indeed the water is so brackish and full of sulphur that there is hardly any drinking it.

My reflections and feelings on this frightful and melancholy occasion, are set forth in the following self-discourse.

Where now, oh! vile worm, is all thy boasted fortitude and resolution? What is become of thine arrogance and self sufficiency? Why dost thou tremble and stand aghast? How humble, how helpless, how contemptible you now appear. And for why? The jarring of elements—the discord of clouds? Oh! impotent presumptuous fool! how durst thou offend that Omnipotence, whose nod alone were sufficient to quell the destruction that hovers over thee, or crush thee into atoms? See thy wretched helpless state, and learn to know thyself. Learn to know thy best support. Despise thyself, and adore thy God. How sweet, how unutterably sweet were now, the voice of an approving conscience; Then couldst thou say, hence ye idle alarms, why do I shrink? What have I to fear? A pleasing calm suspense! A short repose from calamity to end in eternal bliss? Let the Earth rend. Let the planets forsake their course. Let the Sun be extinguished and the Heavens burst asunder. Yet what have I to dread? My staff can never be broken—in Omnip[o]tence I trusted.

Thus did I reflect, and thus at every gust of the wind, did I conclude, 'till it pleased the Almighty to allay it. Nor did my emotions proceed either from the suggestions of too much natural fear, or a conscience over-burthened with crimes of an uncommon cast. I thank God, this was not the case. The scenes of horror exhibited around us, naturally awakened such ideas in every thinking breast, and aggravated the deformity of every failing of our lives. It were a lamentable insensibility indeed, not to have had such feelings, and I think inconsistent with human nature.

Our distressed, helpless condition taught us humility and contempt of ourselves. The horrors of the night, the prospect of an immediate, cruel death—or, as one may say, of being crushed by the Almighty in his anger—filled us with terror. And every thing that had tended to weaken our interest with him, upbraided us in the strongest colours, with our baseness and folly. That which, in a calm unruffled temper, we call a natural cause, seemed then like the correction of the Deity. Our imagination represented him as an incensed master, executing vengeance on the crimes of his servants. The father and benefactor were forgot, and in that view, a consciousness of our guilt filled us with despair.

But see, the Lord relents. He hears our prayer. The Lightning ceases. The winds are appeased. The warring elements are reconciled and all things promise peace. The darkness is dispell'd and drooping nature revives at the approaching dawn. Look back Oh! my soul, look back and tremble. Rejoice at thy deliverance, and humble thyself in the presence of thy deliverer.

I am afraid, Sir, you will think this description more the effort of imagination than a true picture of realities. But I can affirm with the greatest truth, that there is not a single circumstance touched upon, which I have not absolutely been an eye witness to.

Our General has issued several very salutary and humane regulations, and both in his publick and private measures, has shewn himself the Man.[6]

THE STUDENT
TURNS
REVOLUTIONARY

★ ★ ★

*H*ugh Knox raised the funds needed to allow young Alexander
to begin formal education in the North American colonies, first at a
Presbyterian school in Elizabethtown, New Jersey, and soon thereafter
at King's College in Manhattan. There he fell in with a politically
engaged group that included Hercules Mulligan, a high-end tailor
who later became a spy for the American colonists, and students who
shared Hamilton's emerging views about the unjust nature of British
rule in the colonies.

The illegal destruction of nearly £10,000 (approximately $2 mil-
lion in modern dollars) worth of tea in Boston Harbor—the Boston
Tea Party—was a recent memory, and the punitive Coercive Acts,
which the colonists called the Intolerable Acts, had been Britain's harsh
and ill-advised response. Hamilton established himself as an orator
and a leader of the cause for greater self-determination in a sponta-
neous, impassioned speech at a mass meeting to protest the Intolerable
Acts. The speech took place in July 1774 on an open field near King's
College where an enormous pole with the word "Liberty" at the top
had been erected.

In response, the colonies formed the First Continental Congress,
which proposed a boycott of British trade. A Loyalist Anglican minister

named Samuel Seabury, writing as A. W. Farmer, issued a pro-
royalist pamphlet with the title Free Thoughts on the Proceedings
of the Continental Congress, Held at Philadelphia, Sept 5, 1774:
Wherein Their Errors are exhibited, their Reasonings Confuted, and the fatal Tendency of their Non-Importation, Non-
Exportation, and Non-Consumption Measures, are laid open to
the plainest Understandings; and the Only Means pointed out
for Preserving and Securing Our present Happy Constitution: In
a Letter to the Farmers and other inhabitants of North America
in General, and to those of the Province of New-York in Particular. By a Farmer. Hear me, for I Will speak! *Seabury argued, in*
essence, that the boycott proposed by the Continental Congress would
bring economic ruin on the colonies.

The merits of his arguments aside, Seabury's biggest error in judg-
ment was an unwitting one: he had engaged the emerging colonial
leader Alexander Hamilton as his interlocutor. Hamilton's brilliant,
bombastic, and forcefully repetitive thirty-five-page response, published
in December 1774 under the name "Friend to America," laid out many
of the key tenets of the revolutionary cause, chief among them that the
British parliament had no right to impose taxes on the colonists without
their consent and representation in the government. Hamilton mock-
ingly titled his pamphlet A Full Vindication of the Measures of the
Congress, from the Calumnies of their Enemies; In Answer to
A Letter, Under the Signature of A. W. Farmer. Whereby His
Sophistry is exposed, his Cavils confuted, his Artifices detected,
and his Wit ridiculed; in a General Address To the Inhabitants
of America, And A Particular Address To the Farmers of the
Province of New-York. Veritas magna est & prœvalebit. Truth
is powerful, and will prevail.

The only distinction between freedom and slavery consists in this: In the former state, a man is governed by the laws to which he has given his consent, either in person, or by his representative: In the latter, he is governed by the will of another. In the one case his life and property are his own, in the other, they depend upon the pleasure of a master. It is easy to discern which of these two states is preferable. No man in his senses can hesitate in choosing to be free, rather than a slave.

That Americans are intitled to freedom, is incontestaible upon every rational principle. All men have one common original: they participate in one common nature, and consequently have one common right. No reason can be assigned why one man should exercise any power, or pre-eminence over his fellow creatures more than another; unless they have voluntarily vested him with it. Since then, Americans have not by any act of their's impowered the British Parliament to make laws for them, it follows they can have no just authority to do it.

Besides the clear voice of natural justice in this respect, the fundamental principles of the English constitution are in our favour. It has been repeatedly demonstrated, that the idea of legislation, or taxation, when the subject is not represented, is inconsistent with *that*. Nor is this all, our charters, the express conditions on which our progenitors relinquished their native countries, and came to settle in this, preclude every claim of ruling and taxing us without our assent.

Every subterfuge that sophistry has been able to invent, to evade or obscure this truth, has been refuted by the most conclusive reasonings; so that we may pronounce it a matter of undeniable certainty, that the pretensions of Parliament are contradictory to the law of nature, subversive of the British constitution, and destructive of the faith of the most solemn compacts.

What then is the subject of our controversy with the mother country? It is this, whether we shall preserve that security to our lives and properties, which the law of nature, the genius of the British constitution, and our charters afford us; or whether we shall resign them into the hands of the British House of Commons, which is no more privileged to dispose of them than the Grand Mogul? What can actuate those men, who labour to delude any of us into an opinion, that the object of contention between the parent state and the colonies is only three pence duty upon tea? or that the commotions in America originate in a plan, formed by some turbulent men to erect it into a republican government? The parliament claims a right to tax us in all cases whatsoever: Its late acts are in virtue of that claim. How ridiculous then is it to affirm, that we are quarrelling for the trifling sum of three pence a pound on tea; when it is evidently the principle against which we contend.

The design of electing members to represent us in general congress, was, that the wisdom of America might be collected in devising the most proper and expedient means to repel this atrocious invasion of our rights. It has been accordingly done. Their decrees are binding upon all, and demand a religious observance.

We did not, especially in this province, circumscribe them by any fixed boundary, and therefore as they cannot be said to have exceeded the limits of their authority, their act must be esteemed the act of their constituents. If it should be objected, that they have not answered the end of their election; but have fallen upon an improper and ruinous mode of proceeding: I reply, by asking, Who shall be the judge? Shall any individual oppose his private sentiment to the united counsels of men, in whom America has reposed so high a confidence? The attempt must argue no small degree of arrogance and self-sufficiency.[1]

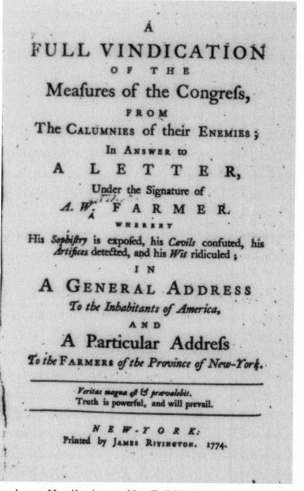

Cover sheet to Hamilton's pamphlet, *Full Vindication of the Measures of Congress*, published in 1774.

When Seabury published a refutation of A Full Vindication, *Hamilton immediately responded with* The Farmer Refuted *(February 23, 1775), a jeremiad that showcases Hamilton's rapidly evolving political outlook as well as his rhetorical abilities. After dismissing the older man's arguments as "puerile and fallacious," Hamilton goes for the jugular in a most ruthlessly entertaining manner—a cocksure and precocious showboating attorney, though his induction into that profession was still years in his future. He is clearly having fun.*

Candour obliges me to acknowledge, that you possess every accomplishment of a polemical writer, which may serve to dazzle and mislead superficial and vulgar minds; a peremptory dictatorial air, a pert vivacity of expression, an inordinate passion for conceit, and a noble disdain of being fettered by the laws of truth.

Hamilton goes on to deny the obligation of the North American colonists to the British parliament on the basis of natural law:

Man, in a state of nature (you say) may be considered, as perfectly free from all restraints of *law* and *government*, and, then, the weak must submit to the strong...

...There is so strong a similitude between your political principles and those maintained by Mr. Hobbs [Thomas Hobbes, the influential political philosopher], that, in judging from them, a person might very easily *mistake* you for a disciple of his. His opinion was, exactly, coincident with yours, relative to man in a state of nature. He held, as you do, that he was, then, perfectly free from all restraint of *law* and *government*. Moral obligation, according to him, is derived from the introduction of civil society; and there is no virtue, but what is purely artificial, the mere contrivance of politicians, for the maintenance of social intercourse....

...Good and wise men, in all ages, have embraced a very dissimilar theory. They have supposed, that the deity, from the relations, we stand in, to himself and to each other, has constituted an eternal and immutable law, which is, indispensibly, obligatory upon all mankind, prior to any human institution whatever.

This is what is called the law of nature, "which, being coeval with mankind, and dictated by God himself, is, of course, superior in obligation to any other. It is binding over all the globe, in all countries, and at all times. No human laws are of any validity, if contrary to this; and such of them as are valid, derive all their authority, mediately, or immediately, from this original."...

...Hence also, the origin of all civil government, justly established, must be a voluntary compact, between the rulers and the ruled; and must be liable to such limitations, as are necessary for the security of the *absolute rights* of the latter; for what original title can any man or set of men have, to govern others, except their own consent? To usurp dominion over a people, in their own despite, or to grasp at a more extensive power than they are willing to entrust, is to violate that law of nature, which gives every man a right to his personal liberty; and can, therefore, confer no obligation to obedience.

Hamilton puts forth a legalistic argument that the only obligation of colonists to Great Britain is to the monarch—the grantor of the original colonial charter—and parses other legal and technical issues. It is an exhaustive tour de force.

He also turns a perceived disadvantage of the colonists, military inferiority to the imposing British force, into an advantage. In an impressive display of insight, Hamilton anticipates the military strategy adopted by General Washington, wearing the enemy down by opportunistically harassing them rather than in the traditional European form of open-field engagement.

Let it be remembered, that there are no large plains, for the two armies to meet in, and decide the contest, by some decisive stroke, where any advantage gained, by either side, might be prosecuted, 'till a complete victory was obtained. The circumstances of our country put it in our power, to evade a pitched battle. It will be better policy, to harrass and exhaust the soldiery, by frequent skirmishes and incursions, than to take the open field with them, by which means, they would have the full benefit of their superior regularity and skill. Americans are better qualified, for that kind of fighting, which is most adapted to this country, than regular troops. Should the soldiery advance into the country, as they would be obliged to do, if they had any inclination to subdue us, their discipline would be of little use to them. We should, in that case, be at least upon an equality with them, in any respect; and as we should have the advantage, on many accounts, they would be likely to gain nothing by their attempts.

Summarizing, Hamilton asserts the purity of his motives as much as the rightness of his cause.

Whatever opinion may be entertained of my sentiments and intentions, I attest that being, whose all-seeing eye penetrates the inmost recesses of the heart, that I am not influenced (in the part I take) by any unworthy motive—that, if I am in an error, it is my judgment, not my heart, that errs. That I earnestly lament the unnatural quarrel, between the parent state and the colonies; and most ardently wish for a speedy reconciliation, a perpetual and *mutually* beneficial union, that I am a warm advocate for limitted monarchy, and an unfeigned well-wisher to the present Royal Family.

But on the other hand, I am inviolably attached to the essential rights of mankind, and the true interests of society. I consider civil liberty, in a genuine unadulterated sense, as the greatest of terrestrial blessings. I am convinced, that the whole human race is intitled to it; and, that it can be wrested from no part of them, without the blackest and most aggravated guilt.

I verily believe also, that the best way to secure a permanent and happy union, between Great-Britain and the colonies, is to permit the latter to be as free, as they desire. To abridge their liberties, or to exercise any power over them, which they are unwilling to submit to, would be a perpetual source of discontent and animosity. A continual jealousy would exist on both sides. This would lead to tyranny, on the one hand, and to sedition and rebellion, on the other. Impositions, not really grievous in themselves, would be thought so; and the murmurs arising from thence, would be considered as the effect of a turbulent ungovernable spirit. These jarring principles would, at length, throw all things into disorder; and be productive of an irreparable breach, and a total disunion.[2]

By 1775, Hamilton was unambiguously a proponent of the Patriot cause. Yet when a New York leader of the Sons of Liberty recruited horsemen from Connecticut to attack the print shop of James Rivington, a vocal and highly visible Tory, Hamilton saw this violence as the wrong solution. In this letter, written when he was just twenty, he reveals a fully developed fear of the mob mentality, even in support of his own cause, and an abiding belief in the rule of law—even as he was agitating to break the prevailing (British) law of the land. Hamilton asks John Jay, a member of the First and Second Continental Congresses, to send troops from New Jersey and Philadelphia to maintain order in New York, and keep the rival New Englanders out.

To John Jay:

[New York, November 26, 1775]

I take the liberty to trouble you with some remarks on a matter which to me appears of not a little importance; doubting not that you will use your influence in Congress to procure a remedy for the evil I shall mention, if you think the considerations I shall urge are of that weight they seem in my judgment to possess.

You will probably ere this reaches you have heard of the late incursion made into this city by a number of horsemen from New England under the command of Capt Sears, who took away Mr. Rivington's types, and a Couteau or two. Though I am fully sensible how dangerous and pernicious Rivington's press has been, and how detestable the character of the man is in every respect, yet I cannot help disapproving and condemning this step.

In times of such commotion as the present, while the passions of men are worked up to an uncommon pitch there is great danger of fatal extremes. The same state of the passions which fits the multitude, who have not a sufficient stock of reason and knowlege to guide them, for opposition to tyranny and oppression, very naturally leads them to a contempt and disregard of all authority. The due medium is hardly to be found among the more intelligent, it is almost impossible among the unthinking populace.

When the minds of these are loosened from their attachment to ancient establishments and courses, they seem to grow giddy and are apt more or less to run into anarchy. These principles, too true in themselves, and confirmed to me both by reading and my own experience, deserve extremely the attention of those, who have the direction of public affairs. In such tempestuous times, it requires the greatest skill in the political pilots to keep men steady and within proper bounds, on which account I am always more or less alarmed at every thing which is done of mere will and pleasure, without any proper authority.

It's doubtful whether Hamilton knew at the time that Rivington might not have been quite the Tory he seemed: late in the war, it was revealed that he had been a vital member of a spy ring that supplied vital British plans to the Continental Army. Later in the letter, Hamilton alludes to a regional rivalry, a reminder that in the context of the time, one identified one's "country" as one's home colony or region.

Moreover, New England is very populous and powerful. It is not safe to trust to the virtue of any people. Such proceedings will serve to produce and encourage a spirit of encroachment and arrogance in them. I like not to see potent neighbours indulged in the practice of making inroads at pleasure into this or any other province.

You well know too, sir, that antipathies and prejudices have long subsisted between this province and New England. To this may be attributed a principal part of the disaffection now prevalent among us. Measures of the present nature, however they may serve to intimidate, will secretly revive and increase those ancient animosities, which though smothered for a while will break out when there is a favorable opportunity....

...All the good purposes that could be expected from such a step will be answered; and many ill consequences will be prevented if your body gently interposes a check for the future. Rivington will be intimidated & the tories will be convinced that the other colonies will not tamely see the general cause betrayed by the Yorkers. A favourable idea will be impressed of your justice & impartiality in discouraging the encroachments of any one province on another; and the apprehensions of prudent men respecting the ill-effects of an ungoverned spirit in the people of New England will be quieted. Believe me sir it is a matter of consequence and deserves serious attention.[3]

SOLDIER AND STATESMAN

★ ★ ★

*I*n *February 1776, the rebellious colonists succeeded in ousting the government in New York, and Hamilton turned his focus to the colony's new rebel government, to the Continental Congress, which included all of the colonies, and to the military. He was appointed to the New York Provincial Company of Artillery, bringing along thirty of his King's College peers (a requirement for the appointment), as well as his friend Hercules Mulligan. The company saw action in the Battles of Long Island, White Plains, and Trenton—among the demoralizing defeats for the ragtag colonists' army early in the war. But Hamilton distinguished himself for his bravery as well as his administrative and leadership abilities. In this letter to the New York Provincial Congress, exhibiting a characteristic protectiveness of his men, he requests pay for them equal to that received by the Continental artillery, citing the latter's newly increased rates. Interestingly, he buttresses his case by alluding to his men's willingness to fight outside of their native colony, an element of intercolonial unity not always evident in the provincial militias.*

By compairing these with my pay rolls, you will discover a considerable difference, and I doubt not you will be easily sensible that such a difference should not exist. I am not personally interested in having an augmentation agreeable to the above rates, because my own pay will remain the same that it now is; but I make this application on behalf of the company, as I am fully convinced such a disadvantageous distinction will have a very pernicious effect on the minds and behaviour of the men. They do the same duty with the other companies and think themselves entitled to the same pay. They have been already comparing accounts and many marks of discontent have lately appeared on this score. As to the circumstance of our being confined to the defence of the Colony, it will have little or no weight, for there are but few in the company who would not as willingly leave the Colony on any necessary expedition as stay in it; and they will not therefore think it reasonable to have their pay curtailed on such a consideration.[1]

Hamilton's talents caught the eye of several of the Continental Army's top leaders, but he resisted their entreaties to become attached to any one of them until General George Washington asked Hamilton to become his aide-de-camp in early 1777. He took the oath of allegiance to Washington on March 1, 1777. Hamilton immediately took over communications on behalf of the general, and his exceptional strategic and administrative abilities frequently came into play. In early 1778, when morale in the Continental Army was at a low point, Hamilton advised Washington on measures for maintaining troop discipline, enumerating eight fairly conventional regulations governing desertion, dereliction of duty, furloughs, and the like. In the ninth, and final, proposed regulation, Hamilton's zeal, and his experience as a soldier in the field, are on display. With customary zeal, he identifies a problem with current procedures, and without solicitation, proposes a solution in this letter written to Washington during the winter of 1778.

To George Washington:

[Valley Forge, before January 29, 1778]

Nothing being more disgraceful to the service, nor dangerous for the army, than for the advanced posts to be surprised by the enemy; it is necessary that every possible precaution should be taken, to prevent an accident so dishonourable to the officer who commands at such a post. And as the instruction given in the chapter on the service of the guard, in the Regulations, is not full and explicit, it is thought necessary to add the following article:

As soon as an officer, commanding a detachment, arrives at the post he is to occupy, he must endeavour to procure some inhabitant on whom he can depend, to show him all the roads, footpaths, and other avenues leading to the post. These he must himself reconnoitre, and then determine the number of guards necessary for his security, as well in front, as on the flanks and in the rear of the post. He must then divide his detachment into three parts, one of which must be always on guard; another, act as reserve picket; and the third, be off duty.

The part destined for guard, must be divided into as many guards as the officer may think necessary: always observing, that the guards are so proportioned as that one-third of each guard may always be on sentry at the same time.

These guards should be posted at three or four hundred paces from the main post, and the sentinels form a chain round it. They must be within sight of each other during the day, and within call during the night.

The commanding officer having himself posted these guards and sentinels, and well instructed the officers and sergeants in their duty, will fix the place where he means to defend himself in case of an attack; as a house, a height, or behind some bridge or fence, which he will strengthen as much as possible, by an abatis ditch, or anything his genius may direct him for that purpose.

The reserve pickets are on no account to stir from the main post, or take off their accoutrements; but must be ready to parade under arms at any moment of the day or night; though, during the day, they may be permitted to lay down and sleep. Every man must have his haversack under his head; and if the post is dangerous, his arms in his hand.

The Reserve will furnish a guard of a sergeant and from six to twelve men, to furnish from two to four sentinels round the house, or wherever they are posted, to give notice of all that approach, or of any alarm. One of these sentries must always be before the arms.

That part of the detachment off duty, may undress and repose themselves. They must cook for the guard and picket, and fetch the wood and water necessary for the post; but they must not do this before the roll-call in the morning, when the commanding officer receives the reports of all the guard. If the post is near the enemy, this part of the detachment must not undress during the night.

As the guard form a chain of sentinels round the post, no soldier must pass the chain without a non-commissioned officer; nor any stranger be permitted to enter, without being conducted to, and examined by, the commanding officer.

After roll-call in the evening, no soldier must be permitted to go more than forty paces from the place of arms. The officers, it is expected, always remain with their men.[2]

A painting showing Hamilton in the uniform of the New York Artillery,
which saw action in the battles of White Plains and Trenton early in the war.

Here Hamilton's Revolutionary War correspondence takes a fascinating
turn, far beyond the scope of combat. He and his friend John Laurens,
whose slave-owning father succeeded John Hancock as president of the
Continental Congress, devised a strategy for regaining the upper hand
in the deep South following the loss of Georgia a few months earlier:
organizing battalions of enslaved black men. Hamilton here outlines
this idealistic plan for John Jay, a trusted advisor who had just succeeded the elder Laurens as president of the Continental Congress. This
letter makes clear Hamilton's support for the younger Laurens's plan
to emancipate slaves who joined forces with the Patriots. Moreover,

he voices surprisingly progressive views on race and slavery for the period—contrary to those of Thomas Jefferson, for example—that blacks possess "natural faculties" equal to those of whites.

To John Jay:

[Middlebrook, New Jersey, March 14, 1779]

Col Laurens...is on his way to South Carolina, on a project, which I think, in the present situation of affairs there, is a very good one and deserves every kind of support and encouragement. This is to raise two three or four batalions of negroes; with the assistance of the government of that state, by contributions from the owners in proportion to the number they possess. If you should think proper to enter upon the subject with him, he will give you a detail of his plan. He wishes to have it recommended by Congress to the state; and, as an inducement, that they would engage to take those batalions into Continental pay.

It appears to me, that an expedient of this kind, in the present state of Southern affairs, is the most rational, that can be adopted, and promises very important advantages. Indeed, I hardly see how a sufficient force can be collected in that quarter without it; and the enemy's operations there are growing infinitely serious and formidable. I have not the least doubt, that the negroes will make very excellent soldiers, with proper management; and I will venture to pronounce, that they cannot be put in better hands than those of Mr. Laurens. He has all the zeal, intelligence, enterprise, and every other qualification requisite to succeed in such an undertaking....I frequently hear it objected to the scheme of embodying negroes that they are too stupid to make soldiers. This is so far from appearing to me a valid objection that I think

their want of cultivation (for their natural faculties are probably
as good as ours) joined to that habit of subordination which they
acquire from a life of servitude, will make them sooner became
soldiers than our White inhabitants....

I foresee that this project will have to combat much opposition from prejudice and self-interest. The contempt we have
been taught to entertain for the blacks, makes us fancy many
things that are founded neither in reason nor experience; and
an unwillingness to part with property of so valuable a kind will
furnish a thousand arguments to show the impracticability or
pernicious tendency of a scheme which requires such a sacrifice.
But it should be considered, that if we do not make use of them
in this way, the enemy probably will; and that the best way to
counteract the temptations they will hold out will be to offer
them ourselves. An essential part of the plan is to give them
their freedom with their muskets. This will secure their fidelity,
animate their courage, and I believe will have a good influence
upon those who remain, by opening a door to their emancipation.
This circumstance, I confess, has no small weight in inducing me
to wish the success of the project; for the dictates of humanity
and true policy equally interest me in favour of this unfortunate
class of men.[3]

*Hamilton's role as General Washington's chief aide did not prevent
him from contemplating political the problems facing the colonies. In
September 1780, he diagnosed the weaknesses of the present system of
government in a letter to his friend James Duane. Hamilton proposed
remedy: a strong central government with control of a national military force, the ability to raise revenue, and the ability to mint money
and obtain foreign loans.*

To James Duane:

[September 3, 1780]

I sit down to give you my ideas of the defects of our present system, and the changes necessary to save us from ruin. They may perhaps be the reveries of a projector rather than the sober views of a politician. You will judge of them, and make what use you please of them.

The fundamental defect is a want of power in Congress. It is hardly...universally acknowleged, [and] may however be said that it has originated from three causes—an excess of the spirit of liberty which has made the particular states show a jealousy of all power not in their own hands; and this jealousy has led them to exercise a right of judging in the last resort of the measures recommended by Congress, and of acting according to their own opinions of their propriety or necessity, a diffidence in Congress of their own powers, by which they have been timid and indecisive in their resolutions, constantly making concessions to the states, till they have scarcely left themselves the shadow of power; a want of sufficient means at their disposal to answer the public exigencies and of vigor to draw forth those means; which have occasioned them to depend on the states individually to fulfill their engagements with the army, and the consequence of which has been to ruin their influence and credit with the army, to establish its dependence on each state separately rather than *on them*, that is rather than on the whole collectively....

Anticipating objections to his plan from colonial leaders naturally suspicious of a strong central authority, Hamilton contrasts the circumstances of the colonies with those of the European powers.

There is a wide difference between our situation and that of an empire under one simple form of government, distributed into counties provinces or districts, which have no legisla[tures] but merely magistratical bodies to execute the laws of a common sovereign. Here the danger is that the sove[re]ign will have too much power to oppress the parts of which it is composed. In our case, that of an empire composed of confederated states each with a government completely organised within itself, having all the means to draw its subjects to a close dependence on itself—the danger is directly the reverse. It is that the common sovereign will not have power sufficient to unite the different members together, and direct the common forces to the interest and happiness of the whole....

...[Our] confederation too gives the power of the purse too intirely to the state legislatures. It should provide perpetual funds in the disposal of Congress—by a land tax, poll tax, or the like. All imposts upon commerce ought to be laid by Congress and appropriated to their use, for without certain revenues, a government can have no power; that power, which holds the purse strings absolutely, must rule. This seems to be a medium, which without making Congress altogether independent will tend to give reality to its authority.

Another defect in our system is want of method and energy in the administration. This has partly resulted from the other defect, but in a great degree from prejudice and the want of a proper executive. Congress have kept the power too much into their own hands and have meddled too much with details of every sort. Congress is properly a deliberative corps and it forgets itself when it attempts to play the executive....

...Without a speedy change the army must dissolve; it is now a mob, rather than an army, without cloathing, without pay, without provision, without morals, without discipline. We begin to hate the country for its neglect of us; the country begins to hate us for our oppressions of them. Congress have long been jealous of us; we have now lost all confidence in them, and give the worst construction to all they do. Held together by the slenderest ties we are ripening for a dissolution....

...The confederation in my opinion should give Congress complete sovereignty; except as to that part of internal police, which relates to the rights of property and life among individuals and to raising money by internal taxes. It is necessary, that every thing, belonging to this, should be regulated by the state legislatures. Congress should have complete sovereignty in all that relates to war, peace, trade, finance, and to the management of foreign affairs, the right of declaring war of raising armies, officering, paying them, directing their motions in every respect, of equipping fleets and doing the same with them, of building fortifications arsenals magazines &c. &c., of making peace on such conditions as they think proper, of regulating trade, determining with what countries it shall be carried on, granting indulgencies laying prohibitions on all the articles of export or import, imposing duties granting bounties & premiums for raising exporting importing and applying to their own use the product of these duties, only giving credit to the states on whom they are raised in the general account of revenues and expences, instituting Admiralty courts &c., of coining money, establishing banks on such terms, and with such privileges as they think proper, appropriating funds and doing whatever else relates to the operations of finance, transacting every thing with foreign nations, making alliances offensive and defensive, treaties of commerce, &c. &c.

Hamilton, being Hamilton, could not pass up an opportunity to promote the beneficial qualities of a national debt, first faulting the current Congress for failing to leverage a loan from France or Spain in their eagerness to compete with Britain.

I have good reason to believe, that measures were not taken in earnest early enough, to procure a loan abroad. I give you my honor that from our first outset, I thought as I do now and wished for a foreign loan not only because I foresaw it would be essential but because I considered it as a tie upon the nation from which it was derived and as a mean to prop our cause in Europe.[4]

Hamilton continues his letter to Duane by proposing a constitutional convention involving all of the colonial assemblies; the appointment of ministers (rather than cumbersome boards) to key posts, such as foreign affairs, war, and finance (recommending individuals for those posts); the raising of an army under congressional authority; and the creation of a national bank. With Hamiltonian fervor, he concludes his seven-thousand-plus-word letter to a friend—presumably written in the scant off-hours permitted by his role as the chief aide to the commander-in-chief of an army engaged in war—by telling him "I have only skimmed the surface of the different subjects I have introduced."

Even with one eye set on affairs of state, Hamilton grew restless in his administrative role under General Washington—vital as it was to the revolutionary effort, and advantageous as it was for him to have unfettered access to the most influential men in America.

It was also not without excitement, as this October 1780 letter to Joshua Mersereau, a spy in the employ of the Continental Army shows in its secretive ("In your way you will call upon the Commanding officer") and urgent tone.

To Joshua Mersereau:

[September 3, 1780]

By intelligence just received from New York, we have reason to believe the enemy have some attempt in view by way of Staten Island, the execution of which will probably take place on thursday evening; if so the troops from New York will probably be past upon Staten Island thursday morning. [The] General wishes you to have [one] trusty person over on the [Is]land, to ascertain, whether any troops do come from New York and whether there are any movemen[ts] more than common among the enemy on the Island. He mu[st] leave the Island thursday morning so as to meet you at some convenient place that you may have time to get the intelligence and bring it to Head Quarters by Thursday evening six oClock. In your way you will call upon the Commanding officer of the troops near *Cranes Gap* [in the Watchung range of New Jersey], as it is possible the design may be against them. It is of great importance you should be punctual.[5]

Still, Hamilton longed for the glory that could only be won on a battlefield, and petitioned Washington for a field command only a few weeks later, in November 1780.

To George Washington:

[November 22, 1780]

Sometime last fall when I spoke to your Excellency about going to the Southward, I explained to you candidly my feelings with respect to military reputation, and how much it was my object to act a conspicuous part in some enterprise that might perhaps raise my character as a soldier above mediocrity. You were so good as to say you would be glad to furnish me with an occasion. When the expedition to Staten Island was on foot a favourable one seemed to offer. There was a batalion without a field officer, the command of which I thought, as it was accidental, might be given to me without inconvenience. I made an application for it through the Marquis [de Lafayette], who informed me of your refusal on two principles—one that giving me a whole batalion might be a subject of dissatisfaction [to other officers], the other that if an accident should happen to me, in the present state of your [military] family, you would be embarrassed for the necessary assistance.

The project you now have in contemplation [an attack on British positions in northern Manhattan] affords another opportunity.

Trying to short-circuit any potential objections, Hamilton points out that his knowledge of the terrain in that area provides the perfect pretext for giving him the command, and then continues with great self-confidence.

I flatter myself also that my military character stands so well in the army as to reconcile the officers in general to the measure. All circumstances considered, I venture to say any exceptions which might be taken would be unreasonable.

I take this method of making the request to avoid the embarrassment of a personal explanation; I shall only add that however much I have the matter at heart, I wish your Excellency entirely to consult your own inclination; and not from a disposition to oblige me, to do any thing, that may be disagreeable to you.

[It will, nevertheless, make me singularly] happy if your wishes correspond with mine.[6]

In July 1781, Washington succumbed to Hamilton's badgering and assigned him to be the commander of a New York light infantry battalion. Hamilton's unit was among the key players in the assault on the British stronghold in Yorktown, Virginia. On October 19, General Charles Cornwallis surrendered to Washington in what proved to be a pivotal defeat for British forces.

After the victory at Yorktown, Hamilton resigned his commission and became a civilian in time to be present for the birth of his first child, Philip. With end of the war in sight, Hamilton turned his full attention to the political arena. The previous month, he had been elected to the Congress of the Confederation. Publicly and privately, he continued to hone his vision of the emergent American nation and pour forth his views in a torrent of letters, speeches, and pamphlets. He turned down an offer from Robert Morris (the recently appointed superintendent of finance) to become the continental receiver of taxes, perceiving it to be an exercise in futility under the Articles of Confederation. Instead, Hamilton chose to focus his energies on reforming the articles themselves. In this December 1782 report, he forcefully describes the consequences of a lack of funds for the Confederation, rebutting Rhode Island speaker William Bradford, a staunch opponent of import duties.

The truth is that no Federal constitution can exist without powers, that in their exercise affect the internal police of the component members. It is equally true that no government can exist without a right to appoint officers for those purposes which proceed from and concenter in itself; and therefore the confeder-

*Lithograph depicting the surrender of General Charles Cornwallis to French
and American forces in Yorktown, Virginia in October 1781.*

ation has expressly declared that Congress shall have authority to
appoint all such "civil officers as may be necessary for managing
the general affairs of The United States under their direction."
All that can be required is that the Federal government confine
its appointments to such as it is empowered to make by the
original act of union, or by the subsequent consent of the parties. Unless there should be express words of exclusion in the
constitution of a state, there can be no reason to doubt, that it
is within the compass of legislative discretion to communicate
that authority.

*Hamilton then sought to reassure legislators who remained leery of a
strong, centralized government with powers of taxation—evocative,
in their time, of a European monarchy.*

The truth is the security intended to the general liberty in the confederation consists in the frequent election and in the rotation of the members of Congress, by which there is a constant and an effectual check upon them. This is the security which the people in every state enjoy against the usurpations of their internal governments; and it is the true source of security in a representative republic. The government so constituted ought to have the means necessary to answer the end of its institution. By weakening its hands too much it may be rendered incapable of providing for the interior harmony or the exterior defence of the state.

Finally, he turns to the nuts and bolts of the matter: there is a war that must be paid for.

The conduct of the war is intrusted to Congress and the public expectation turned upon them without any competent means at their command to satisfy the important trust. After the most full and solemn deliberation under a collective view of all the public difficulties, they recommend a measure, which appears to them the corner stone of the public safety: They see this measure suspended for near two years—partially complied with by some of the states, rejected by one of them and in danger on that account to be frustrated; the public embarrassments every day increasing, the dissatisfaction of the army growing more serious, the other creditors of the public clamouring for justice, both irritated by the delay of measures for their present relief or future security, the hopes of our enemies encouraged to protract the war, the zeal of our friends depressed by an appearance of remissness and want of exertion on our part, Congress harrassed, the national character suffering and the national safety at the mercy of events.

This state of things cannot but be extremely painful to Congress and appear to your Committee to make it their duty to be urgent to obviate the evils with which it is pregnant.[7]

Hamilton was not bluffing about this last point, though true to form, he saw opportunity in a challenging situation. A few months later, in February 1783, he laid out both the diagnosis of the ills in the army and the potential cure in a letter to General Washington.
   To George Washington

[Philadelphia, February 13, 1783]

If the war continues it would seem that the army must in June subsist itself *to defend the* country; if peace should take place it *will* subsist itself to procure *justice to itself.* It appears to be a prevailing opinion in the army that the disposition to recompence their services will cease with the necessity for them; and that if they once lay down their arms, they part with the means of obtaining justice. It is to be lamented that appearances afford to much ground for their distrust.

The claims of the army urged with moderation, but with firmness, may operate on those weak minds which are influenced by their apprehensions more than by their judgments, so as to produce a concurrence in the measures which the exigencies of affairs demand. They may add weight to the applications of Congress to the several states. So far an useful turn may be given to them. But the difficulty will be to keep a *complaining* and *suffering* army within the bounds of moderation.

This Your Excellency's influence must effect—In order to it, it will be adviseable not to discountenance their endeavours to procure redress, but rather by the intervention of confidential and prudent persons, to *take the direction of them*. This however must not appear: it is of moment to the public tranquillity that your Excellency should preserve the confidence of the army without losing that of the people. This will enable you in case of extremity to guide the torrent, and to bring order perhaps even good, out of confusion. 'Tis a part that requires address; but 'tis one, which your own situation as well as the welfare of the community points out.

With exquisite tact, Hamilton cautions Washington about his own vulnerability vis-à-vis his men.

I will not conceal from Your Excellency a truth which it is necessary you should know. An idea is propagated in the army that delicacy carried to an extreme prevents your espousing its interests with sufficient warmth. The falsehood of this opinion no one can be better acquainted with than myself; but it is not the less mischievous for being false. Its tendency is to impair that influence, which you may exert with advantage, should any commotions unhappily ensue, to moderate the pretensions of the army and make their conduct correspond with their duty.[8]

Within weeks, a mutinous faction of the army was threatening to retain arms until they were fully compensated—the prospect of an impending peace with Britain paradoxically giving urgency to their demands. Hamilton's predictions had been accurate, a fact that he lamented in a despairing letter to Washington dated March 25, 1783.

To George Washington:

[Philadelphia, March 25, 1783]

The [e]nclosed I write more in a public than in a private capacity—Here I write as a citizen zealous for the true happiness of this country—as a soldier who feels what is due to an army which has suffered every thing and done much for the safety of America.

I sincer[e]ly wish *ingratitude* was not so natural to the human heart as it is—I sincerely wish there were no seeds of it in those who direct the councils of the United States. But while I urge the army to moderation, and advise Your Excellency to take the direction of their discontents, and endeavour to confine them within the bounds of duty, I cannot as an honest man conceal from you, that I am afraid their distrusts have too much foundation....

...But supposing the Country ungrateful what can the army do? It must submit to its hard fate To seek redress by its arms would end in its ruin. The army would moulder by its own weight and for want of the means of keeping together—the soldiery would abandon their officers—There would be no chance of success without having recourse to means that would reverse our revolution. I make these observations not that I imagine Your Excellency can want motives to continue your influence in the path of moderation; but merely to show why I cannot myself enter into the views of coercion which some Gentlemen entertain for I confess could force avail I should almost wish to see it employed. I have an indifferent opinion of the honesty of this country, and ill-forebodings as to its future system.

Your Excellency will perceive I have written with sensations of chagrin and will make allowance for colouring; but the general picture is too true—God send us all more wisdom.[9]

The inability of Congress to both effectively satisfy the demands of the army and to quell its unrest resulted in one of the most embarrassing episodes in American history: the surrounding of congressional head-quarters in Philadelphia by drunken, unruly soldiers demanding their back pay, and the ignominious retreat of Congress to friendlier confines in Princeton, New Jersey. If Hamilton harbored any doubts about the need for centralized authority as a counterbalance to anarchy—in Hamilton's mind, the inevitable result of unfettered democracy—this event had swept them away.

NATION
BUILDER

★ ★ ★

For the next three and a half years, Hamilton maintained what was for him an arms-length involvement in public life. He turned his attention to building his law practice in New York and to his family.

True to his contrarian personality, one of the pillars of his law practice centered on defending individuals who had been Loyalists during the war. Many had been stripped of their property and worse under the punitive New York Trespass Act. Hamilton viewed this as a test of the character of the new republic to rise above this kind of retribution, but most New Yorkers did not agree. It would be neither the first nor last time Hamilton championed an unpopular cause that he believed to be morally right.

In 1784, Hamilton cofounded the first financial firm in New York, singlehandedly drafting its charter. His constitution for the Bank of New York became the blueprint for similar financial institutions and established many of the underlying principles of the American banking system.

As part of the delegation from New York to the Annapolis Convention, which had been organized to address the increasing number of trade disputes between states, Hamilton was one of those who quickly saw the opportunity to address the systemic problems underlying those disputes. The assembled delegates voted to organize a convention to amend the Articles of Confederation the following May in Philadelphia. In the meantime, Hamilton addressed monarchist concerns in a speech delivered in January 1787 to the New York State Assembly. The speech was a response to a statement by Governor George Clinton, who argued against reform and was emerging as a powerful opponent of centralized authority.

I cannot forbear remarking, that it is a common artifice to endeavour to insinuate a resemblance between the king under the former government, and Congress; though no two things can be more unlike each other. Nothing can be more dissimilar than a monarch, permanent, hereditary, the source of honor and emolument; and a republican body composed of a number of individuals appointed annually, liable to be recalled within the year, and subject to a continual rotation, which with few exceptions, is the fountain neither of honor nor emolument. If we will exercise our judgments we shall plainly see that no such resemblance exists, and that all inferences deducted from the comparison must be false.

Upon every occasion, however foreign such observations may be, we hear a loud cry raised about the danger of intrusting power to Congress, we are told it is dangerous to trust power any where; that *power* is liable to *abuse* with a variety of trite maxims of the same kind. General propositions of this nature are easily framed, the truth of which cannot be denied, but they rarely convey any precise idea. To these we might oppose other propositions equally true and equally indefinite. It might be said that too little power is as dangerous as too much, that it leads to anarchy, and from anarchy to despotism. But the question still recurs, what is this *too much or too little?* where is the measure or standard to ascertain the happy mean?[1]

A month later, Hamilton delivered another speech opposing Governor Clinton yet again, in favoring a bill allowing a continental impost (tax) by invoking the importance of paying down foreign debt. After establishing the legal foundation within the New York constitution for delegating power to the federal government, Hamilton turns to a familiar theme: national character and the importance of honoring debt. Competing state governments, he argues, have so far undermined and prevented the United States from being an honorable (and powerful) player on the world stage. And the fear of a strong centralized government, he continues, is a construct—an imaginary fear.

The causes taken notice of as securing the attachment of the people to their local governments, present us with another important truth—the natural imbecility of federal governments, and the danger that they will never be able to exercise power enough to manage the general affairs of the union. Though the states will have a common interest; yet they will also have a particular interest. For example, as a part of the union, it will be the interest of every state, that the general government should be supplied with the revenues necessary for the national purposes; but it will be the particular interest of each state to pay as little itself and to let its neighbours pay as much as possible. Particular interests have always more influence upon men than general. The several states therefore consulting their immediate advantage may be considered as so many eccentric powers tending in a contrary direction to the government of the union; and as they will generally carry the people along with them, the confederacy will be in continual danger of dissolution.

This, Mr. Chairman is the real rock upon which the happiness of this country is likely to split—this is the point to which our fears and cares should be directed—to guard against this and not to terrify ourselves with imaginary dangers from the spectre of power in Congress will be our true wisdom.

And, Hamilton tactfully points out, the states do not have a very promising track record when it comes to honoring their debts.

The universal delinquency of the states during the war, shall be passed over with the bare mention of it. The public embarrassments were a plausible apology for that delinquency; and [if] it was hoped the peace would produce greater punctuality the experiment has disappointed that hope to a degree, which confounds the least sanguine.

Finally, he depicts a dark future in which state governments continue to operate independently, without a federal authority, citing the example of the ancient Roman republic. The results would be similar: wars and conflict among the states, and wars and conflict between states and other nations.

If these states are not united under a federal government, they will infalliably have wars with each other; and their divisions will subject them to all the mischiefs of foreign influence and intrigue. The human passions will never want objects of hospitality. The western territory is an obvious and fruitful source of contest. Let us also cast our eye upon the mass of this state, intersected from one extremity to the other by a large navigable river. In the event of a rupture with them, what is to hinder our metropolis from becoming a prey to our neighbours? Is it even supposable that they would suffer it to remain the nursery of wealth to a distinct community?

These subjects are delicate, but it is necessary to contemplate them to teach us to form a true estimate of our situation.

Wars with each other would beget standing armies—a source of more real danger to our liberties than all the power that could be conferred upon the representatives of the union. And wars with each other would lead to opposite alliances with foreign powers, and plunge us into all the labyrinths of European politics.

The Romans in their progress to universal dominion, when they conceived the project of subduing the refractory spirit of the Grecian Republics, which composed the famous Achaian league, began by sowing dissensions among them, and instilling jealousies of each other, and of the common head, and finished by making them a province of the Roman empire.

The application is easy; if there are any foreign enemies, if there are any domestic foes to this country, all their arts and artifices will be employed to effect a dissolution of the union. This cannot be better done than by sowing jealousies of the federal head and cultivating in each state an undue attachment to its own power.[2]

When the states' delegates convened in Philadelphia during the scorching summer of 1787, several states submitted competing plans for federal constitutions. Virginia's and New Jersey's were the two leading plans, the former favoring larger states with two chambers of

A head-and-shoulders portrait of a stern-looking Hamilton
painted around 1904.

proportional representation but in many respects recognizable as the
framework of government set forth in the US Constitution; the latter
favoring smaller states, proposing the continuation of states' sovereignty
with modest modifications to the Articles of Confederation. Hamilton
uncharacteristically bit his tongue, wisely understanding his junior
status among New York's delegation. After remaining silent for the
first weeks of the convention, however, he let loose in a five-hour speech
that haunted him for the rest of his career, exposing him to charges that
he was both a monarchist and an apologist for British rule. Hamilton
praised the British parliamentary system for maintaining the rule of
law. Additionally, he proposed that the executive branch be headed
by an "elected monarch," to serve during good behavior, and a senate

similarly elected for life terms during good behavior. His notes from
the speech suggest that he considered proposing—but never publicly or
privately did—a hereditary chief executive!

Hamilton left Philadelphia for a period in July feeling discouraged,
as he reports in a letter to George Washington.

To George Washington:

[New York, July 3, 1787]

I own to you Sir that I am seriously and deeply distressed at the
aspect of the Councils which prevailed when I left Philadelphia.
I fear that we shall let slip the golden opportunity of rescuing the
American empire from disunion anarchy and misery. No motley
or feeble measure can answer the end or will finally receive the
public support. Decision is true wisdom and will be not less
reputable to the Convention than salutary to the community.[3]

By September, after the delegates negotiated the modifications to the
Virginia plan that ultimately became the core of the Constitution,
Hamilton threw himself into the task of getting it ratified. He did so
using the moniker "Publius," and it resulted in perhaps his greatest
contribution to American political discourse: The Federalist Papers.
Hamilton conceived of these essays as a campaign for ratification,
framing out their content, selecting the writers, and managing their
publication. Hamilton wrote fifty-one of the eighty-five essays, includ-
ing Federalist No. 1, which laid out the issues and set the stage for the
public debate and is worth reproducing in its entirety.

To the People of the State of New York: [27 October 1787]

After an unequivocal experience of the inefficacy of the subsisting
Fœderal Government, you are called upon to deliberate on a new

Constitution for the United States of America. The subject speaks its own importance; comprehending in its consequences, nothing less than the existence of the UNION, the safety and welfare of the parts of which it is composed, the fate of an empire, in many respects, the most interesting the world. It has been frequently remarked, that it seems to have been reserved to the people of this country, by their conduct and example, to decide the important question, whether societies of men are really capable or not, of establishing good government from ref[l]ection and choice, or whether they are forever destined to depend, for their political constitutions, on accident and force. If there be any truth in the remark, the crisis, at which we are arrived, may with propriety be regarded as the æra in which that decision is to be made; and a wrong election of the part we shall act, may, in this view, deserve to be considered as the general misfortune of mankind.

This idea will add the inducements of philanthropy to those of patriotism to heighten the sollicitude, which all considerate and good men must feel for the event. Happy will it be if our choice should be directed by a judicious estimate of our true interests, unperplexed and unbiassed by considerations not connected with the public good. But this is a thing more ardently to be wished, than seriously to be expected. The plan offered to our deliberations, affects too many particular interests, innovates upon too many local institutions, not to involve in its discussion a variety of objects foreign to its merits, and of views, passions and prejudices little favourable to the discovery of truth.

Among the most formidable of the obstacles which the new Constitution will have to encounter, may readily be distinguished the obvious interest of a certain class of men in every State to resist all changes which may hazard a diminution of the power, emolument and consequence of the offices they hold under the State-establishments—and the perverted ambition of another class of men, who will either hope to aggrandise themselves by the confusions of their country, or will flatter themselves with fairer prospects of elevation from the subdivision of the empire into several partial confederacies, than from its union under one government.

It is not, however, my design to dwell upon observations of this nature. I am well aware that it would be disingenuous to resolve indiscriminately the opposition of any set of men (merely because their situations might subject them to suspicion) into interested or ambitious views: Candour will oblige us to admit, that even such men may be actuated by upright intentions; and it cannot be doubted, that much of the opposition which has made its appearance, or may hereafter make its appearance, will spring from sources, blameless at least, if not respectable, the honest errors of minds led astray by preconceived jealousies and fears. So numerous indeed and so powerful are the causes, which serve to give a false bias to the judgment, that we upon many occasions, see wise and good men on the wrong as well as on the right side of questions, of the first magnitude to society. This circumstance, if duly attended to, would furnish a lesson of moderation of those, who are ever so much persuaded of their being in the right, in any controversy. And a further reason for caution, in this respect, might be drawn from the reflection, that we are not always sure, that those who advocate the truth are influenced by purer principles than their antagonists. Ambition, avarice, personal animosity, party opposition, and many other motives, not more laudable than these, are apt to operate as well upon those who support as upon those who oppose the right side of a question. Were there not even these inducements to moderation, nothing could be more illjudged than that intolerant spirit, which has, at all times, characterised political parties. For, in politics as in religion, it is equally absurd to aim at making proselytes by fire and sword. Heresies in either can rarely be cured by persecution.

And yet however just these sentiments will be allowed to be, we have already sufficient indications, that it will happen in this as in all former cases of great national discussion. A torrent of angry and malignant passions will be let loose. To judge from the conduct of the opposite parties, we shall be led to conclude, that they will mutually hope to evince the justness of their opinions, and to increase the number of their converts by the loudness of their declamations, and by the bitterness of their invectives. An enlightened zeal for the energy and efficiency of government will be stigmatised, as the off-spring of a temper fond of despotic power and hostile to the principles of liberty. An overscrupulous jealousy of danger to the rights of the people, which is more commonly the fault of the head than of the heart, will be represented as mere pretence and artifice; the bait for popularity at the expence of public good. It will be forgotten, on the one hand, that jealousy is the usual concomitant of violent love, and that the noble enthusiasm of liberty is too apt to be infected with a spirit of narrow and illiberal distrust. On the other hand, it will be equally forgotten, that the vigour of government is essential to the security of liberty; that, in the contemplation of a sound and well informed judgment, their interest can never be separated; and that a dangerous ambition more often lurks behind the specious mask of zeal for the rights of the people, than under the forbidding appearance of zeal for the firmness and efficiency of government. History will teach us, that the former has been found a much more certain road to the introduction of despotism, than the latter, and that of those men who have overturned the liberties of republics the greatest number have begun their carreer, by paying an obsequious court to the people, commencing Demagogues and ending Tyrants.

In the course of the preceeding observations I have had an eye, my Fellow Citizens, to putting you upon your guard against all attempts, from whatever quarter, to influence your decision in a matter of the utmost moment to your welfare by any impressions other than those which may result from the evidence of truth. You will, no doubt, at the same time, have collected from the general scope of them that they proceed from a source not unfriendly to the new Constitution. Yes, my Countrymen, I own to you, that, after having given it an attentive consideration, I am clearly of opinion, it is your interest to adopt it. I am convinced, that this is the safest course for your liberty, your dignity, and your happiness. I effect not reserves, which I do not feel. I will not amuse you with an appearance of deliberation, when I have decided. I frankly acknowledge to you my convictions, and I will freely lay before you the reasons on which they are founded. The consciousness of good intentions disdains ambiguity. I shall not however multiply professions on this head. My motives must remain in the depository of my own breast: My arguments will be open to all, and may be judged of by all. They shall at least be offered in a spirit, which will not disgrace the cause of truth.

I propose in a series of papers to discuss the following interesting particulars—*The utility of the UNION to your political prosperity—The insufficiency of the present Confederation to preserve that Union—The necessity of a government at least equally energetic with the one proposed to the attainment of this object—The conformity of the proposed constitution to the true principles of republican govern-ment—Its analogy to your own state constitution—and lastly, The additional security, which its adoption will afford to the preservation of that species of government, to liberty and to property.*

In the progress of this discussion I shall endeavour to give a satisfactory answer to all the objections which shall have made their appearance that may seem to have any claim to your attention.

It may perhaps be thought superfluous to offer arguments to prove the utility of the UNION, a point, no doubt, deeply engraved on the hearts of the great body of the people in every state, and one, which it may be imagined has no adversaries. But the fact is, that we already hear it whispered in the private circles of those who oppose the new constitution, that the Thirteen States are of too great extent for any general system, and that we must of necessity resort to separate confederacies of distinct portions of the whole. This doctrine will, in all probability, be gradually propagated, till it has votaries enough to countenance an open avowal of it. For nothing can be more evident, to those who are able to take an enlarged view of the subject than the alternative of an adoption of the new Constitution, or a dismemberment of the Union. It will therefore be of use to begin by examining the advantages of that Union, the certain evils and the probable dangers, to which every State will be exposed from its dissolution. This shall accordingly constitute the subject of my next address.

PUBLIUS.[4]
In the earliest Federalist Papers, Hamilton enumerates the by-now-familiar shortcomings of the Articles of Confederation. He considers

the many ways in which the current squabbles between the states can escalate into trade wars, violent disputes, and worse. Perhaps nowhere does he paint a more dramatic picture of the actual state of affairs for the nation at present than in Federalist No. 15.

We may indeed with propriety be said to have reached almost the last stage of national humiliation. There is scarcely any thing that can wound the pride, or degrade the character of an independent nation, which we do not experience. Are there engagements to the performance of which we are held by every tie respectable among men? These are the subjects of constant and unblushing violation. Do we owe debts to foreigners and to our own citizens contracted in a time of imminent peril, for the preservation of our political existence? These remain without any proper or satisfactory provision for their discharge. Have we valuable territories and important posts in the possession of a foreign power, which by express stipulations ought long since to have been surrendered? These are still retained, to the prejudice of our interests not less than of our rights. Are we in a condition to resent, or to repel the aggression? We have neither troops nor treasury nor government. Are we even in a condition to remonstrate with dignity? The just imputations on our own faith, in respect to the same treaty, ought first to be removed. Are we entitled by nature and compact to a free participation in the navigation of the Mississippi? Spain excludes us from it. Is public credit an indispensable resource in time of public danger? We seem to have abandoned its cause as desperate and irretrievable. Is commerce of importance to national wealth? Ours is at the lowest point of declension. Is respectability in the eyes of foreign powers a safe guard against foreign encroachments? The imbecility of our Government even forbids them to treat with us: Our ambassadors abroad are the mere pageants of mimic sovereignty. Is a violent and unnatural decrease in the value of land a symptom of national distress? The price of improved land in most parts of the country is much lower than can be accounted for by the quantity of waste land at market, and can only be fully explained by that want of private and public confidence, which are so alarmingly prevalent among all ranks and which have a direct tendency to depreciate property of every kind. Is private credit the friend and patron of industry? That most useful kind which relates to borrowing and lending is reduced within the narrowest limits, and this still more from an opinion of insecurity than from the scarcity of money. To shorten an enumeration of particulars which can afford neither pleasure nor instruction it may in general be demanded, what indication is there of national disorder, poverty and insignificance that could befal a community so peculiarly blessed with natural advantages as we are, which does not form a part of the dark catalogue of our public misfortunes?[5]

The current system's serious shortcomings laid bare, Hamilton turns to a more prescriptive mode. His natural proclivities made him perfectly suited to argue for a strong executive branch of government, as proposed in the new constitution, against a fresh round of criticism from republicans. He dismisses their concerns about a monarchist executive, managing a swipe along the way at Governor Clinton, a staunch opponent of the new Constitution, and a personal nemesis of Hamilton's.

Here the writers against the Constitution seem to have taken pains to signalize their talent of misrepresentation, calculating

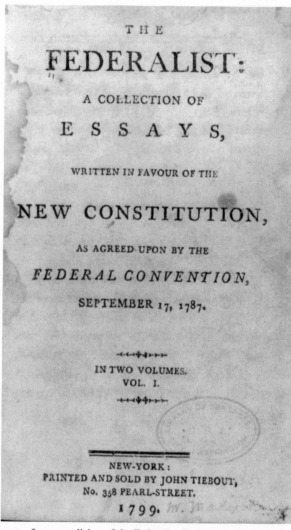

THE

FEDERALIST:

A COLLECTION OF

E S S A Y S,

WRITTEN IN FAVOUR OF THE

NEW CONSTITUTION,

AS AGREED-UPON BY THE

FEDERAL CONVENTION,

SEPTEMBER 17, 1787.

IN TWO VOLUMES.
VOL. I.

NEW-YORK:
PRINTED AND SOLD BY JOHN TIEBOUT,
No. 358 PEARL-STREET.
1799.

Title page from an edition of the Federalist Papers reprinted in 1799,
during the Adams administration.

upon the aversion of the people to monarchy, they have endeavoured to inlist all their jealousies and apprehensions in opposition to the intended President of the United States; not merely as the embryo but as the full grown progeny of that detested parent. To establish the pretended affinity they have not scrupled to draw resources even from the regions of fiction. The authorities of a magistrate, in few instances greater, and in some instances less, than those of a Governor of New-York, have been magnified into more than royal prerogatives. He has been decorated with attributes superior in dignity and splendor to those of a King of Great-Britain.[6]

In Federalist No. 68, Hamilton turns to the proposed system of electing a chief magistrate. Electors chosen by voters in each state select the president and vice president—not voters voting directly. The Framers saw this as a way to combat factionalism and demagogues who master what Hamilton derisively refers to as "the little arts of popularity."

This process of election affords a moral certainty, that the office of president, will seldom fall to the lot of any man, who is not in an eminent degree endowed with the requisite qualifications. Talents for low intrigue and the little arts of popularity may alone suffice to elevate a man to the first honors in a single state; but it will require other talents and a different kind of merit to establish him in the esteem and confidence of the whole union, or of so considerable a portion of it as would be necessary to make him a successful candidate for the distinguished office of president of the United States. It will not be too strong to say, that there will be a constant probability of seeing the station filled by characters preeminent for ability and virtue. And this will be thought no inconsiderable recommendation of the constitution, by those, who are able to estimate the share, which the executive in every government must necessarily have in its good or ill administration. Though we cannot acquiesce in the political heresy of the poet who says—

> *"For forms of government let fools contest—*
> *"That which is best administered is best."*

—yet we may safely pronounce, that the true test of a good government is its aptitude and tendency to produce a good administration.[7]

No aspect of Hamilton's Federalist Papers writing is cited more frequently today than his arguments in favor of an independent judiciary with lifelong appointments.

According to the plan of the convention, all the judges who may be appointed by the United States are to hold their offices *during good behaviour,* which is conformable to the most approved of the state constitutions; and among the rest, to that of this state. Its propriety having been drawn into question by the adversaries of that plan, is no light symptom of the rage for objection which disorders their imaginations and judgments. The standard of good behaviour for the continuance in office of the judicial magistracy is certainly one of the most valuable of the modern improvements in the practice of government. In a monarchy it is an excellent barrier to the despotism of the prince: In a republic it is a no less excellent barrier to the encroachments and oppressions of the representative body. And it is the best expedient which can be devised in any government, to secure a steady, upright and impartial administration of the laws.

He next efficiently and elegantly defines the limits of judiciary power vis-à-vis the other branches of government.

The judiciary on the contrary has no influence over either the sword or the purse, no direction either of the strength or of the wealth of the society, and can take no active resolution whatever. It may truly be said to have neither FORCE nor WILL, but merely judgment; and must ultimately depend upon the aid of the executive arm even for the efficacy of its judgments.

Then Hamilton goes on to delineate the concept of judicial review more clearly and emphatically than is done in the Constitution itself.

There is no position which depends on clearer principles, than that every act of a delegated authority, contrary to the tenor of the commission under which it is exercised, is void. No legislative act therefore contrary to the constitution can be valid. To deny this would be to affirm that the deputy is greater than his principal; that the servant is above his master; that the representatives of the people are superior to the people themselves; that men acting by virtue of powers may do not only what their powers do not authorise, but what they forbid.

If it be said that the legislative body are themselves the constitutional judges of their own powers, and that the construction they put upon them is conclusive upon the other departments, it may be answered, that this cannot be the natural presumption, where it is not to be collected from any particular provision in the constitution. It is not otherwise to be supposed that the constitution could intend to enable the representatives of the people to substitute their *will* to that of their constituents. It is far more rational to suppose that the courts were designed to be an intermediate body between the people and the legislature, in order, among other things, to keep the latter within the limits assigned to their authority. The interpretation of the laws is the proper and peculiar province of the courts. A constitution is in fact, and must be, regarded by the judges as a fundamental law. It therefore belongs to them to ascertain its meaning as well as the meaning of any particular act proceeding from the legislative body. If there should happen to be an irreconcileable variance between the two, that which has the superior obligation and validity ought of course to be preferred; or in other words, the constitution ought to be preferred to the statute, the intention of the people to the intention of their agents.

Nor does this conclusion by any means suppose a superiority of the judicial to the legislative power. It only supposes that the power of the people is superior to both; and that where the will of the legislature declared in its statutes, stands in opposition to that of the people declared in the constitution, the judges ought to be governed by the latter, rather than the former. They ought to regulate their decisions by the fundamental laws, rather than by those which are not fundamental.[8]

One of the factions at the convention, fearful of centralized power, added to the proposed Constitution a series of amendments that its members insisted were necessary to guarantee individual liberties.

Most of us today would unthinkingly agree: the proposed amendments are now known as the Bill of Rights. Surprisingly, Hamilton opposed these in Federalist No. 84, partly for political reasons, and partly because he believed they opened the door to mischief. His argument is precise and persuasive.

I go further, and affirm that bills of rights, in the sense and in the extent in which they are contended for, are not only unnecessary in the proposed constitution, but would even be dangerous. They would contain various exceptions to powers which are not granted; and on this very account, would afford a colourable pretext to claim more than were granted. For why declare that things shall not be done which there is no power to do? Why for instance, should it be said, that the liberty of the press shall not be restrained, when no power is given by which restrictions may be imposed? I will not contend that such a provision would confer a regulating power; but it is evident that it would furnish, to men disposed to usurp, a plausible pretence for claiming that power.[9]

Hamilton's closing argument, as it were, in the final installment of the Federalist Papers, is as self-assured and folksy as any delivered by a self-confident and accomplished New York attorney.

Thus have I, my fellow citizens, executed the task I had assigned to myself; with what success, your conduct must determine. I trust at least you will admit, that I have not failed in the assurance I gave you respecting the spirit with which my endeavours should be conducted. I have addressed myself purely to your judgments, and have studiously avoided those asperities which are too apt to disgrace political disputants of all parties, and which have been not a little provoked by the language and conduct of the opponents of the constitution. The charge of a conspiracy against the liberties of the people, which has been indiscriminately brought against the advocates of the plan, has something in it too wanton and too malignant not to excite the indignation of every man who feels in his own bosom a refutation of the calumny. The perpetual changes which have been rung upon the wealthy, the well-born and the great, have been such as to inspire the disgust of all sensible men. And the unwarrantable concealments and misrepresentations which have been in various ways practiced to keep the truth from the public eye, have been of a nature to demand the reprobation of all honest men. It is not impossible that these circumstance may have occasionally betrayed me into intemperances of expression which I did not intend: It is certain that I have frequently felt a struggle between sensibility and moderation, and if the former has in some instances prevailed, it must be my excuse that it has been neither often nor much.

Let us now pause and ask ourselves whether, in the course of these papers, the proposed constitution has not been satisfactorily vindicated from the aspersions thrown upon it, and whether it has not been shewn to be worthy of the public approbation, and necessary to the public safety and prosperity. Every man is bound to answer these questions to himself, according to the best of his conscience and understanding, and to act agreeably to the genuine and sober dictates of his judgment. This is a duty, from which nothing can give him a dispensation. 'Tis one that he is called upon, nay, constrained by all the obligations that form the bands of society, to discharge sincerely and honestly. No partial motive, no particular interest, no pride of opinion, no temporary passion or prejudice, will justify to himself, to his country or to his posterity, an improper election of the part he is to act. Let him beware of an obstinate adherence to party. Let him reflect that the object upon which he is to decide is not a particular interest of the community, but the very existence of the nation. And let him remember that a majority of America has already given its sanction to the plan, which he is to approve or reject....

...I answer in the next place, that I should esteem it the extreme of imprudence to prolong the precarious state of our national affairs, and to expose the union to the jeopardy of successive experiments, in the chimerical pursuit of a perfect plan. I never expect to see a perfect work from imperfect man. The result of the deliberations of all collective bodies must necessarily be a compound as well of the errors and prejudices, as of the good sense and wisdom of the individuals of whom they are composed. The compacts which are to embrace thirteen distinct states, in a common bond of amity and union, must as necessarily be a compromise of as many dissimilar interests and inclinations. How can perfection spring from such materials?

Hamilton quotes the Scottish philosopher David Hume to provide a sense of perspective about what is being attempted with the Constitution.

"To balance a large state or society (says he [Hume]) whether monarchical or republican, on general laws, is a work of so great difficulty, that no human genius, however comprehensive, is able by the mere dint of reason and reflection, to effect it. The judgments of many must unite in the work: EXPERIENCE must guide their labour: Time must bring it to perfection: And the FEELING of inconveniences must correct the mistakes which they *inevitably* fall into, in their first trials and experiments."

Hamilton concludes by arguing emphatically that the nation had come too far in the process of self-determination (only two more states were needed for ratification), at great effort and cost, to turn back now.

A NATION without a NATIONAL GOVERNMENT is, in my view, an awful spectacle. The establishment of a constitution, in time of profound peace, by the voluntary consent of a whole people, is a PRODIGY, to the completion of which I look forward with trembling anxiety. I can reconcile it to no rules of prudence to let go the hold we now have, in so arduous an enterprise, upon seven out of the thirteen states; and after having passed over so considerable a part of the ground to recommence the course.[10]

On June 25, 1788, New Hampshire ratified the Constitution and was the ninth state to do so, which made it the law of the land. The vote had been a true cliffhanger—so close, in fact, it wasn't until a few days later when Virginia became the tenth state to (barely) vote for ratification that Hamilton and the New York Federalists felt secure that the Clintonites would not lead a movement to secede from the Union. People flooded the streets of New York City, which had the highest concentration of Federalists in the state, in a celebratory parade. The adoring throng singled out Hamilton for recognition, launching a miniature frigate down Broadway, pulled by ten horses, dubbed the "Federal Ship Hamilton."

Hamilton and the Federalists had gotten the centralized government that they wanted. Now it was up to them to make it work.

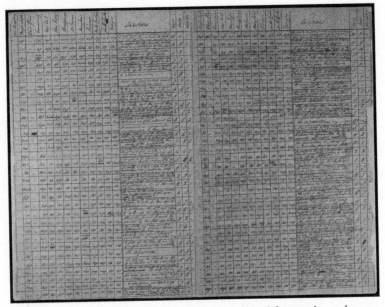

The page recording the final vote of the Constitutional Convention, taken on September 15, 1787. Delegates signed the proposed Constitution two days later.

THE SECRETARY

★ ★ ★

For Alexander Hamilton, the single factor that would most increase the chances for the success of the new system of government was to insure that George Washington was installed as the head of state to guide the nation through this rocky period. Washington's popularity and integrity made him all but unbeatable in a general election, but he needed to be persuaded to come out of his well-deserved retirement in Mount Vernon. In this September 1788 letter, Hamilton implores his former commander and mentor to postpone his retirement in order to become the nation's first president.

To George Washington:

[New York, September 1788]

I should be deeply pained my Dear Sir if your scruples in regard to a certain station should be matured into a resolution to decline it; though I am neither surprised at their existence nor can I but agree in opinion that the caution you observe in deferring an ultimate determination is prudent. I have however reflected maturely on the subject and have come to a conclusion, (in which I feel no hesitation) that every public and personal consideration will demand from you an acquiescence in what will *certainly* be the unanimous wish of your country. The absolute retreat which you meditated at the close of the late war was natural and proper. Had the government produced by the revolution gone on in a *tolerable* train, it would have been most adviseable to have persisted in that retreat. But I am clearly of opinion that the crisis which brought you again into public view left you no alterative but to comply—and I am equally clear in the opinion that you are by that act *pledged* to take a part in the execution of the government....

It cannot be considered as a compliment to say that on your acceptance of the office of President the success of the new government in its commencement may materially depend. Your agency and influence will be not less important in preserving it from the future attacks of its enemies than they have been in recommending it in the first instance to the adoption of the people. Independent of all considerations drawn from this source the point of light in which you stand at home and abroad will make an infinite difference in the respectability with which the government will begin its operations in the alternative of your being or not being at the head of it. I forbear to urge considerations which might have a more personal application. What I have said will suffice for the inferences I mean to draw....

I have taken the liberty to express these sentiments to lay before you my view of the subject. I doubt not the considerations mentioned have fully occurred to you, and I trust they will finally produce in your mind the same result, which exists in mine. I flatter myself the frankness with which I have delivered myself will not be displeasing to you. It has been prompted by motives which you would not disapprove.[1]

The Constitution granted each presidential elector two votes, the recipient of the greatest number of votes becoming president, the second-place candidate becoming vice president. When Washington agreed to run, Hamilton, never one to trust in providence to effect outcomes, immediately lobbied a handful of electors to withhold votes for John Adams, Washington's closest rival. Hamilton laid out his strategy in this letter to James Wilson, an elector from Pennsylvania.

   To James Wilson:

[January 25, 1789]

A degree of anxiety about a matter of primary importance to the new government induces me to trouble you with this letter. I mean the election of the President. We all feel of how much moment it is that Washington should be the man; and I own I cannot think there is material room to doubt that this will be the unanimous sense. But as a failure in this object would be attended with the worst consequences I cannot help concluding that even possibilities should be guarded against.

   Every body is aware of that defect in the constitution which renders it possible that the man intended for Vice President may in fact turn up President. Every body sees that unanimity in Adams as Vice President and a few votes insidiously witheld from Washington might substitute the former to the latter. And every body must perceive that there is something to fear from machinations of Antifederal malignity. What in this situation is wise?

Hamilton projects the likely regional breakdown of the voting, and concludes that there is a possibility that Adams could win over Washington. He proposes "throwing away" votes for Adams, risking his place being taken by an anti-Federalist, rather than risking the possibility that Adams finish with more votes than Washington.

Hence I conclude it will be prudent to throw away a few votes say 7 or 8; giving these to persons not otherwise thought of. Under this impression I have proposed to friends in Connecticut to throw away two to others in Jersey to throw away an equal number & I submit it to you whether it will not be well to lose three or four in Pennsylvania. Your advices from the South will serve you as the best guide; but for God's sake let not our zeal for a secondary object defeat or endanger a first. I admit that in several important views and particularly to avoid disgust to a man who would be a formidable head to Antifederalists—it is much to be desired that Adams may have the plurality of suffrages for Vice President; but if risk is to be run on one side or on the other can we hesitate where it ought to be preferred?

If there appears to you to be any danger, will it not be well for you to write to Maryland to *qualify* matters there?[2]

Hamilton's caution had been unnecessary—Washington received the votes of every elector, while Adams received a total of 34. But Hamilton's strategy had the unintended consequence of beginning a deep and long-running enmity with John Adams, which would return to haunt him when his mentor and protector, George Washington, exited the political stage.

Equally damaging was Hamilton's ongoing feud with New York governor George Clinton. His fiefdom threatened under the new system by the primacy of the federal customs collector over that of the state, Clinton stepped up his attacks on Hamilton, which had turned personal during the struggle over ratification. Hamilton, relishing a good fight, here shows mastery of the twin arts of insinuation and character assassination in a series of published "letters" he wrote under the alias "H.G." in support of Judge Robert Yates—an ally of Hamilton's father-in-law's, and a friend to the Constitution—over the incumbent, Clinton, in the forthcoming gubernatorial election.

The present Governor was bred to the law, under William Smith, Esquire, formerly of this city. Some time before the late revolution, he resided in Ulster county, and there followed his profession with reputation, though not with distinction. He was not supposed to possess considerable talents; but upon the whole, stood fair on the score of probity. It must however be confessed, that he early got the character with many of being a very *artful* man; and it is not to be wondered at, if that impression, on the minds in which it prevailed, deducted something from the opinion of his integrity. But it would be refining too much to admit such a consequence to be a just one. There certainly are characters (tho' they may be rare) which unite a great degree of address, and even a large portion of what is best expressed by the word CUNNING, with a pretty exact adherence, in the main, to the principles of integrity.[3]

In a later article, Hamilton, writing as H.G., takes the art of insinuation even further, disparaging Clinton's courage and war service.

That Mr. Clinton is a man of courage, there is no reason to doubt. That he was upon most occasions active and vigorous cannot be justly disputed. In his capacity of governor he was ever ready to promote the common cause—prompt in affording the aid of the militia, when requisite, and scrupling not, when he thought his presence might be of use, to put himself at the head of them. But here his praise as a soldier ends. Beyond this he has no pretension to the wreath of military renown. No man can tell when or where he gave proofs of generalship, either in council or in the field. After diligent enquiry, I have not been able to learn that he was ever more than once in actual combat. This was at Fort Montgomery, where he commanded in person; and which, after a feeble and unskilful defence, was carried by storm. That post strongly fortified by nature, almost inaccessible in itself, and sufficiently manned, was capable of being rendered a much more difficult morsel to the assailants than they found it to be. This I own was not the common idea at the time; but it is not the less true. To embellish military exploits, and varnish military disgraces, is no unusual policy. Besides, governor Clinton was then at the zenith of his popularity, a circumstance which disposed men's minds to take a great deal for granted. One particular in this affair deserves to be noticed. It is certain that the governor made a well-timed retreat, (I mean personally, for the greatest part of the garrison were captured), a thing which must have occasioned no small conflict in the breast of a commander nice in military punctilio.[4]

Washington was sworn in on the steps of Federal Hall in New York as the first president on April 30, 1780, to great fanfare. Seeking to strike a balance between European formality and American casualness, he was noticeably uncomfortable during his inauguration speech to Congress. He asked Hamilton to draw up guidelines on the comportment of a United States president. The guidelines reveal both Hamilton's acumen as a stage manager and his intuitive aristocratic leanings—an irony, given his humble origins. He makes no bones about the fact that he is modeling the president's environment and behavior on those of the European courts.

The public good requires as a primary object that the dignity of the office should be supported. Whatever is essential to this ought to be pursued though at the risk of partial or momentary dissatisfaction. But care will be necessary to avoid extensive disgust or discontent. Men's minds are prepared for a pretty high tone in the demeanour of the Executive; but I doubt whether for so high a tone as in the abstract might be desireable. The notions of equality are yet in my opinion too general and too strong to admit of such a distance being placed between the President and other branches of the government as might even be consistent with a due proportion. The following plan will I think steer clear of extremes and involve no very material inconveniences.

I. The President to have a levee day once a week for receiving visits. An hour to be fixed at which it shall be understood that he will appear and consequently that the visitors are previously to be assembled. The President to remain half an hour, in which time he may converse cursorily on indifferent subjects with such persons as shall strike his attention, and at the end of that half hour disappear. Some regulation will be hereafter necessary to designate those who may visit. A mode of introduction through particular officers will be indispensable. No visits to be returned.

II. The President to accept no invitations: and to give formal entertainments only twice or four times a year on the anniversaries of important events in the revolution. If twice, the day of the declaration of Independence, and that of the inauguration of the President, which completed the organization of the Constitution, to be preferred; if four times, the day of the treaty of alliance with france & that of the definitive treaty with Britain to be added. The members of the two houses of the legislature

Principal officers of the Government Foreign ministers and other distinguished strangers only to be invited. The numbers form in my mind an objection—But there may be separate tables in separate rooms. This is practiced in some European Courts. I see no other method in which foreign Ministers can with propriety be included in any attentions of the table which the President may think fit to pay.

III. The President on the levée days either by himself or some Gentleman of his household to give informal invitations to family dinners on the days of invitation. Not more than six or eight to be invited at a time & the matter to be confined essentially to members of the legislature and other official characters. The President never to remain long at table.

It is an important point to consider what persons may have access to Your Excellency on business. The heads of departments will of course have this privilege. Foreign Ministers of some descriptions will also be intitled to it. In Europe I am informed ambassadors only have direct access to the Chief Magistrate. Something very *near* what prevails there would in my opinion be right. The distinction of rank between diplomatic characters requires attention and the door of access ought not to be too wide to that class of persons. I have thought that the members of the Senate should also have a right of *individual* access on matters relative to the *public administration*. In England & France Peers of the realm have this right. We have none such in this Country, but I believe that it will be satisfactory to the people to know that there is some body of men in the state who have a right of continual communication with the President. It will be considered as a safeguard against secret combinations to deceive him.

I have asked myself—will not the representatives expect the same privilege and be offended if they are not allowed to participate with the Senate? There is sufficient danger of this, to merit consideration. But there is a reason for the distinction in the constitution. The Senate are coupled with the President in certain executive functions; treaties and appointments. This makes them in a degree his constitutional counsellors and gives them a *peculiar* claim to the right of access. On the whole, I think the discrimination will be proper & may be hazarded.

I have chosen this method of communication, because I understood Your Excellency, that it would be most convenient to you. The unstudied and unceremonious manner of it will I hope not render it the less acceptable. And if in the execution of your commands at any time I consult frankness and simplicity more than ceremony or profession, I flatter myself you will not on that account distrust the sincerity of the assurance I now give of my cordial wishes for your personal happiness and the success of your administration.[5]

After a period of uncertainty (Washington had initially courted Robert Morris, who had been the superintendent of finance under the Articles of Confederation, but who was about to go spectacularly broke—and who recommended Hamilton in his place), Hamilton was sworn in as the first Treasury secretary on September 11, 1789. Hamilton wasted no time in getting to work. Knowing that import duties were the federal government's primary source of revenue, he immediately established contact with the collectors of customs in the form of a circular letter.

*Hamilton's commission as the first treasury secretary of the United States
signed by George Washington in 1789.*

[September 14, 1789]

The exigencies of Government require that I should without
delay be informed of the amount of the Duties which have
accrued in the several States, and of the Monies which have
been already received in payment of them, and the periods at
which the remainder will fall due. In this absolute precision is not
expected, but a General Statement accurate enough in the main
to be relied on. I request your answer as speedily as possible.[6]

*With typical pragmatism, and undoubtedly informed by his experiences
as a shipping clerk as a teenager, Hamilton saw the collectors both as*

valuable sources of intelligence and as agents in need of instruction. He advised them to take the complaints of merchants with a grain of salt but to take them seriously, as they, too, were valuable sources of information.

As in the first establishiment of Revenue systems, imperfections and inconveniencies will naturally present themselves in practice, which could not have been foreseen in their formation; it is of the greatest moment, that the best information should be collected for the use of the Government as to the operation of those, which may have been adopted.

To the obtaining this information, as it respects the plan for the imposition and collection of the duties, the situation of the collectors and naval Officers of the several Ports is in a peculiar manner favourable, and no arguments need be used to shew that it is equally their duty and their interest to make the best use of their opportunities for that purpose.

Not doubting that their inclination will coincide with both; I am to request that they will carefully note and from time to time communicate to me whatever may serve to discover the merits or defects of that plan, and to point out the means of improving it.

Though the complaints of the Merchants will not always be infallible indications of defects, yet they will always merit attention, and when they occur, I shall be glad to be particularly informed of them.

You will doubtless have observed, that it was in the contemplation of Congress to employ Boats for the security of the Revenue against contraband. I shall be glad to have your Ideas, as to the expediency of employing them in your quarter, and (if any appear to you necessary) of the number and kind you deem requisite; their equipments, and the probable expence. Should any have been in use under the State regulations, I desire they may be continued, and that I may be advised with accuracy of the nature of their establishment.

It has been very much apprehended that the number of Ports in several of the States would conduce to great evasions of the duties. It is my wish to be informed how far experience has justified this apprehension, and what can be done to correct the Mischeifs, which may have ensued, avoiding as much as possible the inconveniencies which the multiplication of Ports was designed to obviate.

In hinting these particulars it is not my aim to confine your attention to them only; It will give me pleasure to find that your observation has been as diffusive as the object is extensive.[7]

While setting the machinery of the Treasury Department in motion, Hamilton began work on the first major report of his administration, the Report on Public Credit. *This was the first of several monumental reports that together formed the basis of the United States financial system. First, Hamilton makes universal the case for the necessity of a reliable source of credit. He praises the House observation "That an adequate provision for the support of the Public Credit, is a matter of high importance to the honor and prosperity of the United States."*

In the opinion of the Secretary, the wisdom of the House, in giving their explicit sanction to the proposition which has been stated, cannot but be applauded by all, who will seriously consider, and trace through their obvious consequences, these plain and undeniable truths.

That exigencies are to be expected to occur, in the affairs of nations, in which there will be a necessity for borrowing.

That loans in times of public danger, especially from foreign war, are found an indispensable resource, even to the wealthiest of them.

And that in a country, which, like this, is possessed of little active wealth, or in other words, little monied capital, the necessity for that resource, must, in such emergencies, be proportionably urgent.

And as on the one hand, the necessity for borrowing in particular emergencies cannot be doubted, so on the other, it is equally evident, that to be able to borrow upon *good terms*, it is essential that the credit of a nation should be well established.

For when the credit of a country is in any degree questionable, it never fails to give an extravagant premium, in one shape or another, upon all the loans it has occasion to make. Nor does the evil end here; the same disadvantage must be sustained upon whatever is to be bought on terms of future payment.

From this constant necessity of *borrowing* and *buying dear*, it is easy to conceive how immensely the expences of a nation, in a course of time, will be augmented by an unsound state of the public credit....

If the maintenance of public credit, then, be truly so important, the next enquiry which suggests itself is, by what means it is to be effected? The ready answer to which question is, by good faith, by a punctual performance of contracts. States, like individuals, who observe their engagements, are respected and trusted: while the reverse is the fate of those, who pursue an opposite conduct.

Hamilton expands on the benefits of a properly funded public debt, arguing for the conversion of previously incurred debt in its myriad

*forms, into interest-bearing, government-backed bonds. He argues that
a virtuous circle is created between private enterprise and the federal
government when government debt is funded in this way.*

It is a well known fact, that in countries in which the national
debt is properly funded, and an object of established confidence,
it answers most of the purposes of money. Transfers of stock
or public debt are there equivalent to payments in specie; or
in other words, stock, in the principal transactions of business,
passes current as specie. The same thing would, in all probability
happen here, under the like circumstances.

The benefits of this are various and obvious.

First. Trade is extended by it; because there is a larger capital
to carry it on, and the merchant can at the same time, afford to
trade for smaller profits; as his stock, which, when unemployed,
brings him in an interest from the government, serves him also
as money, when he has a call for it in his commercial operations.

Secondly. Agriculture and manufactures are also promoted by
it: For the like reason, that more capital can be commanded to be
employed in both; and because the merchant, whose enterprize
in foreign trade, gives to them activity and extension, has greater
means for enterprize.

Thirdly. The interest of money will be lowered by it; for this is
always in a ratio, to the quantity of money, and to the quickness
of circulation. This circumstance will enable both the public and
individuals to borrow on easier and cheaper terms.

And from the combination of these effects, additional aids
will be furnished to labour, to industry, and to arts of every kind.

But these good effects of a public debt are only to be looked
for, when, by being well funded, it has acquired an *adequate* and

stable value. Till then, it has rather a contrary tendency. The fluctuation and insecurity incident to it in an unfunded state, render it a mere commodity, and a precarious one. As such, being only an object of occasional and particular speculation, all the money applied to it is so much diverted from the more useful channels of circulation, for which the thing itself affords no substitute: So that, in fact, one serious inconvenience of an unfunded debt is, that it contributes to the scarcity of money.[8]

Resentment of the speculators who had bought up much of the domestic government debt at bargain prices, in many cases from Revolutionary War veterans who had fallen on hard times, motivated a movement to limit the payouts to the speculators while endeavoring to reward the original holders of the debt. Hamilton saw this as a flawed plan on practical grounds—how would the Treasury Department ever locate all of the original holders, let alone sort their claims?—as well as on moral grounds. A debt is a debt, and the holder of legally acquired paper is entitled to a full payout, no matter, according to Hamilton, if the acquisition could be considered predatory or not.

The Secretary, after the most mature reflection on the force of this argument, is induced to reject the doctrine it contains, as equally unjust and impolitic, as highly injurious, even to the original holders of public securities; as ruinous to public credit.

It is inconsistent with justice, because in the first place, it is a breach of contract; in violation of the rights of a fair purchaser.

The nature of the contract in its origin, is, that the public will pay the sum expressed in the security, to the first holder, or his *assignee*. The *intent*, in making the security assignable, is, that the proprietor may be able to make use of his property, by selling it for as much as it *may be worth in the market*, and that the buyer may be *safe* in the purchase.

Every buyer therefore stands exactly in the place of the seller, has the same right with him to the identical sum expressed in the security, and having acquired that right, by fair purchase, and in conformity to the original *agreement* and *intention* of the government, his claim cannot be disputed, without manifest injustice.

That he is to be considered as a fair purchaser, results from this: Whatever necessity the seller may have been under, was occasioned by the government, in not making a proper provision for its debts. The buyer had no agency in it, and therefore ought not to suffer. He is not even chargeable with having taken an undue advantage. He paid what the commodity was worth in the market, and took the risks of reimbursement upon himself. He of course gave a fair equivalent, and ought to reap the benefit of his hazard; a hazard which was far from inconsiderable, and which, perhaps, turned on little less than a revolution in government.

That the case of those, who parted with their securities from necessity, is a hard one, cannot be denied. But whatever complaint of injury, or claim of redress, they may have, respects the government solely. They have not only nothing to object to the persons who relieved their necessities, by giving them the current price of their property, but they are even under an implied condition to contribute to the reimbursement of those persons. They knew, that by the terms of the contract with themselves, the public were bound to pay to those, to whom they should convey their title, the sums stipulated to be paid to them; and, that as citizens of the United States, they were to bear their proportion of the contribution for that purpose. This, by the act of assignment, they tacitly engage to do; and if they had an option, they could not, with integrity or good faith, refuse to do it, without the consent of those to whom they sold.

Hamilton's most controversial recommendation concerned the federal assumption of states' debts. Seemingly a boon to the states' treasuries, assumption raised a red flag to states protective of their hegemony, and the hackles of states that had essentially paid their debts. The latter included Virginia. This issue would dominate Hamilton's efforts for the first year of his term at the helm of the Treasury.

The Secretary, after mature reflection on this point, entertains a full conviction, that an assumption of the debts of the particular states by the union, and a like provision for them, as for those of the union, will be a measure of sound policy and substantial justice.

It would, in the opinion of the Secretary, contribute, in an eminent degree, to an orderly, stable and satisfactory arrangement of the national finances.

Admitting, as ought to be the case, that a provision must be made in some way or other, for the entire debt; it will follow, that no greater revenues will be required, whether that provision be made wholly by the United States, or partly by them, and partly by the states separately.

The principal question then must be, whether such a provision cannot be more conveniently and effectually made, by one general plan issuing from one authority, than by different plans originating in different authorities.

In the first case there can be no competition for resources; in the last, there must be such a competition. The consequences of this, without the greatest caution on both sides, might be interfering regulations, and thence collision and confusion. Particular branches of industry might also be oppressed by it. The most productive objects of revenue are not numerous. Either these must be wholly engrossed by one side, which might lessen the efficacy of the provisions by the other; or both must have recourse to the same objects in different modes, which might occasion an accumulation upon them, beyond what they could properly bear....

If all the public creditors receive their dues from one source, distributed with an equal hand, their interest will be the same. And having the same interests, they will unite in the support of the fiscal arrangements of the government: As these, too, can be made with more convenience, where there is no competition: These circumstances combined will insure to the revenue laws a more ready and more satisfactory execution....

There are several reasons, which render it probable, that the situation of the state creditors would be worse, than that of the creditors of the union, if there be not a national assumption of the state debts. Of these it will be sufficient to mention two; one, that a principal branch of revenue is exclusively vested in the union; the other, that a state must always be checked in the imposition of taxes on articles of consumption, from the want of power to extend the same regulation to the other states, and from the tendency of partial duties to injure its industry and commerce. Should the state creditors stand upon a less eligible footing than the others, it is unnatural to expect they would see with pleasure a provision for them. The influence which their dissatisfaction might have, could not but operate injuriously, both for the creditors, and the credit, of the United States.

Hence it is even the interest of the creditors of the union, that those of the individual states should be comprehended in a general provision. Any attempt to secure to the former either exclusive or peculiar advantages, would materially hazard their interests.

Hamilton's recommendations raised an inevitable question, still familiar in the halls of Congress today: where will the money come from? The money to pay domestic creditors from the old system was to be funded by the new government securities he argued for above. Here his answer pertains to interest payments on the foreign debt. Ironically, the chief sources of revenue he proposes are the very taxes that started American colonists and Hamilton on the path to revolution: taxes on whiskey, tea, and coffee.

This sum may, in the opinion of the Secretary, be obtained from the present duties on imports and tonnage, with the additions, which, without any possible disadvantage either to trade, or agriculture, may be made on wines, spirits, including those distilled within the United States, teas and coffee.

The Secretary conceives, that it will be sound policy, to carry the duties upon articles of this kind, as high as will be consistent with the practicability of a safe collection. This will lessen the necessity, both of having recourse to direct taxation, and of accumulating duties where they would be more inconvenient to trade, and upon objects, which are more to be regarded as necessaries of life.

That the articles which have been enumerated, will, better than most others, bear high duties, can hardly be a question. They are all of them, in reality—luxuries—the greatest part of them foreign luxuries; some of them, in the excess in which they are used, pernicious luxuries. And there is, perhaps, none of them, which is not consumed in so great abundance, as may, justly, denominate it, a source of national extravagance and impoverishment. The consumption of ardent spirits particularly, no doubt very much on account of their cheapness, is carried to an extreme, which is truly to be regretted, as well in regard to the health and the morals, as to the economy of the community.

Should the increase of duties tend to a decrease of the consumption of those articles, the effect would be, in every respect desirable. The saving which it would occasion, would leave individuals more at their ease, and promote a more favourable balance of trade. As far as this decrease might be applicable to distilled spirits, it would encourage the substitution of ciyder and malt liquors, benefit agriculture, and open a new and productive source of revenue.

It is not however, probable, that this decrease would be in a degree, which would frustrate the expected benefit to the revenue from raising the duties. Experience has shewn, that luxuries of every kind, lay the strongest hold on the attachments of mankind, which, especially when confirmed by habit, are not easily alienated from them.

Hamilton warns against profligacy before suggesting one further source of revenue for the government: the post office.

Persuaded as the Secretary is, that the proper funding of the present debt, will render it a national blessing: Yet he is so far from acceding to the position, in the latitude in which it is sometimes laid down, that "public debts are public benefits," a position inviting to prodigality, and liable to dangerous abuse,—that he ardently wishes to see it incorporated, as a fundamental maxim, in the system of public credit of the United States, that the creation of debt should always be accompanied with the means of extinguishment. This he regards as the true secret for rendering public credit immortal. And he presumes, that it is difficult to conceive a situation, in which there may not be an adherence to the maxim. At least he feels an unfeigned solicitude, that this may be attempted by the United States, and that they may commence their measures for the establishment of credit, with the observance of it.

Under this impression, the Secretary proposes, that the nett product of the post-office, to a sum not exceeding one million of dollars, be vested in commissioners, to consist of the Vice-President of the United States or President of the Senate, the Speaker of the House of Representatives, the Chief Justice, Secretary of the Treasury and Attorney-General of the United States, for the time being, in trust, to be applied, by them, or any three of them, to the discharge of the existing public debt, either by purchases of stock in the market, or by payments on account of the principal, as shall appear to them most adviseable, in conformity to the public engagements; to continue so vested, until the whole of the debt shall be discharged.[9]

Hamilton was surprised by the vehemence of opposition by his former ally James Madison to the federal assumption of states' debts. Hamilton might have been equally surprised by the softer stance of the enigmatic Thomas Jefferson. Jefferson had recently returned from his post as minister to France to become the first secretary of state, and Hamilton had given an enthusiastic reception to Jefferson's proposal for a system of standardized weights and measures—a pet project of the multidiscipline inventor. What followed was one of the most pivotal,

A stipple engraving of Thomas Jefferson (1743–1826) from 1800, the year
that Jefferson was elected to the presidency.

fabled, and mysterious events in American history: a private dinner
of the three men at Jefferson's home during which Hamilton persuaded
Madison to accept federal assumption in exchange for relocating the
nation's capitol to the mouth of the Potomac River, the northern border
of both Madison and Jefferson's home state of Virginia. (Many New
Yorkers believed that Hamilton had given away the store.)

The linchpin of Hamilton's plan was in place. Now he needed a
central bank in order to maintain and augment the flow of capital.
So Hamilton followed the first report on public credit with the report
on a national bank. Essentially, Hamilton argues that the developed
countries of the day use central banks to enhance the amount and flow
of capital, keep interest rates down, and serve as reserves available to
the government in the event of a war or other calamity.

It is a fact well understood, that public Banks have found admission and patronage among the principal and most enlightened commercial nations. They have successively obtained in Italy, Germany, Holland, England and France, as well as in the United States. And it is a circumstance, which cannot but have considerable weight, in a candid estimate of their tendency, that after an experience of centuries, there exists not a question about their util[ity] in the countries in which they have been so long established. Theorists and men of business unite in the acknowlegment of it....

The following are among the principal advantages of a Bank.

First. The augmentation of the active or productive capital of a country. Gold and Silver, when they are employed merely as the instruments of exchange and alienation, have been not improperly denominated dead Stock; but when deposited in Banks, to become the basis of a paper circulation, which takes their character and place, as the signs or representatives of value, they then acquire life, or, in other words, an active and productive quality. This idea, which appears rather subtil and abstract, in a general form, may be made obvious and palpable, by entering into a few particulars. It is evident, for instance, that the money, which a merchant keeps in his chest, waiting for a favourable opportunity to employ it, produces nothing 'till that opportunity arrives. But if instead of locking it up in this manner, he either deposits it in a Bank, or invests it in the Stock of a Bank, it yields a profit, during the interval; in which he partakes, or not, according to the choice he may have made of being a depositor or a proprietor; and when any advantageous speculation offers, in order to be able to embrace it, he has only to withdraw his money, if a depositor, or if a proprietor to obtain a loan from the Bank, or to dispose of his Stock; an alternative seldom or never attended with difficulty, when the affairs of the institution are in a prosperous train. His money thus deposited or invested, is a fund, upon which himself and others can borrow to a much larger amount....

The same circumstances illustrate the truth of the position, that it is one of the properties of Banks to increase the active capital of a country. This, in other words is the sum of them. The money of one individual, while he is waiting for an opportunity to employ it, by being either deposited in the Bank for safe keeping, or invested in its Stock, is in a condition to administer to the wants of others, without being put out of his own reach, when occasion presents. This yields an extra profit, arising from what is paid for the use of his money by others, when he could not himself make use of it; and keeps the money itself in a state of incessant activity. In the almost infinite vicissitudes and competitions of mercantile enterprise, there never can be danger of an intermission of demand, or that the money will remain for a moment idle in the vaults of the Bank. This additional employment given to money, and the faculty of a bank to lend and circulate a greater sum than the amount of its stock in coin are to all the purposes of trade and industry an absolute increase of capital. Purchases and undertakings, in general, can be carried on by any given sum of bank paper or credit, as effectually as by an equal sum of gold and silver. And thus by contributing to enlarge the mass of industrious and commercial enterprise, banks become nurseries of national wealth: a consequence, as satisfactorily verified by experience, as it is clearly deducible in theory.

Secondly. Greater facility to the Government in obtaining pecuniary aids, especially in sudden emergencies. This is another and an undisputed advantage of public banks: one, which as already remarked, has been realised in signal instances, among ourselves. The reason is obvious: The capitals of a great number of individuals are, by this operation, collected to a point, and placed under one direction. The mass, formed by this union, is in a certain sense magnified by the credit attached to it: And while this mass is always ready, and can at once be put in motion, in aid of the Government, the interest of the bank to afford that aid, independent of regard to the public safety and welfare, is a sure pledge for its disposition to go as far in its compliances, as can in prudence be desired. There is in the nature of things, as will be more particularly noticed in another place, an intimate connection of interest between the government and the Bank of a Nation.

Interestingly, Hamilton argues against government control of the national bank.

Considerations of public advantage suggest a further wish, which is, that the Bank could be established upon principles, that would cause the profits of it to redound to the immediate benefit of the State. This is contemplated by many, who speak of a National Bank, but the idea seems liable to insuperable objections. To attach full confidence to an institution of this nature, it appears to be an essential ingredient in its structure, that it shall be under a *private* not a *public* Direction, under the guidance of *individual interest*, not of *public policy;* which would be supposed to be, and in certain emergencies, under a feeble or too sanguine administration would, really, be, liable to being too much influenced by *public necessity.* The suspicion of this would most probably be a canker, that would continually corrode the vitals of the credit of the Bank, and would be most likely to prove fatal in those situations, in which the public good would require, that they should be most sound and vigorous. It would indeed be little less, than a miracle, should the credit of the Bank be at the disposal of the Government, if in a long series of time, there was not experienced a calamitous abuse of it. It is true, that it would be the real interest of the Government not to abuse it; its genuine policy to husband and cherish it with the most guarded circumspection as an inestimable treasure. But what Government ever uniformly consulted its true interest, in opposition to the temptations of momentary exigencies? What nation was ever blessed with a constant succession of upright and wise Administrators?

The keen, steady, and, as it were, magnetic sense, of their own interest, as proprietors, in the Directors of a Bank, pointing invariably to its true pole, the prosperity of the institution, is the only security, that can always be relied upon, for a careful and prudent administration. It is therefore the only basis on which an enlightened, unqualified and permanent confidence can be expected to be erected and maintained.[10]

Two of President Washington's cabinet members—Attorney General Edmund Randolph and Secretary of State Thomas Jefferson, together with Jefferson's close ally James Madison—challenged the constitutionality of Hamilton's bank plan on the grounds that no provision had been made in the Constitution for creating corporations, and further, that a national bank was an incursion into the affairs of the individual states. They advised Washington to veto it. Hamilton responded with "An Opinion on the Constitutionality of an Act to Establish a Bank," a fifteen-thousand-word essay dashed off by Hamilton in a few nights.

In it he established the principle of "implied powers" in constitutional law. Unsurprisingly, Hamilton argues for a "liberal latitude to the exercise of the specified powers" of the federal government.

In entering upon the argument it ought to be premised, that the objections of the Secretary of State and Attorney General are founded on a general denial of the authority of the United States to erect corporations. The latter indeed expressly admits, that if there be any thing in the bill which is not warranted by the constitution, it is the clause of incorporation.

Now it appears to the Secretary of the Treasury, that this *general principle* is *inherent* in the very *definition* of *Government* and *essential* to every step of the progress to be made by that of the United States; namely—that every power vested in a Government is in its nature *sovereign*, and includes by *force* of the *term*, a right to employ all the *means* requisite, and fairly *applicable* to the attainment of the *ends* of such power; and which are not precluded by restrictions & exceptions specified in the constitution; or not immoral, or not contrary to the essential ends of political society.

This principle in its application to Government in general would be admitted as an axiom. And it will be incumbent upon those, who may incline to deny it, to *prove* a distinction; and to shew that a rule which in the general system of things is essential to the preservation of the social order is inapplicable to the United States.

The circumstances that the powers of sovereignty are in this country divided between the National and State Governments, does not afford the distinction required. It does not follow from this, that each of the *portions* of powers delegated to the one or to the other is not sovereign *with regard to its proper objects*. It will only *follow* from it, that each has sovereign power as to *certain things*, and not as to *other things*. To deny that the Government of the United States has sovereign power as to its declared purposes & trusts, because its power does not extend to all cases, would be equally to deny, that the State Governments have sovereign power in any case; because their power does not extend to every case. The tenth section of the first article of the constitution exhibits a long list of very important things which they may not do. And thus the United States would furnish the singular spectacle of a *political society* without *sovereignty*, or of a people *governed* without *government*....

It is certain, that neither the grammatical, nor popular sense of the term requires that construction. According to both, *necessary* often means no more than *needful, requisite, incidental, useful*, or *conducive to*. It is a common mode of expression to say, that it is *necessary* for a government or a person to do this or that thing, when nothing more is intended or understood, than that the interests of the government or person require, or will be promoted, by the doing of this or that thing. The imagination can be at no loss for exemplifications of the use of the word in this sense.

And it is the true one in which it is to be understood as used in the constitution. The whole turn of the clause containing it, indicates, that it was the intent of the convention, by that clause to give a liberal latitude to the exercise of the specified powers. The expressions have peculiar comprehensiveness. They are—"to make *all laws*, necessary & proper for *carrying into execution* the foregoing powers & all *other powers* vested by the constitution in the *government* of the United States, or in any *department* or *officer* thereof." To understand the word as the Secretary of State does, would be to depart from its obvious & popular sense, and to give it a *restrictive* operation; an idea never before entertained. It would be to give it the same force as if the word *absolutely* or *indispensibly* had been prefixed to it.

Such a construction would beget endless uncertainty & embarassment. The cases must be palpable & extreme in which it could be pronounced with certainty, that a measure was absolutely necessary, or one without which the exercise of a given power would be nugatory. There are few measures of any government, which would stand so severe a test. To insist upon it, would be to make the criterion of the exercise of any implied power a *case of extreme necessity;* which is rather a rule to justify the overleaping of the bounds of constitutional authority, than to govern the ordinary exercise of it.

It may be truly said of every government, as well as of that of the United States, that it has only a right, to pass such laws as are necessary & proper to accomplish the objects intrusted to it. For no government has a right to do *merely what it pleases.* Hence by a process of reasoning similar to that of the Secretary of State, it might be proved, that neither of the State governments has a right to incorporate a bank. It might be shewn, that all the public business of the State, could be performed without a bank, and inferring thence that it was unnecessary it might be argued that it could not be done, because it is against the rule which has been just mentioned. A like mode of reasoning would prove, that there was no power to incorporate the Inhabitants of a town, with a view to a more perfect police: For it is certain, that an incorporation may be dispensed with, though it is better to have one. It is to be remembered, that there is no *express* power in any State constitution to erect corporations.

The *degree* in which a measure is necessary, can never be a test of the *legal* right to adopt it. That must ever be a matter of opinion; and can only be a test of expediency. The *relation* between the *measure* and the *end*, between the *nature* of *the mean* employed towards the execution of a power and the object of that power, must be the criterion of constitutionality not the more or less of *necessity* or *utility*.[11]

On February 25, 1791, Washington signed the bill creating the national bank into law. Dogged in his efforts to ensure the nation's economic future, Hamilton drafted a report on creating a national mint about a week after his defense of the constitutionality of a national bank. The mint was created by an act of Congress in early 1792, closely following Hamilton's plans. Next, Hamilton turned his attention to another subject near to his heart: commerce.

The "Report on the Subject of Manufactures," issued December 5, 1791, was the result of an intensive, yearlong effort by Hamilton to survey the state of existing industries in the United States. Hamilton reasoned that in order to survive and compete with the European powers, it was in the United States' interest to develop a strong manufacturing base. Here he seeks to assuage the fears of agrarian interests with a promise of a general and mutual prosperity—a rising tide will lift all boats.

It is not uncommon to meet with an opin[ion] that though the promoting of manufactures may be the interest of a part of the Union, it is contrary to that of another part. The Northern & southern regions are sometimes represented as having adverse interests in this respect. Those are called Manufacturing, these Agricultural states; and a species of opposition is imagined to subsist between the Manufacturing [and] Agricultural interests.

This idea of an opposition between those two interests is the common error of the early periods of every country, but experience gradually dissipates it. Indeed they are perceived so often to succour and to befriend each other, that they come at length to be considered as one: a supposition which has been frequently abused and is not universally true. Particular encouragements of particular manufactures may be of a Nature to sacrifice the interests of landholders to those of manufacturers; But it is nevertheless a maxim well established by experience, and generally acknowledged, where there has been sufficient experience, that the *aggregate* prosperity of manufactures, and the *aggregate* prosperity of Agriculture are intimately connected. In the Course of the discussion which has had place, various weighty considerations have been adduced operating in support of that maxim. Perhaps the superior steadiness of the demand of a domestic market for the surplus produce of the soil, is alone a convincing argument of its truth.

Ideas of a contrariety of interests between the Northern and southern regions of the Union, are in the Main as unfounded as they are mischievous. The diversity of Circumstances on which such contrariety is usually predicated, authorises a directly contrary conclusion. Mutual wants constitute one of the strongest links of political connection, and the extent of the[se] bears a natural proportion to the diversity in the means of mutual supply.

Suggestions of an opposite complexion are ever to be deplored, as unfriendly to the steady pursuit of one great common cause, and to the perfect harmony of all the parts.

In proportion as the mind is accustomed to trace the intimate connexion of interest, which subsists between all the parts of a Society united under the *same* government—the infinite variety of channels which serve to Circulate the prosper[ity] of each to and through the rest—in that proportion will it be little apt to be disturbed by solicitudes and Apprehensions which originate in local discriminations. It is a truth as important as it is agreeable, and one to which it is not easy to imagine exceptions, that every thing tending to establish *substantial* and *permanent order*, in the affairs of a Country, to increase the total mass of industry and opulence, is ultimately beneficial to every part of it. On the Credit of this great truth, an acquiescence may safely be accorded, from every quarter, to all institutions & arrangements, which promise a confirmation of public order, and an augmentation of National Resource.

Hamilton enumerates eleven points for the cultivation of industry in the United States, many of which have become standard features of the American financial system. Among them are instituting prohibitions on the export of the materials of manufacturing (that is, proprietary machinery and methods); the exemption of these materials from import duties; the "encouragement of inventions and discoveries," particularly those pertaining to machinery (that is, through what eventually became a patent office); and a system of regulations and inspections governing manufactured goods. Perhaps none had greater impact on the development of the economy than his call for improving inland transportation.

The symptoms of attention to the improvement of inland Navigation, which have lately appeared in some quarters, must fill with pleasure every breast warmed with a true Zeal for the prosperity of the Country. These examples, it is to be hoped, will stimulate the exertions of the Government and the Citizens of every state. There can certainly be no object, more worthy of the cares of the local administrations; and it were to be wished, that there was no doubt of the power of the national Government to lend its direct aid, on a comprehensive plan. This is one of those improvements, which could be prosecuted with more efficacy by the whole, than by any part or parts of the Union. There are cases in which the general interest will be in danger to be sacrificed to the collission of some supposed local interests. Jealousies, in matters of this kind, are as apt to exist, as they are apt to be erroneous.

The following remarks are sufficiently judicious and pertinent to deserve a literal quotation. "Good roads, canals, and navigable rivers, by diminishing the expence of carriage, put the *remote parts of a country* more nearly upon a level with those in the neighborhood of the town. They are *upon that account* the greatest of all improvements. They encourage the cultivation of the remote, which must always be the most extensive circle of the country. They are advantageous to the Town by breaking down the monopoly of the country in its neighborhood. They are advantageous *even to that part of the Country.* Though they introduce some rival commodities into the old Market, they open many new markets to its produce. Monopoly besides is a great enemy to good management, which can never be universally established, but in consequence of that free and universal competition, which forces every body to have recourse to it for the sake of self defence. It is not more than Fifty years ago that *some of the countries in the neighborhood of London petitioned the Parliament, against the extension of the turnpike roads, into the remoter counties.*

Those remoter counties, they pretended, from the cheapness of Labor, would be able to sell their grass and corn cheaper in the London Market, than themselves, and they would thereby reduce their rents and ruin their cultivation. Their rents however have risen and their cultivation has been improved, since that time."

Hamilton details his proposal for a system of protective tariffs and industry-specific subsidies with the goal of nurturing native industries. He presents an almost preposterously thorough, industry-by-industry survey, with specific recommendations for each. The thread that runs through all of them is a vision of abundance and vast potential thanks to a combination of nearly unlimited natural resources and the industriousness of the American people. Here is his proposal for the wool industry:

In a country, the climate of which partakes of so considerable a proportion of winter, as that of a great part of the United States, the woolen branch cannot be regarded, as inferior to any, which relates to the cloathing of the inhabitants.

Household manufactures of this material are carried on, in different parts of the United States, to a very interesting extent; but there is only one branch, which, as a regular business, can be said to have acquired maturity. This is the making of hats.

Hats of wool, and of wool mixed with furr, are made in large quantities, in different States; & nothing seems wanting, but an adequate supply of materials, to render the manufacture commensurate with the demand.

A promising essay, towards the fabrication of cloths, cassimires and other woolen goods, is likewise going on at *Hartford* in Connecticut. Specimens of the different kinds which are made, in the possession of the Secretary, evince that these fabrics have attained a very considerable degree of perfection. Their quality certainly surpasses anything, that could have been looked for, in so short a time, and under so great disadvantages; and conspires with the scantiness of the means, which have been at the command of the directors, to form the eulogium of that public spirit, perseverance and judgment, which have been able to accomplish so much.

To cherish and bring to maturity this precious embryo must engage the most ardent wishes—and proportionable regret, as far as the means of doing it may appear difficult or uncertain.

Measures, which should tend to promote an abundant supply of wool, of good quality, would probably afford the most efficacious aid, that present circumstances permit.

To encourage the raising and improving the breed of sheep, at home, would certainly be the most desireable expedient, for that purpose; but it may not be alone sufficient, especially as it is yet a problem, whether our wool be capable of such a degree of improvement, as to render it fit for the finer fabrics.

Premiums would probably be found the best means of promoting the domestic, and bounties the foreign supply. The first may be within the compass of the institution hereafter to be submitted—The last would require a specific legislative provision. If any bounties are granted they ought of course to be adjusted with an eye to quality, as well as quantity.

Hamilton recognizes that the growth of industry will create the need for more labor. One of his suggested solutions, perfectly acceptable in the context of eighteenth-century mores and practices, might raise a few eyebrows today.

The husbandman himself experiences a new source of profit and support from the encreased industry of his wife and daughters; invited and stimulated by the demands of the neighboring manufactories.

Besides this advantage of occasional employment to classes having different occupations, there is another of a nature allied to it [and] of a similar tendency. This is—the employment of persons who would otherwise be idle (and in many cases a burthen on the community), either from the byass of temper, habit, infirmity of body, or some other cause, indisposing, or disqualifying them for the toils of the Country. It is worthy of particular remark, that, in general, women and Children are rendered more useful and the latter more early useful by manufacturing establishments, than they would otherwise be.[12]

Hamilton's reassurances that nurturing industry would not harm agrarian interests and would, in fact, help them, failed to win over his opponents. The proposal only served to accelerate the rift that was developing between Hamilton on the one hand and Jefferson and Madison—representatives of an agrarian state and region—on the other. Jefferson's antipathy for the national bank in particular was so virulent that he suggested to a state official that any Virginia bank found to be cooperating with Hamilton's First Bank of the United States be charged with treason.

It was abundantly clear to Hamilton that the first order of business was to insure the continued place of George Washington as the head of state. Washington, in ill health, hard of hearing, and never enamored of public life, longed to return to his estate in Mount Vernon. In a letter written in midsummer in 1792, Hamilton used personal charm and political shrewdness to persuade Washington to postpone retirement once again.

To George Washington:

[Philadelphia, July 30–August 3, 1792]

I received the most sincere pleasure at finding in our last conversation, that there was some relaxation in the disposition you had before discovered to decline a reelection. Since your departure, I have lost no opportunity of sounding the opinions of persons, whose opinions were worth knowing, on these two points—1st the effect of your declining upon the public affairs, and upon your own reputation—2dly the effect of your continuing, in reference to the declarations you have made of your disinclination to public life—And I can truly say, that I have not found the least difference of sentiment, on either point. The impression is uniform—that your declining would be to be deplored as the greatest evil, that could befall the country at the present juncture, and as critically hazardous to your own reputation—that your continuance will be justified in the mind of every friend to his country by the evident necessity for it...

I trust, Sir, and I pray God that you will determine to make a further sacrifice of your tranquillity and happiness to the public good. I trust that it need not continue above a year or two more—And I think that it will be more eligibible to retire from office before the expiration of the term of an election, than to decline a reelection.

The sentiments I have delivered upon this occasion, I can truly say, proceed exclusively from an anxious concern for the public welfare and an affectionate personal attachment. These dispositions must continue to govern in every vicissitude.[13]

James Madison (1751–1836), shown in an early nineteenth-century lithograph.

Jefferson stepped up his attacks on Hamilton, frequently through proxies. A newspaper closely allied with Jefferson, the National Gazette, *published a series of attacks on Hamilton and his policies. The publisher of the paper, Philip Freneau, had recently been hired by Thomas Jefferson as a translator for the State Department. Hamilton smelled a rat and wrote as much in a series of pseudonymous letters published between August and October 1792.*

Mr. Freneau is not then, as he would have supposed, the Independent Editor of a News Paper, who though receiving a salary from Government has firmness enough to expose its maladministration. He is the faithful and devoted servant of the head of a party, from whose hand he receives the boon. The whole complexion of his paper is an exact copy of the politics of his employer foreign and domestic, and exhibits a decisive internal evidence of the influence of that patronage under which he acts.

Whether the services rendered by him are an equivalent for the compensation he receives is best known to his employer and himself. There is however some room for doubt. Tis well known that his employer is himself well acquainted with the French language; the only one of which he is the translator; and it may be a question how often his aid is necessary.

It is somewhat singular too that a man acquainted with but one foreign language engaged in a particular trade, which it may be presumed occupies his whole time and attention, the Editor of a News Paper, should be the person selected as the Clerk for foreign languages, in the department of the United States for foreign affairs. Could no person have been found acquainted with more than one foreign language, and who, in so confidential a trust, could have been regularly attached to, in the constant employ of the department and immediately under the eye of the head of it?

But it may be asked—Is it possible that Mr. Jefferson, the head of a principal department of the Government can be the Patron of a Paper, the evident object of which is to decry the Government and its measures? If he disapproves of the Government itself and thinks it deserving of opposition, could he reconcile to his own personal dignity and the principles of probity to hold an office under it and employ the means of official influence in that opposition? If he disapproves of the leading measures, which have been adopted in the course of its administration, could he reconcile it with the principles of delicacy and propriety to continue to hold a place in that administration, and at the same time to be instrumental in vilifying measures which have been adopted by majorities of both branches of the Legislature and *sanctionned by the Chief Magistrate of the Union?*[14]

Washington, frustrated by the growing rift in his cabinet, demanded a stop to the hostilities. Hamilton responded in a letter on September 9, 1792. Hamilton recognizes the burden on Washington of a divided cabinet, and offers to "cheerfully acquiesce" in order to avoid a feud. But he leaves no doubt about whom he considers the injured party to be, and uses his personal relationship with Washington to great advantage.

[Philadelphia, September 9, 1792]

I most sincerely regret the causes of the uneasy sensations you experience. It is my most anxious wish, as far as may depend upon me, to smooth the path of your administration, and to render it prosperous and happy. And if any prospect shall open of healing or terminating the differences which exist, I shall most chearfully embrace it; though I consider myself as the deeply injured party. The recommendation of such a spirit is worthy of the moderation and wisdom which dictated it; and if your endeavours should prove unsuccessful, I do not hesitate to say that in my opinion the period is not remote when the public good will require *substitutes* for the *differing members* of your administration. The continuance of a division there must destroy the energy of Government, which will be little enough with the strictest Union. On my part there will be a most chearful acquiescence in such a result.

I trust, Sir, that the greatest frankness has always marked and will always mark every step of my conduct towards you.

In this disposition, I cannot conceal from you that I have had some instrumentality of late in the retaliations which have fallen upon certain public characters and that I find myself placed in a situation not to be able to recede *for the present*.

I considered myself as compelled to this conduct by reasons public as well as personal of the most cogent nature. I *know* that I have been an object of uniform opposition from Mr. Jefferson, from the first moment of his coming to the City of New York to enter upon his present office. I *know*, from the most authentic sources, that I have been the frequent subject of the most unkind whispers and insinuating from the same quarter. I have long seen a formed party in the Legislature, under his auspices, bent upon my subversion. I cannot doubt, from the evidence I possess, that the National Gazette was instituted by him for political purposes and that one leading object of it has been to render me and all the measures connected with my department as odious as possible.

Nevertheless I can truly say, that, except explanations to confidential friends, I never directly or indirectly retaliated or countenanced retaliation till very lately. I can even assure you, that I was instrumental in preventing a very severe and system- atic attack upon Mr. Jefferson, by an association of two or three individuals, in consequence of the persecution, which he brought upon the Vice President, by his indiscreet and light letter to the Printer, transmitting *Paine's* pamphlet....

...Nevertheless I pledge my honor to you Sir, that if you shall here-after form a plan to reunite the members of your administration, upon some steady principle of cooperation, I will faithfully concur in executing it during my continuance in office. And I will not directly or indirectly say or do a thing, that shall endanger a feud.[15]

Hamilton's frame of mind during this period is best depicted in a letter he wrote to his friend and former Continental Army officer, Edward Carrington, near its beginning, in May 1792, before the hostilities had become overt. The letter is notable both for its seemingly frank assessment of Hamilton's emotional duress and for its concise summation of his opinions on the vital issues of the day. Hamilton expresses bewilderment over Madison's apparent change of heart, and interestingly, attributes Jefferson's hostility to Hamilton's plans to his having been absent from the country during the "imbecilities" of the Confederation period and to Jefferson's having lived in France, but seeing the French government "only on the side of its abuses."

To Edward Carrington:

[Philadelphia, May 26, 1792]

Believing that I possess a share of your personal friendship and confidence and yielding to that which I feel towards you—persuaded also that our political creed is the same on *two essential points*, 1st the necessity of *Union* to the respectability and happiness of this Country and 2 the necessity of an *efficient* general government to maintain that Union—I have concluded to unbosom myself to you on the present state of political parties and views. I ask no reply to what I shall say. I only ask that you will be persuaded, the representations I shall make are agreeable to the real and sincere impressions of my mind. You will make the due allowances for the influence of circumstances upon it—you will consult your own observations and you will draw such a conclusion as shall appear to you proper.

When I accepted the Office, I now hold, it was under a full persuasion, that from similarity of thinking, conspiring with per-

sonal goodwill, I should have the firm support of Mr. Madison, in
the *general course* of my administration. Aware of the intrinsic dif-
ficultties of the situation and of the powers of Mr. Madison, I do
not believe I should have accepted under a different supposition.

I have mentioned the similarity of thinking between that
Gentleman and myself. This was relative not merely to the
general principles of National Policy and Government but to
the leading points which were likely to constitute questions in
the administration of the finances. I mean 1 the expediency of
funding the debt 2 the inexpediency of *discrimination* between
original and present holders 3 The expediency of *assuming* the
state Debts....

Under these circumstances, you will naturally imagine that it
must have been [a] matter of surprize to me, when I was apprised,
that it was Mr. Madison's intention to oppose my plan on both
the last mentioned points....

It was not 'till the last session that I became unequivocally
convinced of the following truth—"*That Mr. Madison cooperating with Mr. Jefferson is at the head of a faction decidedly hostile to
me and my administration, and actuated by views in my judgment
subversive of the principles of good government and dangerous to the
union, peace and happiness of the Country.*"...

These are strong expressions; they may pain your friendship
for one or both of the Gentlemen whom I have named. I have not
lightly resolved to hazard them. They are the result of a *Serious
alarm* in my mind for the public welfare, and of a full conviction
that what I have alledged is a truth, and a truth, which ought to
be told and well attended to, by all the friends of Union and efficient National Government. The suggestion will, I hope, at least
awaken attention, free from the byass of former prepossessions.

In various conversations with *foreigners* as well as citizens, [Jefferson] has thrown censure on my *principles* of government and on my measures of administration. He has predicted that the people would not long tolerate my proceedings & that I should not long maintain my ground. Some of those, whom he *immediately* and *notoriously* moves, have *even* whispered suspicions of the rectitude of my motives and conduct. In the question concerning the Bank he not only delivered an opinion in writing against its constitutionality & expediency; but he did it *in a stile and manner* which I felt as partaking of asperity and ill humour towards me....

I find a strong confirmation in the following circumstances. *Freneau* the present Printer of the National Gazette, who was a journeyman with Childs & Swain at New York, was a known anti-federalist. It is reduced to a certainty that he was brought to Philadelphia by Mr. Jefferson to be the conductor of a News Paper. It is notorious that contemporarily with the commencement of his paper he was a Clerk in the department of state for foreign languages. Hence a clear inference that his paper has been set on foot and is conducted under the patronage & not against the views of Mr. Jefferson. What then is the complexion of this paper? Let any impartial man peruse all the numbers down to the present day; and I never was more mistaken, if he does not pronounce that it is a paper devoted to the subversion of me & the measures in which I have had an Agency; and I am little less mistaken if he do not pronounce that it is a paper of a tendency *generally unfriendly* to the Government of the U States....

In respect to our foreign politics the views of these Gentlemen are in my judgment equally unsound & dangerous. *They have a womanish attachment to France and a womanish resentment against Great Britain.* They would draw us into the closest embrace of the former & involve us in all the consequences of her politics, & they would risk the peace of the country in their endeavours to keep us at the greatest possible distance from the latter. This disposition goes to a length particularly in Mr. Jefferson of which, till lately, I had no adequate Idea. Various circumstances prove to me that if these Gentlemen were left to pursue their own course there would be in less than six months *an open War between the U States & Great Britain.*...

Mr. Jefferson, it is known, did not in the first instance cordially acquiesce in the new constitution for the U States; he had many doubts & reserves. He left this Country before we had experienced the imbicillities of the former [that is, government under the Articles of Confederation].

In France he saw government only on the side of its abuses. He drank deeply of the French Philosophy, in Religion, in Science, in politics. He came from France in the moment of a fermentation which he had had a share in exciting, & in the passions and feelings of which he shared both from temperament and situation....

He came electrified *plus* with attachment to France and with the project of knitting together the two Countries in the closest political bands.

Mr. Madison had always entertained an exalted opinion of the talents, knowledge and virtues of Mr. Jefferson. The sentiment was probably reciprocal. A close correspondence subsisted between them during the time of Mr. Jefferson's absence from this country. A close intimacy arose upon his return....

In such a state of mind, both these Gentlemen are prepared to hazard a great deal to effect a change. Most of the important measures of every Government are connected with the Treasury. To subvert the present head of it they deem it expedient to risk

rendering the Government itself odious; perhaps foolishly thinking that they can easily recover the lost affections & confidence of
the people, and not appreciating as they ought to do the natural
resistance to Government which in every community results from
the human passions, the degree to which this is strengthened by
the *organised rivality* of State Governments, & the infinite danger
that the National Government once rendered odious will be kept
so by these powerful & indefatigable enemies.

They forget an old but a very just, though a coarse saying—
That it is much easier to raise the Devil than to lay him....

It is yet to be determined by experience whether [a republican
system] be consistent with that *stability* and *order* in Government
which are essential to public strength & private security and
happiness. On the whole, the only enemy which Republicanism has to fear in this Country is in the Spirit of faction and
anarchy. If this will not permit the ends of Government to be
attained under it—if it engenders disorders in the community,
all regular & orderly minds will wish for a change—and the
demagogues who have produced the disorder will make it for
their own aggrandizement. This is the old Story.

If I were disposed to promote Monarchy & overthrow State
Governments, I would mount the hobby horse of popularity—I
would cry out usurpation—danger to liberty &c. &c—I would
endeavour to prostrate the National Government—raise a ferment—and then "ride in the Whirlwind and direct the Storm."
That there are men acting with Jefferson & Madison who have
this in view I verily believe. I could lay my finger on some of
them. That Madison does *not* mean it I also verily believe, and
I rather believe the same of Jefferson; but I read him upon the
whole thus—"A man of profound ambition & violent passions."[16]

FOREIGN AFFAIRS, AND A FOOLISH ONE

★ ★ ★

In the midst of his campaign to establish a national bank and a manufacturing base in the United States, Hamilton had already begun courting Great Britain as a trading partner, engaging George Beckwith, Britain's unofficial representative (actually an aide to the governor-general of Canada), as early as 1789 and later, her new envoy to the United States, George Hammond. The violent turn that the French Revolution had taken confirmed Hamilton's worst fears about democracy, and in spite of his sympathies for Lafayette and other former French comrades-in-arms, he saw France as a potentially dangerous ally and trading partner for the United States.

With the cabinet and public opinion seeming to conform increasingly to Jefferson's view, and relations with Britain increasingly testy, Hamilton sent a letter to Washington resigning his post effective the following year. But then the tide turned: Following the execution of Louis XVI, the French revolutionary government declared war on Holland, Spain, and Great Britain, and demanded immediate payment of American war debts. At the same time, the French revolutionaries initiated a naval campaign against British merchant vessels engaged in trade with the United States.

Hamilton turned to his friend John Jay for advice, seeking an understanding of what, in this complicated situation, constituted "perfectly neutral" ground. He wished to communicate to the world at large the "pacific position" of the American government, and simultaneously to discourage United States citizens from provocations and hunger for war.

To John Jay:

[April 9, 1793]

The King has been decapitated. Out of this will arise a Regent, acknowledged and supported by the Powers of Europe almost universally—in capacity to Act and who may himself send an Ambassador to the United States. Should we in such case receive both? If we receive one from the Republic & refuse the other, shall we stand on ground perfectly neutral?

If we receive a Minister from the Republic, shall we be afterwards at liberty to say—"We will not decide whether there is a Government in France competent to demand from us the performance of the existing treaties. What the Government in France shall be is the very point *in dispute.* 'Till that is decided the *applicability* of the Treaties is suspended. When that Government is *established* we shall consider whether such changes have been made as to render their continuance incompatible with the interest of the U States." If we shall not have concluded ourselves by any Act, I am of opinion, that we have at least a right to hold the thing suspended till the point in dispute is decided. I doubt whether we could *bona fide* dispute the ultimate obligation of the Treaties. Will the unqualified reception of a Minister conclude us?

If it will ought we so to conclude ourselves?

Ought we not rather to refuse receiving or to receive with qualification—declaring that we receive the person as the representative of the Government *in fact* of the French Nation reserving to ourselves a right to consider the applicability of the Treaties to the *actual situation* of the parties?

These are questions which require our utmost Wisdom. I would give a great deal for a personal discussion with you. *Imprudent things* have been already done; which renders it proportionably important that every succeeding step should be well considered.[1]

Jay advised to say as little as possible and to avoid accepting an emissary from the regent unless and until he became the regent "de facto." The Americans received the revolutionary French government's minister, but neither side got much satisfaction. French privateers kept

An 1889 etching of John Jay (1745–1829).

attacking British ships. Not wishing to lose his chief source of excise revenue, and not wanting to be pulled into a war that the United States could ill afford, Hamilton counseled Washington to chart a course of neutrality in relations with the European powers.

When Washington issued the Neutrality Proclamation in April 1793, congressional Republicans immediately attacked the measure as a violation of the 1778 treaty of alliance with France and executive overreach. Hamilton defended the wisdom and legality of the proclamation, challenging the motives of the Republicans as a demagogic power grab, pure and simple.

The ground which has been so wisely taken by the Executive of the UStates, in regard to the present war of Europe against France, is to be the pretext of this mischievous attempt. The people are if possible to be made to believe, that the Proclamation of neutrality issued by the President of the US was unauthorised illegal and officious—inconsistent with the treaties and plighted faith of the Nation—inconsistent with a due sense of gratitude to France for the services rendered us in our late contest for independence and liberty—inconsistent with a due regard for the progress and success of republican principles. Already the presses begin to groan with invective against the Chief Magistrate of the Union, for that prudent and necessary measure; a measure calculated to manifest to the World the pacific position of the Government and to caution the citizens of the UStates against practices, which would tend to involve us in a War the most unequal and calamitous, in which it is possible for a Country to be engaged—a war which would not be unlikely to prove pregnant with still greater dangers and disasters, than that by which we established our existence as an Independent Nation.

What is the true solution of this extraordinary appearance? Are the professed the real motives of its authors? They are not. The true object is to disparage in the opinion and affections of his fellow citizens that man who at the head of our armies fought so successfully for the Liberty and Independence, which are now our pride and our boast—who during the war supported the hopes, united the hearts and nerved the arm of his countrymen—who at the close of it, unseduced by ambition & the love of power, soothed and appeased the discontents of his suffering companions in arms, and with them left the proud scenes of a victorious field for the modest retreats of private life—who could only have been drawn out of these favourite retreats, to aid in the glorious work of ingrafting that liberty, which his sword had contributed to win, upon a stock of which it stood in need and without which it could not flourish—endure—a firm adequate national Government—who at this moment sacrifices his tranquillity and every favourite pursuit to the peremptory call of his country to aid in giving solidity to a fabric, which he has assisted in rearing—whose whole conduct has been one continued proof of his rectitude moderation disinterestedness and patriotism, who whether the evidence of a uniform course of virtuous public actions be considered, or the motives likely to actuate a man placed precisely in his situation be estimated, it may safely be pronounced, can have no other ambition than that of doing good to his Country & transmitting his fame unimpaired to posterity. For what or for whom is he to hazard that rich harvest of glory, which he has acquired that unexampled veneration and love of his fellow Citizens, which he so eminently possesses?[2]

Hamilton saw the challenge to the proclamation not just as wrong-headed policy, but in its charge of executive overreach, as a challenge to

the Constitution itself. In a series of articles published under the name
"Pacificus," he countered these arguments, elucidating a delineation of
authority between the branches of government that still resonates in
twenty-first-century headlines concerning the use of executive orders
to implement policy. To Hamilton, the arguments for strong executive
authority are so "obvious" (to use his word) that he seems baffled at the
necessity of having to make them. So he painstakingly identifies the rel-
evant sections of the Constitution to make his case.

The inquiry then is—what department of the Government of the
UStates is the prop[er] one to make a declaration of Neutrality
in the cases in which the engagements [of] the Nation permit
and its interests require such a declaration.

A correct and well informed mind will discern at once that it
can belong neit[her] to the Legislative nor Judicial Department
and of course must belong to the Executive.

The Legislative Department is not the *organ* of intercourse
between the UStates and foreign Nations. It is charged neither
with *making* nor *interpreting* Treaties. It is therefore not naturally that Organ of the Government which is to pronounce the
existing condition of the Nation, with regard to foreign Powers,
or to admonish the Citizens of their obligations and duties as
founded upon that condition of things. Still less is it charged
with enforcing the execution and observance of these obligations
and those duties.

It is equally obvious that the act in question is foreign to the
Judiciary Department of the Government. The province of that
Department is to decide litigations in particular cases. It is indeed
charged with the interpretation of treaties; but it exercises this
function only in the litigated cases; that is where contending

parties bring before it a specific controversy. It has no concern
with pronouncing upon the external political relations of Treaties
between Government and Government. This position is too plain
to need being insisted upon.

It must then of necessity belong to the Executive Department
to exercise the function in Question—when a proper case for the
exercise of it occurs.

It appears to be connected with that department in various
capacities, as the *organ* of intercourse between the Nation and foreign Nations—as the interpreter of the National Treaties in those
cases in which the Judiciary is not competent, that is in the cases
between Government and Government—as that Power, which is
charged with the Execution of the Laws, of which Treaties form
a part—as that Power which is charged with the command and
application of the Public Force.

This view of the subject is so natural and obvious—so analo-
gous to general theory and practice—that no doubt can be entertained of its justness, unless such doubt can be deduced from
particular provisions of the Constitution of the UStates.

Let us see then if cause for such doubt is to be found in that
constitution.

The second Article of the Constitution of the UStates, section
1st, establishes this general Proposition, That "The EXECUTIVE
POWER shall be vested in a President of the United States of
America."

The same article in a succeeding Section proceeds to designate particular cases of Executive Power. It declares among
other things that the President shall be Commander in Cheif
of the army and navy of the UStates and of the Militia of the
several states when called into the actual service of the UStates,

that he shall have power by and with the advice of the senate to make treaties; that it shall be his duty to receive ambassadors and other public Ministers and to take care that the laws be faithfully executed.

It would not consist with the rules of sound construction to consider this enumeration of particular authorities as derogating from the more comprehensive grant contained in the general clause, further than as it may be coupled with express restrictions or qualifications; as in regard to the cooperation of the Senate in the appointment of Officers and the making of treaties; which are qualifica[tions] of the general executive powers of appointing officers and making treaties: Because the difficulty of a complete and perfect specification of all the cases of Executive authority would naturally dictate the use of general terms—and would render it improbable that a specification of certain particulars was designed as a substitute for those terms, when antecedently used. The different mode of expression employed in the constitution in regard to the two powers the Legislative and the Executive serves to confirm this inference. In the article which grants the legislative powers of the Governt. the expressions are—*"All Legislative powers herein granted shall be vested in a Congress of the UStates;"* in that which grants the Executive Power the expressions are, as already quoted "The EXECUTIVE PO[WER] shall be vested in a President of the UStates of America."

The enumeration ought rather therefore to be considered as intended by way of greater caution, to specify and regulate the principal articles implied in the definition of Executive Power; leaving the rest to flow from the general grant of that power, interpreted in conformity to other parts [of] the constitution and to the principles of free government.

The general doctrine then of our constitution is, that the EXECUTIVE POWER of the Nation is vested in the President; subject only to the *exceptions* and *qu[a]lifications* which are expressed in the instrument.

Two of these have been already noticed—the participation of the Senate in the appointment of Officers and the making of Treaties. A third remains to be mentioned the right of the Legislature "to declare war and grant letters of marque and reprisal."

With these exceptions the EXECUTIVE POWER of the Union is completely lodged in the President. This mode of construing the Constitution has indeed been recognized by Congress in formal acts, upon full consideration and debate. The power of removal from office is an inportant instance.

And since upon general principles for reasons already given, the issuing of a proclamation of neutrality is merely an Executive Act; since also the general Executive Power of the Union is vested in the President, the conclusion is, that the step, which has been taken by him, is liable to no just exception on the score of authority.

It may be observed that this Inference w[ould] be just if the power of declaring war had [not] been vested in the Legislature, but that [this] power naturally includes the right of judg[ing] whether the Nation is under obligations to m[ake] war or not.

The answer to this is, that however true it may be, that th[e] right of the Legislature to declare wa[r] includes the right of judging whether the N[ation] be under obligations to make War or not—it will not follow that the Executive is in any case excluded from a similar right of Judgment, in the execution of its own functions.

If the Legislature have a right to make war on the one hand—it is on the other the duty of the Executive to preserve Peace till war is declared; and in fulfilling that duty, it must necessarily possess a right of judging what is the nature of the obligations which the treaties of the Country impose on the Government; and when in pursuance of this right it has concluded that there is nothing in them inconsistent with a *state* of neutrality, it becomes both its province and its duty to enforce the laws incident to that state of the Nation. The Executive is charged with the execution of all laws, the laws of Nations as well as the Municipal law, which recognises and adopts those laws. It is consequently bound, by faithfully executing the laws of neutrality, when that is the state of the Nation, to avoid giving a cause of war to foreign Powers.

This is the direct and proper end of the proclamation of neutrality. It declares to the UStates their situation with regard to the Powers at war and makes known to the Community that the laws incident to that situation will be enforced. In doing this, it conforms to an established usage of Nations, the operation of which as before remarked is to obviate a responsibility on the part of the whole Society, for secret and unknown violations of the rights of any of the warring parties by its citizens.[3]

France's provocations and unresolved disputes (including continued raids on American merchant ships) put a strain on American relations with Britain as much as on those with France. With the typical swagger of the world's greatest naval power, Great Britain seized more than 250 American merchant ships trading with French colonies in the Caribbean in March 1794. Aiming to defuse the crisis, Hamilton suggested to Washington that he send John Jay to London as a special envoy. Never one to let events follow their own course, Hamilton sent a letter to Jay encouraging him to negotiate a commercial as well as a military accord.

To George Washington:

[Philadelphia, May 6, 1794]

I see not how it can be disputed with you that this Country in a commercial sense is more important to G Britain than any other. The articles she takes from us are certainly precious to her, important perhaps essential to the ordinary subsistence of her Islands—not unimportant to her own subsistence *occasionally*, always very important to her manufactures, and of real consequence to her revenue. . . . We now consume of her exports from a million to [a] million & a half Sterling more in value than any other foreign country & while the consumption of other countries from obvious causes is likely to be stationary that of this country is increasing and for a long, long, series of years, will increase rapidly. Our manufactures are no doubt progressive. But our population and means progress so much faster, that our demand for manufactured supply far outgoes the progress of our faculty to manufacture. Nor can this cease to be the case for any calculable period of time.

How unwise then in G Britain to suffer such a state of things to remain exposed to the hazard of constant interruption & derangement by not fixing on the basis of a good Treaty the principles on which it should continue?

In an interesting sidenote, after expounding on the issue of neutrality and offering statistics on the volume of trade with Britain, Hamilton floated the idea of allowing British merchant ships access to the Mississippi River as a bargaining chip.

The Navigation of the Mississippi is to us an object of immense consequence. Besides other considerations connected with it, if the Government of the UStates can procure & secure the enjoyment of it to our Western Country, it will be an infinitely strong link of Union between that Country & the Atlantic States. As its preservation will depend on the naval resources of the Atlantic States the Western country cannot but feel that this essential interest depends on its remaining firmly united with them.

If any thing could be done with G Britain to increase our chances for the speedy enjoyment of this right it would be in my judgment a very valuable ingredient in any arrangement you could make. Nor is Britain without a great interest in the Question, if the arrangement shall give to her a participation in that Navigation & a Treaty of Commerce shall admit her advantageously into this large field of commercial adventure.

May it not be possible to obtain a Guarantee of our right in this particular from G Britain on the condition of mutual enjoyment & a trade on the same terms as to our Atlantic Ports?

This is a delicate subject not well matured in my mind. It is the more delicate as there is at this moment a negotiation pending with Spain, in a position I believe not altogether unpromising, and ill use might be made of any overture or intimation on the subject. Indeed in such a posture of the thing an eventual arrangement only could be proper. I throw out the subject merely that you may contemplate it.[4]

Early in 1793, prior to Washington's Neutrality Proclamation, Hamilton had faced a serious challenge to his leadership from Republicans in Congress. Jefferson led the challenge, accusing Hamilton of mismanaging foreign loans. Virginia congressman William Branch

Giles, privately acting on behalf of Jefferson and Madison, made the charges in a series of resolutions he submitted to the House of Representatives. (Giles later courted one of Jefferson's daughters). Though Hamilton's quick and forceful response defeated these resolutions almost immediately, a cloud remained over his tenure as Treasury secretary. Hamilton wanted official exoneration, and before the year ended, he demanded a formal inquiry by the House into his conduct. Hamilton was later exonerated by the House, and it was Jefferson who resigned his post as secretary of state, on December 31.

His position was seemingly solidified, but Hamilton's hopes for a quiet summer were dashed when farmers in western Pennsylvania and Kentucky, like their rebellious predecessors of the 1760s and 1770s, escalated their violent campaign against an impost, Hamilton's excise tax on whiskey. The farmers mounted a full-fledged insurrection, which became known as the Whiskey Rebellion. This kind of brute, uninformed (in Hamilton's view) activism was at the core of his fear of democracy. (Yet of course, it could be argued that this is precisely what he himself had done as a British colonist fomenting revolution in the 1770s.) Here he summarizes the situation for Washington.

To George Washington:

[August 5, 1794]

The disagreeable crisis at which matters have lately arrived in some of the Western counties of Pennsylvania, with regard to the laws laying duties on spirits distilled within the UStates and on Stills, seems to render proper a review of the circumstances which have attended those laws in that scene, from their commencement to the present time and of the conduct which has hitherto been observed on the part of the Government, its motives and effect;

in order to a better judgment of the measures necessary to be pursued in the existing emergency.

The opposition to those laws in the four most Western Counties of Pennsylvania (Alleghany Washington Fayette and Westmoreland) commenced as early as they were known to have been passed. It has continued, with different degrees of violence, in the different counties, and at different periods. But Washington has uniformly distinguished its resistance by a more excessive spirit, than has appeared in the other Counties & seems to have been chiefly instrumental in kindling and keeping alive the flame.

The opposition first manifested itself in the milder shape of the circulation of opinions unfavourable to the law & calculated by the influence of public disesteem to discourage the accepting or holding of Offices under it or the complying with it, by those who might be so disposed; to which was added the show of a discontinuance of the business of distilling. These expedients were shortly after succeeded by private associations to *forbear* compliances with the law. But it was not long before these more negative modes of opposition were perceived to be likely to prove ineffectual. And in proportion as this was the case and as the means of introducing the laws into operation were put into execution, the disposition to resistance became more turbulent and more inclined to adopt and practice violent expedients.

Hamilton goes into the details of the violence with the practiced eye of a gendarme. Small-scale attacks and harassment included cutting off the hair and the tarring and feathering of those thought to be revenue agents.

On the 6th of the same Month of September, the Opposition broke out in an act of violence upon the person & property of Robert Johnson Collector of the Revenue for the Counties of Alleghany & Washington.

A party of men armed and disguised way-laid him at a place on Pidgeon Creek in Washington county—seized tarred and feathered him cut off his hair and deprived him of his horse, obliging him to travel on foot a considerable distance in that mortifying and painful situation.

The case was brought before the District Court of Pennsylvania out of which Processes issued against John Robertson, John Hamilton & Thomas McComb: three of the persons concerned in the outrage.

The serving of These processes was confided by the then Marshall Clement Biddle to his Deputy Joseph Fox, who in the month of October went into Alleghany County for the purpose of serving them.

The appearances & circumstances which Mr. Fox observed himself in the course of his journey, & learnt afterwards upon his arrival at Pittsburgh, had the effect of deterring him from the service of the processes and unfortunately led to adopting the injudicious and fruitless expedient of sending them to the parties by a private Messenger under cover.

The Deputy's Report to the Marshall states a number of particulars evincing a considerable fermentation in the part of the country, to which he was sent, and inducing a belief on his part that he could not with safety have executed the processes. The Marshall transmitting this report to the District Atty makes the following observations upon it "I am sorry to add that he (the Deputy) found the people in general in the Western part of the

State, and particularly beyond the Alleghany Mountain, in such a ferment, on account of the Act of Congress for laying a duty on distilled spirits & so much opposed to the execution of the said Act, and from a variety of threats to himself personally, although he took the utmost precaution to conceal his errand, that he was not only convinced of the impossibility of serving the process, but that any attempt to effect it would have occasionned the most violent opposition from the greater part of the Inhabitants, & he declares that if he had attempted it, he believes he should not have returned alive. I spared no expence nor pains to have the process of the Court executed & have not the least doubt that my Deputy would have accomplished it, if it could have been done."[5]

Washington requested Hamilton's recommendation for dealing with the rebellion, and Hamilton gave this reply in a letter dated August 1794. An aggressive show of military force would be necessary, he wrote to the president.

To George Washington:

[August 2, 1794]

The case upon which an Opinion is required is summarily as follows. The four most Western Counties of Pennsylvania since the Commencement of those laws a period of more than three Years, have been in steady and Violent Opposition to them. By formal public meetings of influential individuals, whose resolutions and proceedings had for undisguised objects, to render the laws odious, to discountenance a compliance with them, and to intimidate individuals from accepting and executing Offices under them—by a general Spirit of Opposition (thus fomented) among the Inhabitants—by repeated instances of armed parties going in disguise to the houses of the Officers of the Revenue and inflicting upon them personal violence and outrage—by general combinations to forbear a compliance with the requisitions of the laws by examples of injury to the Property and insult to the persons of individuals who have shewn by their conduct a disposition to comply and by an almost universal noncompliance with the laws—their execution within the Counties in question has been completely frustrated.

Various Alterations have been made in the laws by the Legislature to obviate as far as possible the objections of the Inhabitants of those Counties.

The executive, on its part has been far from deficient in forbearance lenity or a Spirit of Accomodation.

But neither the Legislative nor the Executive accomodations have had any effect in producing compliance with the laws.

The Opposition has continued and matured, till it has at length broke out in Acts which are presumed to amount to Treason...

It appears to me that the very existence of Government demands this course and that a duty of the highest nature urges the Chief Magistrate to pursue it. The Constitution and laws of the United States, contemplate and provide for it.

What force of Militia shall be called out, and from What State or States?

The force ought if attainable to be an imposing one, such if practicable, as will deter from opposition, save the effusion of the blood of Citizens and secure the object to be accomplished.

The quantum must of course be regulated by the resistance to be expected. Tis computed, that the four opposing Counties contain upwards of sixteen thousand males of 16 years and more, that of these about seven thousand may be expected to be armed. Tis possible that the union of the nieghbouring Counties of Virginia may augment this force. Tis not impossible, that it may receive an accession from some adjacent Counties of this state on this side of the Alleghany Mountain.

To be prepared for the worst, I am of opinion, that twelve thousand Militia ought to be ordered to assemble; 9000 foot and 3000 horse. I should not propose so many horse, but for the probability, that this description of Militia, will be more easily procured for the service.

From what State or States shall these come?

The Law contemplates that the Militia of a State, in which an insurrection happens, if willing & sufficient shall first be employed, but gives power to employ the Milita of other States in the case either of refusal or insufficiency.

The Governor of Pennsylvania in an Official conference this day, gave it explicitly as his opinion to the President, that the Militia of Pennsylvania alone would be found incompetent to the suppression of the insurrection.

This Opinion of the Chief Magistrate of the State is presumed to be a sufficient foundation for calling in, in the first instance, the aid of the Militia of the Neighbouring States.

I would submit then, that Pennsylvania be required to furnish 6000 men of whom 1000 to be horse, New-Jersey 2000 of whom 800 to be horse, Maryland 2000 of whom 600 to be horse, Virginia 2000, of whom 600 to be horse.

Or perhaps it may be as eligible to call upon each State for such a number of Troops, leaving to itself the proportion of horse and foot according to convenience. The Militia called for to rendezvous at Carlisle in Pensylvania & Cumberland Fort in Virginia on the 10th of September next.

The law requires that previous to the using of force a Proclamation shall issue, commanding the Insurgents to disperse and return peaceably to their respective abodes within a limited time. This step must of course be taken.

Predictably, the state militias met with limited success. When the insurrection was still unresolved in September, Hamilton, in his own mind the person most directly responsible for the rebellion, urged Washington to grant him permission to accompany the force sent to quell the rebels.

To George Washington:

[Philadelphia, September 19, 1794]

Upon full reflection I entertain an opinion, that it is adviseable for me, on public ground, considering the connection between the immediate ostensible cause of the insurrection in the Western Country and my department, to go out upon the expedition against the insurgents. In a government like ours, it cannot but have a good effect for the person who is understood to be the adviser or proposer of a measure, which involves danger to his fellow citizens, to partake in that danger: While, not to do it, might have a bad effect. I therefore request your permission for the purpose.[6]

Washington acquiesced, and initially commanded the federalized militia forces himself. After handing over the command of the troops to Governor Henry Lee of Virginia, Washington asked Hamilton to issue these instructions to Lee.

To Henry Lee:

[Bedford, Pennsylvania, October 20, 1794]

I have it in special instruction from the President of the United States, now at this place, to convey to you on his behalf, the following instructions for the general direction of your conduct in the command of the Militia army, with which you are charged.

The objects for which the militia have been called forth are.

1. To suppress the combinations which exist in some of the western counties in Pennsylvania in opposition to the laws laying duties upon spirits distilled within the United States and upon Stills.
2. To cause the laws to be executed.

These objects are to be effected in two ways—

1. By military force.
2. By judiciary process, and other civil proceedings.

The objects of the military force are twofold.

1. To overcome any armed opposition which may exist.
2. To countenance and support the civil officers in the means of executing the laws.

With a view to the first of these two objects, you will proceed as speedily as may be, with the army under your command, into the insurgent counties to attack, and as far as shall be in your

power subdue, all persons whom you may find in arms, in opposition to the laws above mentioned. You will march your army in
two columns, from the places where they are now assembled, by
the most convenient routes, having regard to the nature of the
roads, the convenience of supply, and the facility of co-operation
and union; and bearing in mind, that you ought to act, till the
contrary shall be fully develloped, on the general principle of having to contend with the whole force of the Counties of Fayette,
Westmoreland, Washington and Alleghany, and of that part of
Bedford which lies westward of the town of Bedford; and that
you are to put as little as possible to hazard. The approximation,
therefore, of your columns, is to be sought, and the subdivision of
them, so as to place the parts out of mutual supporting distance,
to be avoided as far as local circumstances will permit. Parkinson's
Ferry appears to be a proper point, towards which to direct the
march of the column for the purpose of ulterior measures.

When arrived within the insurgent Country, if an armed
opposItion appear, it may be proper to publish a proclamation,
inviting all good citizens, friends of the Constitution and laws,
to join the standard of the United States. If no armed opposition
exist, it may still be proper to publish a proclamation, exhorting
to a peaceable and dutiful demeanour, and giving assurances
of performing, with good faith and liberality, whatsoever may
have been promised by the Commissioners to those who have
complied with the conditions prescribed by them, and who have
not forfeited their title by subsequent misconduct.

Of those persons in arms, if any, whom you may make prisoners;
leaders, including all persons in command, are to be delivered up to
the civil magistrate: the rest to be disarmed, admonished and sent
home (except such as may have been particularly violent and also

influential) causing their own recognizances for their good behaviour to be taken, in the cases in which it may be deemed expedient.

With a view to the second point, namely, "the countenance and support of the civil officers, in the means of executing the laws," you will make such dispositions as shall appear proper to countenance and protect, and, if necessary and required by them, to support and aid the civil officers in the execution of their respective duties; for bringing offenders and delinquents to justice; for seizing the stills of delinquent distillers, as far as the same shall be deemed eligible by the supervisor of the Revenue, or chief-officer of Inspection; and also for conveying to places of safe custody, such persons as may be apprehended and not admitted to bail.

The objects of judiciary process and other civil proceedings, will be,

1. To bring offenders to Justice.
2. To enforce penalties on delinquent distillers by suit.
3. To enforce the penalty of forfeiture on the same persons by seizure of their stills and spirits.

The better to effect these purposes, the Judge of the District, Richard Peters Esquire, and the Attorney of the district, William Rawle Esquire, accompany the army.

You are aware that the Judge cannot be controuled in his functions. But I count on his disposition to cooperate in such a general plan as shall appear to you consistent with the policy of the case. But your method of giving a direction to legal proceedings, according to your general plan, will be by instruction to the District Attorney.

He ought particularly to be instructed, (with due regard to time and circumstance)—1st to procure to be arrested, all influential actors in riots and unlawful assemblies, relating to the insurrection, and combinations to resist the laws; or having for object to abet that insurrection, and those combinations; and who shall not have complied with the terms offered by the Commisioners; or manifested their repentance in some other way, which you may deem satisfactory. 2dly. To cause process to issue for enforcing penalties on delinquent distillers. 3d. To cause *offenders*, who may be arrested, to be conveyed to goals where there will be no danger of rescue: those for misdemeanors to the goals of York and Lancaster; those for capital offences to the goal of Philadelphia, as more secure than the others. 4th. To prosecute indictable offences in the Courts of the United States—those for penalties on delinquents, under the laws beforementioned, in the courts of Pennsylvania.

As a guide in the case, the District Attorney has with him a list of the persons who have availed themselves of the offers of the Commissioners on the day appointed.

The seizure of Stills is the province of the Supervisor and other officers of Inspection. It is difficult to chalk out the precise line concerning it. There are opposite considerations which will require to be nicely balanced, and which must be judged of by those officers on the spot. It may be found useful to confine the seizures to stills of the most leading and refactory distillers. It may be adviseable to extend them far in the most refractory County.

When the insurrection is subdued, and the requisite means have been put in execution to secure obedience to the laws, so as to render it proper for the army to retire (an event which you will accelerate as much as shall be consistent with the object) you will endeavour to make an arrangement for detaching such a force as you deem adequate; to be stationed within the disaffected Country, in such manner as best to afford protection to well-disposed Citizens, and to the officers of the revenue, and to repress by their presence, the spirit of riot & opposition to the laws.

But before you withdraw the army, you will promise on behalf of the President a general pardon to all such as shall not have been arrested, with such exceptions as you shall deem proper. The promise must be so guarded as not to affect pecuniary claims under the revenue laws. In this measure, it is adviseable there should be a cooperation with the Governor of Pennsylvania.[7]

The insurrection subdued and his plans for the United States Treasury largely in place, Hamilton decided to step down from his post as secretary of the Treasury, effective early in 1795. Late in 1794, he wrote this warning about the developments in France, citing the "excesses" of the revolutionary government, but never published it. "[T]he time must come," he concludes, "when it will have been a disgrace to have advocated the Revolution of France in its late stages."

In the early periods of the French Revolution, a warm zeal for its success was in this Country *a sentiment truly universal.* The love of Liberty is here the ruling passion *of the Citizens of the UStates* pervading every class [,] animating every bosom. As long therefore as the Revolution of France bore the marks of being the cause of liberty it united all hearts concentered [,] all opinions. But this unanimity of approbation has been for a considerable time decreasing. The excesses which have constantly multiplied, with greater and greater aggravations have successively though slowly detached reflecting men from their partiality for an object which has appeared less and less to merit their regard. Their reluctance to abandon it has however been proportioned to the ardor and fondness with which they embraced it. They were willing to overlook many faults—to apologise for some enormities—to hope that better justifications existed than were seen—to look forward to more calm and greater moderation, after the first shocks of the political earthquake had subsided. But instead of this, they have been witnesses to one volcano succeeding another, the last still more dreadful than the former, spreading ruin and devastation far and wide—subverting the foundations of right security and property, of order, morality and religion—sparing neither sex nor age, confounding innocence with guilt, involving the old and the young, the sage and the madman, the long tried friend of virtue and his country and the upstart pretender to purity and patriotism—the bold projector of new treasons with the obscure in indiscriminate and profuse destruction. They have found themselves driven to the painful alternative of renouncing an object dear to their wishes or of becoming by the continuance of their affection for it accomplices with Vice Anarchy Depotism and Impiety...

It is not among the least perplexing phenomina of the present times, that a people like that of the UStates—exemplary for humanity and moderation surpassed by no other in the love of order and a knowlege of the true principles of liberty, distinguished for purity of morals and a just reverence for Religion should so long perservere in partiality for a state of things the most cruel sanguinary and violent that ever stained the annuals of mankind, a state of things which annihilates the foundations of social order and true liberty, confounds all moral distinctions and *substitutes to* the mild & beneficent religion of the Gospel a gloomy persecuting and desolating atheism. To the eye of a wise man, this partiality is the most inauspicious circumstance, that has appeared in the affairs of this country. It leads involuntarily and irresistibly to apprehensions concerning the soundness of our principles and the stability of our welfare. It is natural to fear that the transition may not be difficult from the approbation of bad things to the imitation of them; a fear which can only be mitigated by a careful estimate of the extraneous causes that have served to mislead the public judgment.

But though we may find in these causes a solution of the fact calculated to abate our solicitude for the consequences; yet we can not consider the public happiness as out of the reach of danger so long as our principles continue to be exposed to the debauching influence of admiration for an example which, it will not be too strong to say, presents the caricature of human depravity. And the pride of national character at least can find no alleviation for the wound which must be inflicted by so ill-judged so unfortunate a partiality.

If there be any thing solid in virtue—the time must come when it will have been a disgrace to have advocated the Revolution of France in its late stages.[8]

On January 31, 1795, Hamilton tendered his resignation to President Washington, who responded with a deep and succinct expression of respect:

From George Washington:

[February 2, 1795]

In every relation, which you have borne to me, I have found that my confidence in your talents, exertions and integrity, has been well placed. I the more freely render this testimony of my approbation, because I speak from opportunities of information wch cannot deceive me, and which furnish satisfactory proof of your title to public regard.[9]

Hamilton responded to Washington the next day:
   To George Washington:

[February 3, 1795]

My particular acknowledgements are due for your very kind letter of yesterday. As often as I may recall the vexations I have endured, your approbation will be a great and precious consolation.

It was not without a struggle, that I yielded to the very urgent motives, which impelled me to relinquish a station, in which I could hope to be in any degree instrumental in promoting the success of an administration under your direction; a struggle which would have been far greater, had I supposed that the prospect of future usefulness was proportioned to the sacrifices to be made.

Whatsoever may be my destination hereafter, I entreat you to be persuaded (not the less for my having been sparing in professions) that I shall never cease to render a just tribute to those eminent and excellent qualities which have been already productive of so many blessings to your country—that you will always have my fervent wishes for your public and personal felicity, and that it will be my pride to cultivate a continuance of that esteem regard and friendship, of which you do me the honor to assure me. With true respect and affectionate attachment.[10]

Letter from Alexander Hamilton to George Washington dated February 3, 1795 announcing Hamilton's resignation as secretary of the treasury.

Only a couple of weeks before leaving his post, Hamilton issued a valedictory of sorts, a report on a plan for the further support of public credit. In it, he crystallizes the political implications of public debt and credit. His allusion to immortality resonates on many levels, though it's open to question whether even he imagined that his legacy would remain relevant in the early part of the twenty-first century. Even his skewering of congressional leaders who "clamor for occasions of expense" that happen to be popular, but who are meanwhile "vehement against every plan of taxation" echoes across the intervening centuries.

To extinguish a Debt which exists and to avoid contracting more are ideas almost always favored by public feeling and opinion; but to pay Taxes for the one or the other purpose, which are the only means of avoiding the evil, is always more or less unpopular. These contradictions are in human nature. And the lot of a Country would be enviable indeed, in which there were not always men ready to turn them to the account of their own popularity or to some other sinister account.

Hence it is no uncommon spectacle to see the same men Clamouring for Occasions of expense, when they happen to be in unison with the present humor of the community, whether well or ill directed, declaiming against a Public Debt, and for the reduction of it as an *abstract thesis;* yet vehement against every plan of taxation which is proposed to discharge old debts, or to avoid new by defraying the expences of exigencies as they emerge.

These unhandsome arts throw artificial embarrassment in the way of the administrators of Government; and Co-operating with the desire, which they themselves are too apt to feel to conciliate public favor by declining to lay even necessary burthens, or with the fear of loosing it by imposing them with firmness serve to promote the accumulation of debt; by leaving that which at any time exists without adequate provision for its reimbursement, and by preventing the laying with energy new Taxes when new

Occasions of expense Occur. The consequence is, that the public Debt swells 'till its magnitude becomes enormous, and the Burthens of the people gradually increase 'till their weight becomes intolerable. Of such a state of things great disorders in the whole political economy, convulsions & revolutions of Government are a Natural offspring.

There can be no more sacred obligation, then, on the public Agents of a Nation than to guard with a provident foresight and inflexible perseverance against so mischievous a result. True patriotism and genuine policy cannot, it is respectfully observed, be better demonstrated by those of the United States at the present juncture, than by improveing efficaciously the very favourable situation in which they stand, for extinguishing with reasonable celerity the actual debt of the Country, and for laying the foundations of a system which may shield posterity from the consequences of the usual improvidence and selfishness of its ancestors: And which if possible may give IMMORTALITY to PUBLIC CREDIT.[11]

PRIVATE
CITIZEN,
PUBLIC POWER

★ ★ ★

On the last day of January 1795, Hamilton handed the reigns of the Treasury Department over to his deputy, Oliver Wolcott Jr., who had been a deputy in the department since 1791. Hamilton left Philadelphia in February and turned his attention to reviving his law practice in New York. He remained in regular correspondence with his government colleagues, though, and it was not long before Washington, without a secretary of state since Jefferson's resignation, asked Hamilton to review the unpopular Anglo-American treaty nego-tiated by John Jay. Giving the president an article-by-article review, Hamilton acknowledged that the treaty contained drawbacks, but he urged Washington to sign it anyway.

To these particular views of the different articles of the Treaty The following general view may be added.

The truly important side of this Treaty is that it closes and upon the whole as reasonably as could have been expected the controverted points between the two Countries—and thereby gives us the prospect of repossessing our Western Posts, an object of primary consequence in our affairs—of escaping finally from being implicated in the dreadful war which is ruining Europe—

and of preserving ourselves in a state of peace for a considerable time to come.

Well considered, the greatest interest of this Country in its external relations is that of peace. The more or less of commercial advantages which we may acquire by particular treaties are of far less moment. With peace, the force of circumstances will enable us to make our way sufficiently fast in Trade. War at this time would give a serious wound to our growth and prosperity. Can we escape it for ten or twelve years more, we may then meet it without much inquietude and may advance and support with ener[g]y and effect any just pretensions to greater commercial advantages than we may enjoy.

It follows that the objects contained in the permanent articles are of real and great value to us. The price they will cost us in the article of compensation for the Debts is not likely to bear any proportion to the expences of a single Campaign to enforce our rights. The calculation is therefore a simple and a plain one. The terms are no way inconsistent with national honor.

As to the Commercial arrangements in the Temporary articles, they can be of no great importance either way; if it were only for the circumstance that it is in the power of either party to terminate them within two years after the war. So short a duration renders them unimportant however considered as to intrinsic merit.

Intrinsically considered they have no very positive character of advantage or disadvantage. They will in all probability leave the Trade between the two Countries where it at present is.[1]

The Jay Treaty, as it came to be known, was widely attacked when it was published on July 1, and Hamilton responded with a series of pseudonymous articles to defend it. Hamilton, writing as Hora-

tius, praised it for keeping the United States at a remove from the "Controversies of Europe"—a theme to which he would return in the near future in Washington's farewell address. Additionally, Hamilton accuses the Jeffersonians of possessing a "servile and criminal subserviency to the views of France."

[July 1795]

It is an unquestionable truth, fellow Citizens! and one which it is essential you should understand, that the great and cardinal *sin* of the Treaty in the eyes of its adversaries is that it *puts an end to controversy* with Great Britain. We have a sect of politicians among us, who influenced by a servile and criminal subserviency to the views of France have adopted it as a fundamental tenet that there ought to subsist between us and Great Britain eternal variance and discord...

Reason, Religion, Philosophy, Policy, disavow the spurious and odious doctrine that we ought to cherish and cultivate enmity with any Nation whatever. In reference to a Nation with whom we have such extensive relations of Commerce as with Great Britain—to a power, from her maritime strength, so capable of annoying us—it must be the offspring of treachery or extreme folly. If you consult your true interest Your Motto cannot fail to be "PEACE and TRADE with ALL NATIONS; beyond our present engagements, POLITICAL CONNECTION with NONE" You ought to spurn from you as the box of Pandora—the fatal heresy of CLOSE ALLIANCE, or in the language of *Genet* a true *family compact* with France. This would at once make you a mere satellite of France, and entangle you in all the contests broils, and wars of Europe.

Tis evident that the Controversies of Europe must often grow out of causes intirely foreign to this Country. Why then should we by a close political connection with any power of Europe expose our peace & interest as a matter of course to all the shocks with which their mad rivalships and wicked ambition so frequently convulse the earth? 'Twere insanity to embrace such a system. The avowed and secret partisans of it merit our contempt for their folly or our execration for their depravity.[2]

On July 22, Camillus, another Hamilton pseudonym, began a series of articles known as The Defence. In the first of these, Camillus impugns the motives of the Republicans opposing the treaty, and then appeals to the reason of those whose minds remain open, arguing that "the too probable result of a refusal to ratify is war, or what would be still worse, a disgraceful passiveness under violations of our rights."

To every man who is not an enemy to the national government, who is not a prejudiced partizan, who is capable of comprehending the argument, and passionate enough to attend to it with impartiality, I flatter myself I shall be able to demonstrate satisfactorily in the course of some succeeding papers—

1. That the treaty adjusts in a reasonable manner the points in controversy between the United States and Great-Britain, as well those depending on the inexecution of the treaty of peace, as those growing out of the present European war.
2. That it makes no improper concessions to Great-Britain, no sacrifices on the part of the United States.
3. That it secures to the United States equivalents for what they grant.

4. That it lays upon them no restrictions which are incompatible with their honour or their interest.

5. That in the articles which respect war, it conforms to the laws of nations.

6. That it violates no treaty with, nor duty toward any foreign power.

7. That compared with our other commercial treaties, it is upon the whole, entitled to a preference.

8. That it contains concessions of advantages by Great-Britain to the United States, which no other nation has obtained from the same power.

9. That it gives to her no superiority of advantages over other nations with whom we have treaties.

10. That interests of primary importance to our general welfare, are promoted by it.

11. That the too probable result of a refusal to ratify is war, or what would be still worse, a disgraceful pas[s]iveness under violations of our rights, unredressed and unadjusted; and consequently, that it is the true interest of the United States, that the treaty should go into effect.

It will be understood, that I speak of the treaty as advised to be ratified by the Senate—for this is the true question before the public.[3]

In early 1796, Hamilton was part of a legal team that represented the government before the Supreme Court in Hylton v United States to defend the constitutionality of an annual federal tax on carriages. In one of his most frequently cited briefs, Hamilton argued this was not a direct tax and therefore not subject to apportionment by population, as the Constitution required for taxes on (for example) land. (A direct tax, such as land tax or income tax, is borne exclusively by the taxed entity and cannot be transferred or passed along, as can an indirect tax such as sales tax.) This ruling established the precedent of judicial review of legislative acts, in this case upholding the act of Congress—Marbury v. Madison *famously being the first one in which an act of Congress was overruled.*

As ratification of the Jay Treaty remained mired in Congress, Hamilton provided the rationale for yet another legal precedent in government, this time executive privilege. The Jay Treaty remained unfunded by Congress, with escalating suspicions and recriminations on both sides of the issue. When Congressman Edward Livingston of New York demanded to see executive branch documents pertaining to the treaty, Hamilton advised Washington to refuse, citing what we would now call executive privilege. Were Washington to cooperate with Congress, Hamilton warned the commander-in-chief, the result would be a "new and unpleasant game" that would be "fatal to the negotiating power of the government."

To George Washington:

[New York, March 7, 1796]

Mr. Livingston's motion in the House of Representatives, concerning the production of papers has attracted much attention. The opinion of those who think here is, that if the motion succeeds, it ought not to be complied with. Besides that in a matter of such a nature the production of the papers cannot fail to start [a] new and unpleasant Game—it will be fatal to the Negotiating Power of the Government if it is to be a matter of course for a call of either House of Congress to bring forth all the communication however confidential.

It seems to me that something like the following answer by the President will be advisable.

"A right in the House of Representatives, to demand and have as a matter of course, and without specification of any object all communications respecting a negotiation with a foreign power cannot be admitted without danger of much inconvenience. A discretion in the Executive Department how far and where to comply in such cases is essential to the due conduct of foreign negotiations and is essential to preserve the limits between the Legislative and Executive Departments. The present call is altogether indefinite and without any declared purpose. The Executive has no cases on which to judge of the propriety of a compliance with it and cannot therefore without forming a very dangerous precedent comply.

It does not occur that the view of the papers asked for can be relative to any purpose of the competency of the House of Representatives but that of an impeachment. In every case of a foreign Treaty the grounds for an impeachment must primarily be deduced from the nature of the Instrument itself and from nothing extrinsic. If at any time a Treaty should present such grounds and it shall have been so pronounced by the House of Representatives and a further inquiry shall be necessary to ascertain the culpable person, there being then a declared and ascertained object the President would attend with due respect to any application for necessary information."

This is but a hasty and crude outline of what has struck me as an eligible course. For while a too easy compliance will be mischievous, a too peremptory and unqualified refusal might be liable to just criticism.[4]

By midyear, the realization that Washington's presidential term would soon expire, and that he was in no mind to run for reelection, had set

in. Washington felt that he had done his job shepherding the nation
through its fledgling days, and he was beyond eager to retire to his
Mount Vernon estate. He dusted off the farewell address to the nation
that he had prepared in 1792, and asked for Hamilton's help in revising
it to the current situation. (Hamilton's involvement was a closely held
secret at the time.) The reserved, deliberate, and even-handed nature
of the president, whose voice Hamilton was conjuring, paradoxically
gave Hamilton the license he needed to present his familiar arguments
in a more measured, less hectoring tone than he usually adopted. The
farewell speech is a testament to the power of the symbiotic relationship
that these men shared—one plus one equaling far more than two.

In Hamilton's draft of the speech, Washington first announces that
the time has come for the electorate to choose another "Citizen" to lead
them. Then Hamilton turns the speech to the necessity for vigilance
in the protection of the nation's hard-won liberty, the importance of
maintaining neutrality, and the threat of factions and regional interests
to health of the republic.

Interwoven as is the love of Liberty with every fibre of your hearts
no recommendation is necessary to fortify your attachment to
it. Next to this that unity of Government which constitutes you
one people claims your vigilant care & guardianship—as a main
pillar of your real independence of your peace safety freedom
and happiness.

This being the point in your political fortress against which
the batteries of internal and external enemies will be most constantly and actively however covertly and insidiously levelled, it
is of the utmost importance that you should appreciate in its full
force the immense value of your political Union to your national
and individual happiness—that you should cherish towards it an

affectionate and immoveable attachment and that you should watch for its presservation with jealous solicitude.

For this you have every motive of sympathy and interest. Children for the most part of a common country, that country claims and ought to concentrate your affections. The name of American must always gratify and exalt, the just pride of patriotism more than any denomination which can be derived from local discrimination. You have, with slight shades of difference the same religion manners habits & political institutions &, principles. You have in a common cause fought and triumphed to gether. The independence and liberty you enjoy are the work of joint councils, efforts—dangers sufferings & successes. By your Union you atchieved them, by your union you will most effectually maintain them....

These considerations speak a conclusive language to every virtuous and considerate mind. They place the continuance of our Union among the first objects of patriotic desire. Is there a doubt whether a common government can long embrace so extensive a sphere? Let Time & Experience decide the question. Speculation in such a case ought not to be listened to—And tis rational to hope that the auxiliary agency of the, governments of the subdivisions, with a proper organisation of the whole will secure a favourable issue to the Experiment. Tis allowable to believe that the spirit of party the intrigues of foreign nations, the corruption & the ambition of Individuals are likely to prove more formidable adversaries to the unity of our Empire than any inherent difficulties in the scheme. Tis against these that the guards of national opinion national sympathy national prudence & virtue are to be erected. With such obvious motives to Union there will be always cause from the fact itself to distrust the <u>patriotism</u> of those who in any quarter, may endeavour to weaken its bands. And by all the love I bear you My fellow Citizens I conjure, you as often, as it appears to frown upon the attempt....

To the duration and efficacy of your Union a Government extending over the whole is indispensable. No alliances however strict between the parts could be an adequate substitute. These could not fail to be liable to the infractions and interruptions which all alliances in all times have suffered. Sensible of this important truth you have lately established a Constitution of General Government, better calculated than the former for an intimate union and more adequate to the direction of your common concerns. This Government the offspring of your own choice uninfluenced and unawed, completely free in its principles, in the distribution of its powers uniting energy with safety and containing in itself a provision for its own amendment is well entitled to your confidence and support—, Respect for its authority, compliance with its laws, acquiescence in its measures, are duties dictated by the fundamental maxims of true Liberty. The basis of our political systems is the right of the people to make and to alter their constitutions of Government. But the constitution for the time, and until changed by an explicit and authentic act of the whole people, is sacredly binding upon all. The very idea of the right and power of the people to establish Government presupposes the duty of every individual to obey the established Government....

Tis essentially true that virtue or morality is a main & necessary, spring, of popular or republican Governments. The rule indeed extends with more or less force to all free Governments. Who that is a prudent & sincere friend to them can look with indifference on the ravages which are making in the foundation of the Fabric? Religion? The uncommon means which of late have been directed to this fatal end seem to make it in a particular of manner the duty of the Retiring Chief of a, nation to warn his country against tasting of the poisonous draught.

In Washington's measured, authoritative voice, Hamilton turns to his most venerated topic.

Cherish public Credit as a mean of strength and security. As one method of preserving it, use it as little as possible. Avoid occasions of expence by cultivating peace—remembering always that the preparation against danger, by timely and provident disbursements is often a mean of avoiding greater disbursements to repel it. Avoid the accumulation of debt by avoiding occasions of expence and by vigorous exertions in time of peace to discharge the debts which unavoidable wars may have occasionned—not transferring to posterity the burthen which we ought to bear ourselves. Recollect that towards the payment of debts there must be Revenue, that to have revenue there must be taxes, that it is impossible to devise taxes which are not more or less inconvenient and unpleasant—that they are always a choice of difficulties— that the intrinsic embarrassment which never fails to attend a selection of objects ought to be a motive for a candid construction of the conduct of the Government in making it—and that a spirit of acquiescence in those measures for obtaining revenue which the public exigencies dictate is in an especial manner the duty and interest of the citizens of every State.

He counsels Americans and their leaders to avoid international attachments and alliances, particularly those involving European powers.

In like manner, a passionate attachment of one nation, to another produces multiplied ills. Sympathy for the favourite nations, promoting the illusion of a supposed common interest in cases where it does not exist, and communicating to one the enmities of the one betrays into a participation in its quarrels & wars without adequate inducements or justifications. It leads to the concession of privileges to one nation and to the denial of them to others— which is apt doubly to injure the nation making the concession by an unnecessary yielding of what ought to have been retained and by exciting jealousy ill will and retaliation in the party from whom an equal privilege is witheld. And it gives to ambitious corrupted or deluded citizens, who devote themselves to the views of the favourite foreign power, facility in betraying or sacrificing the interests of their own country even with,without odium & popularity, gilding with the appearance, of a virtuous impulse, he base yieldings, of ambition or corruption....

Europe has a set of primary interests which have none or a very remote relation to us. Hence she must be involved in frequent contests the causes of which will be essentially foreign to us. Hence therefore it must necessarily be unwise on our part to implicate ourselves by an artificial connection, in the ordinary vicissitudes of European politics—in the combination, & collisions of her friendships or enmities.

Our detached and distant situation invites us to a different course & enables us to pursue it. If we remain a united people under an efficient Government the period is not distant when we may defy material injury from external annoyance—when we may take such an attitude as will cause the neutrality we shall at any time resolve to observe to be violated with caution—, when it will be the interest of belligerent nations under the impossibility of making acquisitions upon us to be very careful how either forced us to throw our weight into the opposite scale—when we may choose peace or war as our interest guided by justice shall dictate.

Hamilton's draft speech concludes on a note of humility—an admission of errors, tempered with the reassurance of the purity of Washington's motives. One cannot help but think that this is precisely how Hamilton saw his own best self. Washington had his own ideas regarding a conclusion to the speech, and in the end deleted the following passage in favor of his own.

Though in reviewing the incidents, of my administration I am unconscious of intentional error—I am yet too sensible of my own deficiencies not to think it probable that I have committed many errors. I deprecate the evils to which they may tend—and fervently implore the Almighty to avert or mitigate them. I shall carry with me nevertheless the hope that my motives will continue to be viewed by my Country with indulgence & that after forty five years of my life devoted with an upright zeal to the public service the faults of inadequate abilities will be consigned to oblivion as myself must soon be to the mansions of rest.

Neither Ambition nor interest has been the impelling cause of my actions. I never designedly misused any power confided to me. The fortune with which I came into office is not bettered otherwise than by that improvement in the value of property which the natural progress and peculiar prosperity of our country have produced. I retire with a pure heart, without cause for a blush—, with no alien sentiment to the ardor of those vows for the happiness of his Country which is so natural to a Citizen who sees in it, vows for the native soil of himself, and progenitors for four generations.[5]

Hamilton submitted this annotated draft of Washington's Farewell Address to the President for his review as Washington neared the end of his second term in office in 1796. The address was based on a version created during Washington's first term, written by Washington with the aid of James Madison.

In November 1796, Hamilton also drafted Washington's final annual message to Congress, hitting many of the same thematic notes as were featured in the farewell address.

Meanwhile, he turned his attention to influencing the choice of Washington's replacement, writing private letters urging equal support of John Adams, Washington's vice president, and Thomas Pinckney, a Federalist from South Carolina who had been Washington's minister to Great Britain. Until the Constitution was amended in 1804, electors chosen by voters in each state in turn voted for two presidential candidates; the recipient of the most votes became president, and the runner-up became vice president. Hamilton had hoped that Southern support would put Pinckney over the top and that he would become president. Contrary to Hamilton's wishes, Adams was elected in a narrow victory over Jefferson, who became the vice president. Adams retained many of Washington's cabinet members—Wolcott, who had taken over at Treasury from Hamilton; James McHenry, the secretary of war; and Timothy Pickering, secretary of state—all of whom were accustomed to working alongside Hamilton.

The new year began for Hamilton in typical fashion, influencing, if not running, the government by advising its ministers in an unofficial capacity, and pouring forth a torrent of published opinions. "The Warning," published under the pseudonym "Americus," used the continued seizure of American merchant vessels by French ships as the focus of a broad attack on the French government and, by corollary, France's supporters in the US government.

There are appearances too strong not to excite apprehension that the affairs of this Country are drawing fast to an eventful crisis. Various circumstances dayly unfolding themselves authorise a conclusion that France has adopted a system of conduct towards the neutral maritime nations generally which amount to little less than actual hostility. I mean the total *interruption* of their Trade with the ports of her enemies: A pretension so violent, and at the same time so oppressive humiliating and ruinous to them, that they cannot submit to it, without not only the complete sacrifice of their commerce but their absolute degradation from the rank of sovereign and independent States.

Hamilton directs his next argument in "The Warning" at apologists for France who maintain that the actions of the American government themselves (that is, reneging on the 1778 Treaty of Alliance) are forcing the French to act badly. Hamilton sees a more generalized ruthlessness, aimed at cutting off Britain's supply of revenue from trade. The British, meanwhile, were conducting their own seizures of American vessels and the impressment of American sailors into the Royal Navy—facts Hamilton chooses not to mention.

Did we need a confirmation of this truth, we should find it in the intelligence lately received from Cadiz. We are informed through a respectable channel, that *Danish* and *Swedish* as well as *American* Vessels, carried into that port by French Cruisers, have with their cargoes been condemned and confiscated by the French Consular Tribunal there, on the declared principle of intercepting the Trade of neutrals with the ports of the enemies of France. This indiscriminate spoliation of the commerce of neutral powers is a clear proof that France is actuated not by particular causes of discontent given by our Government but by a general plan of policy.

The practice upon the decree is a comment much broader than the text. The decree purports that France would observe towards neutrals the same conduct which they permitted her enemies to observe towards them. But the practice goes a great deal further. None of the enemies of France, even at the height of their power and presumption, ever pretended totally to cut off the Trade of neutrals, with her ports. This is a pretension reserved for her to increase the catalogue of extraordinary examples, of which her Revolution has been so fruitful.

The allegations of discontent with this Country are evidently a mere colouring to the intended violation of its rights by treaty as well as by the laws of Nations. Some pretext was necessary and this has been seized. It will probably appear hereafter that *Denmark*, and *Sweden* have been mocked with a similar tale of grievances. It is indeed already understood, that Sweden, outraged in the person of her Representative, has been obliged to go the length of withdrawing her Minister from Paris....

Already in certain circles is heared the debasing doctrine that France is determined to reduce us to the alternative of War with her enemies or war with herself and that it is our interest and safety to elect the former.

There was a time when it was believed that a similar alternative would be imposed by Great Britain. At this crisis there was but one sentiment. The firmest friends of moderation and peace no less than the noisiest partisans of violence and war resolved to elect war with that power which should drive us to the election. This resolution was the dictate of morality & honor, of a just regard to national dignity and independence. If any consideration, in any situation, should degrade us into a different resolution, we that instant espouse crime and infamy; we descend from the high ground of an independent people and stoop to the ignominious level of Vassals. I trust there are few Americans who would not cheerfully encounter the worst evils of a Contest with any nation on earth rather than subscribe to so shameful an abdication of their rank as men and citizens.[6]

In the spring of 1797, things took a nasty turn that Hamilton probably should have seen coming. A scandalmonger by the name of James Callender published a series of pamphlets under the title The History of the United States for 1796, *in which he alleged financial misconduct on the part of the former Treasury secretary dating back to 1792. Hamilton by now was fairly accustomed to defending himself from charges of corruption, but Callender had thrown in an additional charge of adultery—a damaging accusation for a public figure championing himself as a paragon of personal virtue, as Hamilton did.*

Rumors of this nature had circulated for years, but Callender's charge of adultery rattled Hamilton to his core because he knew that it was true and that Callender had found the right sources for his story, or they him. So began the Maria Reynolds affair (see page 233), or rather the public phase of it. Hamilton had begun the actual affair during the summer of 1791 and it was over—or so he had fervently hoped—by the middle of 1792.

In fact, Hamilton's entanglement was still in its early stages when the actual affair ended. Maria Reynolds' husband, James Reynolds, had known about the infidelity from its outset and had begun blackmailing Hamilton in the winter of 1791. Subsequently, Reynolds was able to get a message to Republican Virginia congressman Frederick Muhlenberg alleging that Hamilton had secretly been engaging in financial speculation as well as adultery. The congressman and Virginia's two Republican senators, James Monroe and Abraham Venable, investigated. They interviewed Hamilton regarding the charges in December 1792, during which Hamilton made a hand-wringing admission of adultery but an adamant rejection of the charge of official corruption. He also provided the three with a ream of documents— detailed and tawdry correspondence with both Maria and James Reynolds—confirming his version of events. Muhlenberg, Monroe, and Venable exonerated Hamilton of official wrongdoing, swore an oath of silence—and kept the documents.

Particularly troubling to Hamilton now was that the timing of the publication of Callender's story, which included publication of the documents he had surrendered to Muhlenberg, Monroe, and Venable, coincided with the return of James Monroe from Paris. Monroe, allied with Jefferson and the other Virginia Republicans, had recently been recalled from his post as envoy of the Adams administration as a direct result of Republican-Federalist infighting. Since Monroe had been the repository of all documents pertaining to the Reynolds affair, he now became Hamilton's number one suspect as the source of the leak. Angry arguments ensued, leading in July 1797 to a challenge on the field of honor—a duel—that was narrowly averted, though as it turned out, Hamilton was correct about Monroe.

Hamilton's preoccupation with the Reynolds affair might have dented his confidence, but it did not seem to diminish his capacity for work. He continued to run a thriving law practice and pursue other public-minded interests. In January, he was elected a counselor to the New-York Society for Promoting the Manumission of Slaves, an abolitionist organization with which he had been involved since its inception in 1785.

He also continued to correspond and influence the actions of the key cabinet members whom Adams had inherited from Washington— Wolcott at Treasury; Pickering at State; and James McHenry, the secretary of War—in spite of his status as a private citizen. McHenry, in particular, was in need of Hamilton's help. When the president asked for McHenry's advice on dealing with the growing threat of war with France, which had just refused to accept Adams's newly appointed envoy, Charles Pinckney, Hamilton provided the war secretary with a detailed, point-by-point program as though giving a classmate the answers for an exam. Hamilton advised taking a firm but measured stance with France. In Hamilton's words, "The U[nited] States have the strongest motives to avoid war. They may lose a great deal; they can gain nothing."

To The first.　It is difficult to fix the precise point at which indignity or affront from one state to another ceases to be negotiable without absolute humiliation and disgrace. It is for the most part a relative question—relative to the comparitive strength of the parties—the motives for peace or war—the antecedent relations—the circumstances of the moment as well with regard to other nations as to those between whom the question arises. The conduct of France exclusive of the refusal of Mr. Pinckney is no doubt very violent insulting and injurious. The treatment of Mr. Pinckney if it does not pass certainly touches upon the utmost limit of what is tolerable. Yet it is conceived that under all the singular and very extraordinary circumstances of the case further negotiation may be admitted without the absolute humiliation and disgrace which ought perhaps never to be incurred—to avoid which it is probably always wise to put even the political existence of a Nation upon the hazard of the die.

The triumphs of France have been such as to confound and astonish mankind. Several of the principal powers of Europe even England herself have found it necessary or expedient in greater or less degrees to submit to some humiliation from France. At the present juncture the course of her affairs & the situation of her enemies more than ever admonishes those who are in danger of becoming so and who are not able to oppose barriers to her progress to temporise. The mind of mankind tired with the suffering, or spectacle, of a war, fatal beyond example, is prepared to see more than usual forbearance in powers not yet parties to it who may be in danger of being involved. It is prepared to view as only prudent what in other circumstances would be deemed dishonorable submission.

The U States have the strongest motives to avoid war. They may lose a great deal; they can gain nothing. They may be annoyed much and can annoy comparatively little. Tis even a possible event *that they may be left alone to contend with the Conquerors of Europe.* When interests so great invite and dangers so great menace, delicacy is called upon to yield a great deal to prudence. And a considerable degree of humiliation may, without *ignominy*, be encountered to avoid the possibility of much greater and a train of incalculable evils.

To the second—It will be expedient to declare to France that if there be any thing in the Treaty with G Britain which France is desirous of incorporating in the Treaty with her—The U States are ready to do so—having no wish to give to any other power privileges which France may not equally enjoy *on the same terms.* This general offer seems the most unexceptionable & will stop as well the mouth of France as of her partisans among ourselves. The duration of privileges should also be in both cases the same.

To the third.   It does not occur that it will be expedient to *propose* the abolition of any of the articles of our Treaties with France further than may be implied in the above general offer. To propose the abolition of things inconvenient to us would confirm the suspicion that we were disposed to narrow the privileges of France and would do harm there and here.[7]

Hamilton's allies in the Adams cabinet largely adopted his suggested program, but it failed to satisfy the French. The French Directory refused to accept the members of a joint negotiating commission including Pinckney, the Massachusetts congressman Elbridge Gerry (a Republican supporter of the French Revolution), and the Virginia Federalist and jurist John Marshall. The French demanded that the committee pay huge bribes before the French would consider a meeting. They also forced the committee to negotiate with agents to whom they referred as W, X, Y, and Z in official correspondence. When this news reached the United States, the incident became known as the XYZ Affair, and it gave the administration the political cover it needed to stiffen its opposition to France. The administration began engaging France in naval skirmishes that became known as the Quasi War against France. In a series of essays called "The Stand," Hamilton abandoned his calls for neutrality and urged his countrymen to gird for a full-on land war.

This country has doubtless powerful motives to cultivate peace. It was its policy, for the sake of this object, to go a great way in yielding secondary interests, and to meet injury with patience as long as it could be done without the manifest abandonment of essential rights; without absolute dishonor. But to do more than this is suicide in any people who have the least chance of contending with effect. The conduct of our government has corresponded with the cogent inducements to a pacific system. Towards Great-Britain it displayed forbearance—towards France it has shewn humility. In the case of Great Britain, its moderation was attended with success. But the inexorable arrogance and rapacity of the oppressors of unhappy France barr all the avenues to reconciliation as well as to redress, accumulating upon us injury and insult till there is no choice left between resistance and infamy.

My countrymen! can ye hesitate which to prefer? can ye consent to taste the brutalizing cup of disgrace, to wear the livery of foreign masters, to put on the hateful fetters of foreign bondage? Will it make any difference to you that the badge of your servitude is a *cap* rather than an *epaulet?* Will tyranny be less odious because FIVE instead of ONE inflict the rod? What is there to deter from the manful vindication of your rights and your honor?

With an immense ocean rolling between the United States and France—with ample materials for ship building, and a body of hardy seamen more numerous and more expert than France can boast, with a population exceeding five millions, spread over a wide extent of country, offering no one point, the seizure of which, as of the great capitals of Europe, might deside the issue, with a soil liberal of all the productions that give strength and resource, with the rudiments of the most essential manufactures capable of being developed in proportion to our want, with a numerous and in many quarters well appointed militia, with respectable revenues and a flourishing credit, with many of the principle sources of taxation yet untouched, with considerable arsenals and the means of extending them, with experienced officers ready to form an army under the command of the same illustrious chief who before led them to victory and glory, and who, if the occasion should require it, could not hesitate again to obey the summons of his country—what a striking and encouraging contrast does this situation in many respects form, to that in which we defied the thunder of Britain? what is there in it to excuse or palliate the cowardice and baseness of a tame surrender of our rights to France?

The question is unnecessary. The people of America are neither idiots nor dastards. They did not break one yoke to put on another. Tho a portion of them have been hitherto misled; yet not even these, still less the great body of the nation, can be long unaware of the true situation, or blind to the treacherous arts by which they are attempted to be hood winked. The unfaithful and guilty leaders of a foreign faction, unmasked in all their intrinsic deformity, must quickly shrink from the scene, appalled and confounded. The virtuous whom they have led astray will renounce their exotic standard. Honest men of all parties will unite to maintain and defend the honor and the sovereignty of their country.[8]

In the sixth installment of "The Stand," Hamilton paints an alarming picture of a future in which France sets its sights upon the conquest of North America after subduing Europe. Though he admits the prospect is unlikely, he nonetheless urges Americans to support the measure then being considered in Congress to raise a standing army to defend against this possibility.

The inevitable conclusion from the facts which have been presented is, that Revolutionary France has been and continues to be governed by a spirit of proselytism, conquest, domination and rapine. The detail well justifies the position, that we may have to contend at our very doors for our independence and liberty....

...In opposition to this, it is suggested that the interest of France concurring with the difficulty of execution is a safeguard against the enterprize. It is asked what incentives sufficiently potent can stimulate to so unpromising an attempt?

The answer is—the strongest passions of bad hearts—inordinate ambition, the love of domination, that prime characteristick of the despots of France—the spirit of vengeance for the presumption of having thought and acted for ourselves, a spirit which has marked every step of the revolutionary leaders—the fanatical egotism of obliging the rest of the world to adapt their political system to the French standard of perfection—the desire of securing the future controul of our affairs by humbling and ruining the independent supporters of their country and of elevating the partisans and tools of France—the desire of entangling our commerce with preferences and restrictions which would give to her the monopoly—these passions the most imperious, these motives the most enticing to a crooked policy, are sufficient persuasives to undertake the subjugation of this country.

Added to these primary inducements, the desire of finding an outlet for a part of the vast armies which on the termination of the European war are likely to perplex and endanger the men in power would be an auxiliary motive of Great Force. The total loss of the troops sent would be no loss to France. Their cupidity would be readily excited to the undertaking by the prospect of dividing among themselves the fertile lands of this Country. Great Britain once silenced, there would be no insuperable obstacle to the transportation. The divisions among us, which have been urged to our commission[er]s as one motive to a compliance with the unreasonable demands of the Directory would be equally an encouragement to invasion. It would be believed that a sufficient number would flock to the standard of France to render it easy to quell the resistance of the rest. Drunk with success nothing would be thought too arduous to be accomplished....

...Admit, that in our case invasion is upon the whole improbable; yet if there are any circumstances which pronounce that the apprehension of it is not absolutely chimerical, it is the part of wisdom to act as if [it] was likely to happen. What are the inconveniences of preparation compared with the infinite magnitude of the evil if it shall surprise us unprepared? They are lighter than air weighed against the smallest probability of so disastrous a result.

But what is to be done? It is not wiser to compound on any terms than to provoke the consequences of resistance....

...The resolution to raise an army, it is to be feared, is that one of the measures suggested, which will meet with greatest obstacle; and yet it is the one which ought most to unite opinion. Being merely a precaution for internal security, it can in no sense tend to provoke war, and looking to eventual security, in a case, which if it should happen would threaten our very existence as a nation, it is the most important....

...To have a good army on foot will be best of all precautions to prevent as well as to repel invasion.[9]

Perhaps feeling a bit guilty for his public tirades against France, Hamilton sought to explain his position to an old friend and comrade-in-arms, the Marquis de Lafayette, assuring him "that my friendship for you will survive all revolutions & all vicissitudes." In the years following the American Revolution, Lafayette had continued to fight in the French Army. He was captured by the Austrian Army in 1792, and though Hamilton made several attempts to intercede on his behalf, Lafayette was not released until 1797.

To Marquis de Lafayette:

[New York, April 28, 1798]

Your letter implied, as I had before understood, that though your engagements did not permit you to follow the fortunes of the republic [revolutionary France] yet your attachments had never been separated from them. In this, I frankly confess, I have differed from you. The suspension of the King and the massacre of September (of which events a temporary intelligence was received in this Country) cured me of my good will for the French Revolution.

I have never been able to believe that France can make a republic and I have believed that the attempt while it continues can only produce misfortunes.

Among the events of this revolution I regret extremely the misunderstanding which has taken place between your country and ours and which seems to threaten an open rupture. It would be useless to discuss the causes of this state of things. I shall only assure you that a disposition to form an intimate connection with Great Britain, which is charged upon us forms no part of the real Cause, though it has served the purpose of a party to impose the belief of it on france. I give you this assurance on the faith of our former friendship. And the effect will prove to you that I am not wrong. The basis of the policy of the party, of which I am, is to avoid intimate and exclusive connection with any foreign powers.

But away with politics the rest of my letter Shall be dedicated to assure you that my friendship for you will survive all revolutions & all vicissitudes.

No one feels more than I do the motives which this country has to love you, to desire and to promote your happiness. And I Shall not love it, if it does not manifest the sensibility by unequivocal acts. In the present state of our affairs with france, I cannot urge you to us—but until some radical change in france I Shall be sorry to learn you have gone elsewhere. Should the continuation of an evil course of things in your own country lead you to think of a permanent asylum elsewhere you will be sure to find in America a most cordial and welcome reception. The only thing in which our parties agree is to love you.[10]

Hamilton proceeded to recruit the one man he knew had the ability and the political standing to rally states opposed to confronting France, and still more vehemently opposed to a standing army: George Washington. Hamilton presents a dire picture of a subversive internal faction in the American government whose aim was to "make this Country a province of France."

To George Washington:

[New York, May 19, 1798]

At the present dangerous crisis of public affairs, I make no apology for troubling you with a political letter. Your impressions of our situation, I am persuaded, are not different from mine. There is certainly great probability that we may have to enter into a very serious struggle with France; and it is more and more evident that the powerful faction which has for years opposed the Government is determined to go every length with France. I am sincere in declaring my full conviction, as the result of a long course of observation, that they are ready to *new model* our constitution under the *influence* or *coertion* of France—to form with her a perpetual alliance *offensive* and *defensive*—and to give her a monopoly of our Trade by *peculiar* and *exclusive* privileges. This would be in substance, whatever it might be in name to make this Country a province of France. Neither do I doubt, that her standard displayed in this country would be directly or indirectly seconded by them in pursuance of the project I have mentioned.

It is painful and alarming to remark that the Opposition-Faction assumes so much a Geographical complexion. As yet from the South of Maryland nothing has been heared but accents of disapprobation of our Government and approbation of or apology for France. This is a most portentous symptom & demands every human effort to change it.

In such a state of public affairs it is impossible not to look up to you; and to wish that your influence could in some proper mode be brought into direct action. Among the ideas which have passed through my mind for this purpose—I have asked myself whether it might not be expedient for you to make a circuit through Virginia and North Carolina under some pretence of health &c. This would call forth addresses public dinners &c. which would give you an opportunity of expressing sentiments in Answers Toasts &c. which would throw the weight of your character into the scale of the Government and revive an enthusiasm for your person that may be turned into the right channel.

I am aware that the step is delicate & ought to be well considered before it is taken. I have even not settled my own opinion as to its propriety—but I have concluded to bring the general idea under your view, confident that your judgment will make a right choice and that you will take no step which is not well calculated. The conjuncture however is extraordinary & now or very soon will demand extraordinary measures.

You ought also to be aware, My Dear Sir, that in the event of an open rupture with France, the public voice will again call you to command the armies of your Country; and though all who are attached to you will from attachment, as well as public considerations, deplore an occasion which should once more tear you from that repose to which you have so good a right—yet it is the opinion of all those with whom I converse that you will be compelled to make the sacrifice. All your past labour may demand to give it efficacy this further, this very great sacrifice.[11]

Adams, thinking along lines similar to Hamilton's, appointed General Washington to the leadership of an expanded federal army—as it turned out, without the general's knowledge. Hamilton urged Washington to accept.

To George Washington:

[Philadelphia, July 8, 1798]

I was much surprized on my arrival here to discover that your nomination had been without any previous consultation of you. Convinced of the goodness of the motives it would be useless to scan the propriety of the step. It is taken and the question is— what under the circumstances ought to be done? I use the liberty which my attachment to you and to the public authorises to offer my opinion that you should not decline the appointment. It is evident that the public satisfaction at it is lively and universal. It is not to be doubted that the circumstance will give an additional spring to the public mind—will tend much to unite and will facilitate the measures which the conjuncture requires—on the other hand, your declining would certainly produce the opposite effects, would throw a great damp upon the ardor of the Country inspiring the idea that the Crisis was not really serious or alarming.[12]

The newly unretired commander-in-chief insisted on appointing Hamilton to the post of inspector general. Adams acceded to Wash-

ington's request, but appointed Henry Knox and Charles Cotesworth Pinckney, both of whom outranked Hamilton at the close of the Revolutionary War, to positions above him. Adams placed Knox second to Washington in the hierarchy. After a protracted dispute, Washington once again intervened and demanded that Hamilton be made his second-in-command. Like his rivals, Hamilton now had the title of major general.

Hamilton set about reorganizing the army and laying out detailed plans for the fortification of the New York harbor and the environs of the city, on which he collaborated with Ebenezer Stevens, a New York merchant and former officer in the Continental Army—and none other than Aaron Burr.

Alexander Hamilton, Aaron Burr, and Ebenezer Stevens to James McHenry:

[New York, June 14, 1798]

We submit that a plan, the success of which must entirely depend on the degree of enterprise of an enemy, which again depends on national and *individual* character, cannot safely be relied upon, and that it would be inexpedient to exhaust the slender pecuniary means which are hinted at in the execution of such a plan. If great and efficacious obstacles could be opposed to the passage of a fleet to the City, it would be of the greatest importance, and as an ulterior measure, is to be contemplated. But for this, we conceive, much greater means are requisite than seem to be at command and considerable time must be employed in the execution, more than it is imagined we ought to count upon having. The measure as an ulterior one engages our enquiries, and the result if deferred will be communicated. But for the present it has appeared to us on mature reflection, that the best thing to be done with the means already provided is to establish such defences as promise to be effectual to prevent ships from taking and keeping stations near the City, from which they can cannonade and bombard it with effect. To this end it seems to us of primary importance to put the works already begun on *Governor's*, *Bedlow's* and *Oyster Islands* in a condition to be defended, and to annoy—to occupy with small works *Red Hook*, and *Powles Hook*, and to erect four batteries on New-York Island at points which can be indicated.

We beg leave to add, that if the General Government will take the necessary measures in relation to the three first mentioned Islands, and to Red Hook, and Powles Hook, means will be found on the part of this City, provisionally, and in confidence of reimbursement by the General Government, to establish the batteries on New-York Island with the necessary cannon and apparatus.

A few gun-boats may likewise be useful auxiliaries, and it will deserve examination whether the channel between Governor's, and Long Islands, cannot be stopped without too great expence.[13]

As the Quasi War continued, a new crisis emerged on the home front. The legislatures of Virginia and Kentucky both passed resolutions declaring that the federal Alien and Sedition Acts were unconstitutional, a direct challenge to federal authority. The Alien and Sedition Acts were signed into law by President Adams in 1798. In an ill-advised attempt to prevent foreign agents and recent immigrants from stirring civil unrest, the acts criminalized "false, scandalous, and malicious" writing or speech about the United States government and tightened restrictions on citizenship. Hamilton wrote to Theodore Sedgwick, a Massachusetts Congressman:

To Theodore Sedgwick:

[New York, February 2, 1799]

What, My Dear Sir, are you going to do with Virginia? This is a very serious business, which will call for all the wisdom and firmness of the Government. The following are the ideas which occur to me on the occasion.

The first thing in all great operations of such a Government as ours is to secure the opinion of the people. To this end, the proceedings of Virginia and Kentucke with the two laws complained of should be referred to a special Committee. That Committee should make a report exhibiting with great luminousness and particularity the reasons which support the constitutionality and expediency of those laws—the tendency of the doctrines advanced by Virginia and Kentucke to destroy the Constitution of the UStates—and, with calm dignity united with pathos, the full evidence which they afford of a regular conspiracy to overturn the government. And the Report should likewise dwell upon the inevitable effect and probably the intention of these proceedings to encourage a hostile foreign power to decline accommodation and proceed in hostility. The Government must [no]t merely [de]fend itself [bu]t must attack and arraign its enemies. But in all this, there should be great care to distinguish the people of Virginia from the legislature and even the greater part of those who may have concurred in the legislature from the Chiefs; manifesting indeed a strong confidence in the good sense and patriotism of the people, that they will not be the dupes of an insidious plan to disunite the people of America to break down their constitution & expose them to the enterprises of a foreign power. . . .

...In the mean time the measures for raising the Military force should proceed with activity. Tis much to be lamented that so much delay has attended the execution of this measure. In times like the present not a moment ought to have been lost to secure the Government so powerful an auxiliary. Whenever the experiment shall be made to subdue a *refractory* & powerful *state* by Militia, the event will shame the advocates of their sufficiency. In the expedition against the Western Insurgents I trembled every moment lest a great part of the Militia should take it into their heads to return home rather than go forward.

When a clever force has been collected let them be drawn towards Virginia for which there is an obvious pretext—& then let measures be taken to act upon the laws & put Virginia to the Test of resistance.

This plan will give time for the fervour of the moment to subside, for reason to resume the reins, and by dividing its enemies will enable the Government to triumph with ease.[14]

Hamilton immediately dispensed unsolicited advice to his friend Secretary of War McHenry, about the nature of this force.
   To James McHenry:

Private
New York March 18, 1799

Beware, my Dear Sir, of magnifying a riot into an insurrection, by employing in the first instance an inadequate force. Tis better far to err on the other side. Whenever the Government appears in arms it ought to appear like a *Hercules*, and inspire respect by the display of strength. The consideration of expence is of no moment compared with the advantages of energy. Tis true this is always a relative question—but tis always important to make no mistake. I only offer a *principle* and a *caution*.

A large corps of auxiliary cavalry may be had in Jersey New York Delaware Maryland without interfering with farming pursuits.

Will it be inexpedient to put under marching Orders a large force provisionally, as in eventual support of the corps to be employed—to awe the disaffected?

Let all be well considered.[15]

No detail was too small to escape Hamilton's administrative mind. His plan for providing and issuing military supplies, shared in another letter to McHenry, reveals a master at work.

Portrait of Alexander Hamilton by John Trumbull, 1832.

To James McHenry:

[New York, April 8, 1799]

The business of providing shall constitute one distinct branch of service that of issuing another.

The *Purveyor* shall be charged with the procuring of all supplies except those for which contracts are made directly by the Chiefs of the Treasury or War Departments.

The Superintendant of Military Stores shall superintend the issues of all supplies.

The Purveyor shall have near him three *Assistants*, by whatsoever Denomination, one in relation to the supplies which according to past practice fall within the department of Quarter Master General including the means of Transportation—another in relation to the supplies which according to past practice fall within the Department of Commissary of Provisions with the Addition of Medical & Hospital a third in relation to the supplies which according to past practice fall within the Department of Commissary of Military Stores with the addition of cloathing. The person who now resides at the seat of Government in quality of Qr. Master General may perform the duty of the first mentioned Assistant.

The Superintendant of Military Stores shall have near him *three* principal Clerks, each of whom particularly to superintend the issues in one of the abovementioned branches; aided by as many store keepers as may be necessary.

The Purveyor shall have with each army a Deputy to be charged with the procuring of all supplies necessary to be procured with the army.

The Superintendant shall have with each army a Deputy who shall have under him three Assistants, one to superintend the issues of Quarter Master's Stores another to superintend the issues of Provisions—a third to superintend the issue of other Military Stores & Cloathing.

The Purveyor & his Deputies shall deliver over all that they provide to the Superintendant and his Deputies. The actual custody and issuing of articles to be with the Store Keepers pursuant to the written orders of the Superintendant and his deputies. The Quarter Master General with the Main Army & the Deputy Quarter Master General with each separate army shall have the superintendance of the Deputies of the Purveyor with the respective armies; to see that they do their duty according to their instructions from the heads of their respective Branches & the orders of the Commander of the Army.

The Inspector General with the main army & the Deputy Inspector General with each separate army shall have a like charge of the Deputies of the Superintendant of Military Stores.

These Officers to serve as checks upon the respective Deputies & points of Union between the Military & Civil authorities.

The Pay Master General shall reside at the seat of Government and be the fountain of all issues of money for the pay bounty &c. of the Troops.

He shall have a Deputy with each army who shall be charged with the issuing of all monies to the Regimental Pay Masters.

The Quarter Master of each *Division* shall be charged with the procuring of all supplies which may be occasionally necessary for such division in addition to the general Supplies.

The Quarter Master of each Brigade shall be charged with the like duty, when the brigade is detached only, and always with the superintendence of the issues for such brigade and consequently with the direction of all brigade Officers having the custody of supplies.

Each Brigade shall have a Commissary of Forage and another of Provisions to be charged respectively with the issues of those articles.

The Regimental Quarter Master shall receive and issue all supplies for the Regiment except of money or cloathing.

The Regimental Pay Master shall receive and issue all supplies of money and cloathing for the Regiment.[16]

George Washington died on December 14, 1799. Hamilton is sober and reflective in this letter to his Federalist ally Charles Cotesworth Pinckney. He knows all too well that he has lost his protector. He writes, "Perhaps no friend of his has more cause to lament, on personal account, than my self." (See p. 221 for Hamilton's condolence note to Martha Washington.)

To Charles Cotesworth Pinckney:

[Philadelphia, December, 22, 1799]

Sir

The death of our beloved commander in Chief was known to you before it was to me. I can be at no loss to anticipate what have been your feelings. I need not tell you what are mine. Perhaps no friend of his has more cause to lament, on personal account, than my self. The public misfortune is one which all the friends of our Government will view in the same light. I will not dwell on the subject. My Imagination is gloomy my heart sad.[17]

The new century began with what in Hamilton's mind was a terrible threat: the possibility of a Jefferson presidency. Hamilton saw only one possible way to counter this situation, telling Congressman Theodore Sedgwick in a letter, "To support Adams & Pinckney, equally, is the only thing that can possibly save us from the fangs of Jefferson." His hope was to squeeze out Jefferson by mustering enough support to give Adams and Pinckney first- and second-place finishes among the electors, which would give Federalists the presidency and vice presidency under the electoral law of the day.[18] *In another letter, sent a few days later to John Jay, who was now the governor of New York, Hamilton assesses recent losses by Federalist candidates in city and district elections, arguing that the aim of the Republican Party was nothing short of "the overthrow of the government" or "a Revolution after the manner of Bonaparte."*

To John Jay:

[New York, May 7, 1800]

...The moral certainty therefore is that there will be an Antifederal Majority in the Ensuing Legislature, and this very high probability is that this will bring *Jefferson* into the Chief Magistracy; unless it be prevented by the measure which I shall now submit to your consideration, namely the immediate calling together of the existing Legislature.

I am aware that there are weighty objections to the measure; but the reasons for it appear to me to outweigh the objections. And in times like these in which we live, it will not do to be overscrupulous. It is easy to sacrifice the substantial interests of society by a strict adherence to ordinary rules.

In observing this, I shall not be supposed to mean that any thing ought to be done which integrity will forbid—but merely that the scruples of delicacy and propriety, as relative to a common course of things, ought to yield to the extraordinary nature of the crisis. They ought not to hinder the taking of a *legal* and *constitutional* step, to prevent an *Atheist* in Religion and a *Fanatic* in politics from getting possession of the helm of the State.

You Sir know in a great degree the Antifederal party, but I fear that you do not know them as well as I do. Tis a composition indeed of very incongruous materials but all tending to mischief—some of them to the overthrow of the Government by stripping it of its due energies others of them to a Revolution after the manner of Buonaparte. I speak from indubitable facts, not from conjectures & inferences.[19]

Adams soon realized that Hamilton was behind a plot to control his administration, and relations between the two men, which had never been warm, now became hostile. Hamilton correctly predicted that Adams would not appoint him to be Washington's replacement at the head of the army, in spite of his position as the second in command. Adams replaced the cabinet members who were loyal to Hamilton, and demobilized the additional army (a standing army), one of Hamilton's pillars for a strong republic. Further, after the first mission was rebuffed during the Quasi War, Adams sent a second set of emissaries to France without the knowledge of his cabinet, and over Hamilton's vehement opposition. As a result of this growing distrust, Hamilton made a disastrous political misjudgment that haunted him for the rest of his career.

Impetuously reversing his previous strategy of keeping Jefferson out of the presidency at all costs, Hamilton now withdrew his support in the presidential election of 1800 from Adams, the Federalist candidate, in favor of Jefferson. "If we must have an enemy at the head of the

*Government," Hamilton explains in a letter to Sedgwick, "let it be
one whom we can oppose & for whom we are not responsible."*
  To Theodore Sedgwick:

New York May 10, 1800

He [Samuel Dexter, a Federalist Senator from Massachusetts,
loyal to Adams] is I am persuaded much mistaken as to the opinion entertained of Mr Adams by the Federal party. Were I to
determine from my own observation I should say, *most* of the
most influential men of that party consider him as a very *unfit*
and *incapable* character.

  For my individual part my mind is made up. I will never more
be responsible for him by my direct support—even though the
consequence should be the election of *Jefferson*. If we must have an
enemy at the head of the Government, let it be one whom we can
oppose & for whom we are not responsible, who will not involve
our party in the disgrace of his foolish and bad measures. Under
Adams as under *Jefferson* the government will sink. The party in
the hands of whose chief it shall sink will sink with it and the
advantage will all be on the side of his adversaries.

  Tis a notable expedient for keeping the Federal party together
to have at the head of it a man who hates and is dispised by those
men of it who in time past have been its most efficient supporters.

  If the cause is to be sacrificed to a weak and perverse man,
I withdraw from the party & act upon my own ground—never
certainly against my principles but in pursuance of them in my
own way. I am mistaken if others will not do the same.

  The only way to prevent a fatal schism in the Federal party is
to support G Pinckney in good earnest.

188 THE HAMILTON COLLECTION

If I can be perfectly satisfied that Adams & Pinckney will be upheld in the East with entire good faith, on the ground of conformity I will wherever my influence may extend pursue the same plan. If not I will pursue Mr. Pinkny as my single object.[20]

Then the confrontation became direct. As Hamilton was privately undermining Adams, the latter was returning the favor in kind. Adams enjoyed tweaking Hamilton for the circumstances of his birth (calling him a "Creole bastard"), and referred to him as a hypocrite. But in the current political environment, no insult could compare with Adams's deeming Hamilton to be the leader of a "British faction" in the United States government. His honor offended, Hamilton demanded an explanation.

To John Jay:

[New York, August 1, 1800]

It has been repeatedly mentioned to me that you have, on different occasions, asserted the existence of a *British Faction* in this Country, embracing a number of leading or influential characters of the *Federal Party* (as usually denominated) and that you have sometimes named me, at other times plainly alluded to me, as one of this description of persons: And I have likewise been assured that of late some of your warm adherents, for electioneering purposes, have employed a corresponding language.

I must, Sir, take it for granted, that you cannot have made such assertions or insinuations without being willing to avow them, and to assign the reasons to a party who may conceive himself injured by them. I therefore trust that you will not deem it improper that I apply directly to yourself, to ascertain from you, in reference to your own declarations, whether the information, I have received, has been correct or not, and if correct what are the grounds upon which you have founded the suggestion.[21]

Hamilton received no reply, which incensed him further. He weighed the idea of going public with his attack on Adams in this letter to Oliver Wolcott Jr., his replacement at Treasury.
    To Wolcott Jr.:

[New York, August 3, 1800]

I have two days since written to Mr. Adams a *respectful* letter on the subject I heretofore mentioned to you. Occupations at Court prevented its being sooner done.

But I wait with impatience for the statement of facts which you promised me. It is plain that unless we give our reasons in some form or other—Mr. Adam's personal friends seconded by the Jacobins [the most radical and violent of the political groups formed in the aftermath of the French Revolution] will completely *run us down in the public opinion.* Your name in company with mine that of T Pickering &c. is in full circulation as one of the *British Faction* of which Mr. Adams has talked so much [.]

I have serious thoughts of giving to the public my opinion respecting Mr. Adams with my reasons in a letter to a friend with my signature. This seems to me the most authentic way of conveying the information & best suited to the plain dealing of my character. There are however reasons against it and a very strong one is that some of the principal causes of my disapprobation proceed from yourself & other members of the Administration who would be understood to be the sources of my information whatever cover I might give the thing.

What say you to this measure? I could predicate it on the fact that I am abused by the friends of Mr. Adams who ascribe my opposition to pique & disappointment & would give it the shape of a *defence of my self.*

You have doubtless seen The Aurora publications of Treasury Documents & the manner in which my name is connected with it. These publications do harm with the ignorant who are the greatest number. I have thoughts of instituting an action of slander to be tried by a struck jury against the Editor. If I do it I should claim you & the Supervisors Collectors & Loan Officers of all the States from Maryland to N York inclusively as Witnesses to demonstrate completely the malice & falsity of the accusation. What think you of this? You see I am in a very belligerent humour.[22]

Frustrated by the lack of reply from Adams and by a swarm of attacks on his conduct as secretary of the Treasury, Hamilton followed through on his disastrous plan. The Letter from Alexander Hamilton Concerning the Public Conduct and Character of John Adams, Esq. President of the United States *was initially planned as a private letter to influential Federalists. When details of the letter were leaked to a Republican newspaper, Hamilton hurriedly published it as a pamphlet in October 1800. Hamilton first dismisses conjecture that his rift with Adams was caused by the president's refusal to appoint Hamilton to replace Washington at the head of the army. Then he turns to the substance of his attack.*

...While our object is common, our motives are variously dissimilar. A part, well affected to Mr. ADAMS, have no other wish than to take a double chance against Mr. JEFFERSON. Another part, feeling a diminution of confidence in him, still hope that the general tenor of his conduct will be essentially right. Few go as far in their objections as I do. Not denying to Mr. ADAMS patriotism and integrity, and even talents of a certain kind, I should be deficient in candor, were I to conceal the conviction, that he does not possess the talents adapted to the *Administration* of Government, and that there are great and intrinsic defects in his character, which unfit him for the office of Chief Magistrate.

Hamilton offers faint praise of Adams's performance of his duties as an envoy to France.

But this did not hinder me from making careful observations upon his several communications, and endeavoring to derive from them an accurate idea of his talents and character. This scrutiny enhanced my esteem in the main for his moral qualifications, but lessened my respect for his intellectual endowments. I then adopted an opinion, which all my subsequent experience has confirmed, that he is a man of an imagination sublimated and eccentric; propitious neither to the regular display of sound judgment, nor to steady perseverance in a systematic plan of conduct; and I began to perceive what has been since too manifest, that to this defect are added the unfortunate foibles of a vanity without bounds, and a jealousy capable of discoloring every object.

In a rambling, Lear-like monologue, Hamilton reviews Adams's record as president, giving particular attention to warnings not heeded and slights Hamilton himself has suffered along the way. Nearly fourteen thousand words later, he comes to his conclusion:

It is time to conclude—The statement, which has been made, shews that Mr. ADAMS has committed some positive and serious errors of Administration; that in addition to these, he has certain fixed points of character which tend naturally to the detriment of any cause of which he is the chief, of any Administration of which he is the head; that by his ill humors and jealousies he has already divided and distracted the supporters of the Government; that he has furnished deadly weapons to its enemies by unfounded accusations, and has weakened the force of its friends by decrying some of the most influential of them to the utmost of his power; and let it be added, as the necessary effect of such conduct, that he has made great progress in undermining the ground which was gained for the government by his predecessor, and that there is real cause to apprehend, it might totter, if not fall, under his future auspices. A new government, constructed on free principles, is always weak, and must stand in need of the props of a firm and good administration; till time shall have rendered its authority venerable, and fortified it by habits of obedience.

Yet with this opinion of Mr. ADAMS, I have finally resolved not to advise the withholding from him a single vote. The body of Federalists, for want of sufficient knowledge of facts, are not convinced of the expediency of relinquishing him. It is even apparent, that a large proportion still retain the attachment which was once a common sentiment. Those of them, therefore, who are dissatisfied, as far as my information goes, are, generally speaking, willing to forbear opposition, and to acquiesce in the equal support of Mr. ADAMS with Mr. PINCKNEY, whom they prefer. Have they not a claim to equal deference from those who continue attached to the former? Ought not these, in candor, to admit the possibility that the friends who differ from them, act not only from pure motives, but from cogent reasons? Ought they not, by a co-operation in General PINCKNEY, to give a chance for what will be a *safe* issue, supposing that they are right in their preference, and the best issue, should they happen to be mistaken? Especially, since by doing this, they will increase the probability of excluding a third candidate, of whose unfitness all sincere federalists are convinced. If they do not pursue this course, they will certainly incur an immense responsibility to their friends and to the Government.

To promote this co-operation, to defend my own character, to vindicate those friends, who with myself have been unkindly aspersed, are the inducements for writing this letter. Accordingly, it will be my endeavor to regulate the communication of it in such a manner as will not be likely to deprive Mr. ADAMS of a single vote. Indeed, it is much my wish that its circulation could forever be confined within narrow limits. I am sensible of the inconveniences of giving publicity to a similar developement of the character of the Chief Magistrate of our country; and I lament the necessity of taking a step which will involve that result. Yet to suppress truths, the disclosure of which is so interesting to the public welfare as well as to the vindication of my friends and myself, did not appear to me justifiable.

The restraints, to which I submit, are a proof of my disposition to sacrifice to the prepossessions of those, with whom I have heretofore thought and acted, and from whom in the present question I am compelled to differ. To refrain from a decided opposition to Mr. ADAMS'S re-election has been reluctantly sanctioned by my judgment; which has been not a little perplexed between the unqualified conviction of his unfitness for the station contemplated, and a sense of the great importance of cultivating harmony among the supporters of the Government; on whose firm union hereafter will probably depend the preservation of order, tranquillity, liberty, property; the security of every social and domestic blessing.[23]

The impact was immediate and profound. Hamilton had effectively destroyed the Federalist Party and his leadership of it. His tortured condemnation of Adams, dogged, unconvincing vindication of himself, and, ultimately, his contradictory resolution "not to advise the withholding from him [Adams] a single vote" baffled and angered his allies and delighted his foes. For his part, Adams drafted a response, but discarded it, astutely observing that Hamilton had done more damage to himself than to Adams. Historians debate whether the pamphlet contributed to Jefferson's victory in the election, but at minimum it damaged the Federalist cause.

Jefferson's victory was not yet a foregone conclusion when Hamilton set his sights on his next target: his professional colleague and sometime ally in the courtroom Aaron Burr. (See p. 239 for a more detailed account of Hamilton's complicated relationship with Burr.) Hamilton and Burr (together with Henry Brockholst Livingston, an attorney from an influential New York family) had recently succeeded in exonerating a young Manhattan carpenter named Levi Weeks of murder in a high-profile case. But when the 1800 presidential election came down to a deadlock in the House of Representatives between Jefferson and Burr, Hamilton had such severe doubts about Burr's character that he threw his weight behind Jefferson in the election. He set about dismantling Burr's reputation in a handful of private, well-targeted letters, the first to his friend Gouverneur Morris.

To Gouverneur Morris:

[New York, December 26, 1800]

The post of yesterday gave me the pleasure of a letter from you. I thank you for the communication. I trust that a letter which I wrote you the day before the receipt of yours will have duly reached you as it contains some very free & confidential observations ending in two results—1 That The Convention with France ought to be ratified as the least of two evils 2 That *on the same ground Jefferson* ought to be preferred to *Burr.*

I trust the Federalists will not finally be so mad as to vote for the *latter.* I speak with an intimate & accurate knowlege of character. His elevation can only promote the purposes of the desperate and proflicate. [If t]here be [a man] in the world I ought to hate it is Jefferson. With *Burr* I have always been personally well. But the public good must be paramount to every private consideration. My opinion may be freely used with such reserves as you shall think discreet.[24]

Hamilton stepped up his targeted attacks, telling Representative John Rutledge Jr., a Federalist member of the House of Representatives from South Carolina, in a January 1801 letter, "You cannot in my opinion render a greater service to your Country than by exerting your influence to counteract the impolitic and impure idea of raising Mr. Burr to the Chief Magistracy." Lest Rutledge harbor any doubts, Hamilton enclosed a point-by-point indictment of Burr's character, referring to him as "a voluptuary," "insolvent," and "cowardly."

1. He is in every sense a profligate; a voluptuary in the extreme, with uncommon habits of expence; in his profession extortionate to a proverb; suspected on strong grounds of having *corruptly* served the views of the Holland Company, in the capacity of a

member of our legislature*; and understood to have been guilty of several breaches of probity in his pecuniary transactions. His very friends do not insist upon his integrity.

2. He is without doubt insolvent for a large *deficit*. All his visible property is deeply mortgaged, and he is known to owe other large debts, for which there is no specific security. Of the number of these is a Judgment in favour of Mr. Angerstien for a sum which with interest amounts to about 80,000 Dollars.

3. The fair emoluments of any station, under our government, will not equal his expences in that station; still less will they suffice to extricate him from his embarassments & he must therefore from the necessity of his situation have recourse to unworthy expedients. These may be a *bargain* and *sale* with some foreign power, or combinations with public agents in projects of gain by means of the public monies; perhaps and probably, to enlarge the sphere—a *War*.

4. He has no pretensions to the Station from services. He acted in different capacities in the last war finally with the rank of Lt. Col in a Regiment, and gave indications of being a good officer; but without having had the opportunity of performing any distinguished action. At a *critical period* of the War, he resigned his commission, assigning for cause ill-health, and went to reside at *Paramus* in the State of New Jersey. If his health was bad he might without difficulty have obtained a furlough and was not obliged to resign. He was afterwards seen in his usual health. The circumstance excited much jealousy of his motives. In civil life, he has never projected nor aided in producing a single measure of important public utility.

---

*He cooperated in obtaining a law to permit Aliens to hold & convey lands.

5. He has *constantly* sided with the party hostile to *federal* measures before and since the present constitution of the U States. In opposing the adoption of this constitution he was engaged covertly and insidiously; because, as he said at the time "it was too strong and too weak" and he has been uniformly the opposer of the Federal Administration.

6. No mortal can tell what his political principles are. He has talked *all round the compass. At times* he has dealt in all the jargon of Jacobinism; at other times he has proclaimed decidedly the total insufficiency of the Federal Government and the necessity of changes to one far more energetic. The truth seems to be that he has no plan but that of *getting* power by *any* means and *keeping* it by *all* means. It is probable that if he has any theory 'tis that of a simple *despotism*. He has intimated that he thinks the present French constitution not a bad one.

7. He is of a temper bold enough to think no enterprize too hazardous and sanguine enough to think none too difficult. He has censured the leaders of the Federal party as wanting in vigour and enterprise, for not having established a strong Government when they were in possession of the power and influence.

8. Discerning men of all parties agree in ascribing to him an irregular and inordinate ambition. Like *Catiline [a notorious Roman Senator]*, he is indefatigable in courting the *young* and the *profligate*. He knows well the weak sides of human nature, and takes care to play in with the passions of all with whom he has intercourse. By natural disposition, the haughtiest of men, he is at the same time the most creeping to answer his purposes. Cold and collected by nature and habit, he never loses sight of his object and scruples no means of accomplishing it. He is artful and intriguing to an inconceivable degree. In short

all his conduct indicates that he has in view nothing less than the establishment of Supreme Power in his own person. Of this nothing can be a surer index than that having in fact high-toned notions of Government, he has nevertheless constantly opposed the *federal* and courted the *popular* party. As he never can effect his wish by the aid of good men, he will court and employ able and daring scoundrels of every party, and by availing himself of their assistance and of all the bad passions of the Society, he will in all likelihood attempt an usurpation.

Hamilton even takes exception to Burr's wanton participation in dinner table toasts before returning to matters of law and state.

8. Within the last three weeks at his own Table, he drank these toasts successively 1 The French Republic 2 The Commissioners who negotiated the Convention 3 *Buonaparte* 4 *La Fayette;* and he countenanced and seconded the positions openly advanced by one of his guests that it was the interest of this Country to leave it free to the Belligerent Powers to sell their prizes in our ports and to build and equip ships for their respective uses; a doctrine which evidently aims at turning all the naval resources of the UStates into the channel of France; and which by making these states the most pernicious enemy of G Britain would compel her to go to War with us.

9. Though possessing infinite art cunning and address—he is yet to give proofs of great or solid abilities. It is certain that at the Bar he is more remarkable for ingenuity and dexterity than for sound judgment or good logic. From the character of his understanding and heart it is likely that any innovations which he may effect will be such as to serve the turn of his own power,

not such as will issue in establishments favourable to the permanent security and prosperity of the Nation—founded upon the
principles of a *strong free* and *regular* Government.[25]

*Hamilton's next letter, to the Federalist representative James Bayard
of Delaware, might be the one that tipped the election to Jefferson. It
was Bayard who, on the thirty-sixth vote among the sixteen states in
the House, submitted a blank ballot, breaking the deadlock. Bayard
made a deal with Jefferson, who promised to retain the current financial system, honor existing commitments to expand the navy, and keep
Federalist officials below cabinet level in their jobs. Hamilton's letter's
chief criticism of Burr was that he had no moral center; better to have
a man with erroneous beliefs than none at all. He compares Burr to
Catiline, a Roman Senator who plotted the overthrow of the Republic
in the first century BC—in essence, painting him as a traitor.*
    To James A. Bayard:

[New York, January 16, 1801]

The truth is that *Burr* is a man of a very subtile imagination, and
a mind of this make is rarely free from ingenious whimsies. Yet
I admit that he has no fixed theory & that his peculiar notions
will easily give way to his interest. But is it a recommendation to
have *no theory?* Can that man be a systematic or able statesman
who has none? I believe not. *No general principles* will hardly work
much better than erroneous ones....
    Can there be any serious question between the policy of leav-
ing the Antifœderalists to be answerable for the elevation of an
exceptionable man, & that of adopting ourselves & becoming
answerable for a man who on all hands is acknowledged to be

a complete *Cataline* in his practice & principles? 'Tis enough to state the question to indicate the answer, if reason not passion presides in the decision. You may communicate this & my former letter to discreet & confidential friends.[26]

Hamilton's efforts succeeded. Jefferson became the third President of the United States, and Aaron Burr became his vice president. Hamilton was now relegated to the political sideline, though of course, never completely. Wishing to assure himself a continued voice, he founded the New-York Evening Post *(which remains in publication today as the* New York Post*).*

The next week, tragedy struck. Hamilton's eldest son, Philip, now nineteen, was killed in a duel with George Eacker, a Republican attorney and supporter of Burr's who had recently claimed in a speech that Hamilton would not oppose overthrowing the Jefferson administration by force.[27] Months later, Philip and a friend confronted Eacker, and the result was an "interview" (the current euphemism for a duel) on the field of honor—the very same one in Weehawken on which Alexander Hamilton would be killed less than three years later. Hamilton was at Philip's bedside when he died, the day after the duel. To say he was devastated is an understatement. Philip's death altered Hamilton's entire being. (See p. 229 for details of Hamilton's relationship with his eldest son and a letter relating to Philip's death.)

Mourning though he was, Hamilton issued blistering criticism of proposed Jefferson administration policies (delivered by Jefferson to Congress in a written address Hamilton refers to as "The Message"). Hamilton published a series of eighteen articles in the New-York Evening Post *he called "The Examination" under the pseudonym "Lucius Crassus," each refuting an element of Jefferson's proposal. In the second and third of these articles, Hamilton attacks Jefferson's plan to cut domestic taxes, alarmed at what he perceives to be its inevitable detrimental effect on Hamilton's great legacy, public credit. In the process, he lands a few jabs at Jefferson and his supporters, implying that they must either be misrepresenting their motives, or else merely exhibiting "a deficiency of intellect, and...an ignorance of our financial arrangements."*

[New York, December 21, 1801]

The next most prominent feature in the Message, is the proposal to abandon at once all the internal revenue of the country. The motives avowed for this astonishing scheme, are that "there is *reasonable ground of confidence* that this part of the revenue may now be safely dispensed with—that the remaining sources will be sufficient to provide for the support of government, to *pay the interest* of the public debt, and to *discharge the principal* in shorter periods than the *laws* or the *general expectation* had contemplated—and that though wars and untoward events might change this prospect of things, and call for expences which the *impost* could not meet—yet that sound principles would not justify our taxing the industry of our fellow citizens to *accumulate treasure* for wars to happen we know not when, and which might not perhaps happen but from the *temptations offered* by that treasure."

If we allow these to be more than ostensible motives, we shall be driven to ascribe this conduct to a deficiency of intellect, and to an ignorance of our financial arrangements, greater than could have been suspected: if but ostensible, it is then impossible to trace the suggestion to any other source than the culpable desire of gaining or securing popularity at an immediate expence of public utility, equivalent, on a pecuniary scale to a million of dollars annually; and at the greater expence of a very serious invasion of our system of public credit.[28]

Hamilton continues, in the next installment of "The Examination," by presenting the reasons for maintaining the internal revenue. Rather than abolish the duty on American vessels, for example, he proposes lessening them "on some particular articles on which they may press with inconvenient weight."

[New York, December 24, 1801]

Thomas Jefferson, shown in a 1928 lithograph, began his presidency in 1801 by seeking to reverse many of the policies implemented by Hamilton.

But admitting the position that there is an excess of income which ought to be relinquished, still the proposal to surrender the *internal revenue* is impolitic. It ought to be carefully preserved, as not being exposed to the casualties incident to our intercourse with foreign nations, and therefore the most certain. It ought to be preserved, as reaching to descriptions of persons who are not proportionably affected by the impost, and as tending for this reason, to distribute the public burden more equitably. It ought to be preserved, because if revenue can really be spared, it is best to do it in such a manner as will conduce to the relief or advancement of our navigation and commerce. Rather let the tonnage duty on American vessels be abolished, and let the duties be lessened on some particular articles on which they may press with inconvenient weight. Let not the merchant be provoked to attempt to evade the duties, by the sentiment that his ease or interest is disregarded, and that his capital alone is to be clogged and incumbered by the demands of the treasury.

But who and what are the merchants when compared with the patriotic votaries of whiskey in Pennsylvania and Virginia?[29]

In "The Examination Number VI," Hamilton questions the wisdom of Jefferson's plan to eliminate judges at the circuit court level, which had been created to relieve the workload of the Supreme Court in a geographically expanding nation. (They had previously traveled to each district to hear cases.) Adams had filled the circuit court with Federalist judges. Hamilton recognized Jefferson's plan as a challenge to an independent judiciary, or possibly, merely to a judiciary dominated by Federalists.

[New York, January 2, 1802]

Weighing maturely all the very important and very delicate considerations, which appertain to the subject, would a wise or prudent statesman hazard the consequences of immediately unmaking at one session, Courts and Judges which had only been called in into being at the one preceding? Delectable indeed must be the work of disorganization to a mind which can thus rashly advance in its prosecution! Infatuated must that people be, who do not open their eyes to projects so intemperate—so mischievous! Who does not see what is the ultimate object? *"Delenda est Carthago"* ["Carthage must be destroyed]—ill-fated Constitution, which Americans had fondly hoped would continue for ages, the guardian of public liberty, the source of national prosperity![30]

In Hamilton's critique of the liberalized immigration policy proposed by Jefferson, he reveals a deep-seated fear of the effect of "foreigners" on the body politic, whose heterogeneous views, in Hamilton's words, could have a tendency "to change and corrupt the national spirit." Rather ironic coming from a recent immigrant!

[New York, January 12, 1802]

The safety of a republic depends essentially on the energy of a common National sentiment; on a uniformity of principles and habits; on the exemption of the citizens from foreign bias, and prejudice; and on that love of country which will almost invariably be found to be closely connected with birth, education and family....

...[F]oreigners will generally be apt to bring with them attachments to the persons they have left behind; to the country of their nativity, and to its particular customs and manners. They will also entertain opinions on government congenial with those under which they have lived, or if they should be led hither from a preference to ours, how extremely unlikely is it that they will bring with them that *temperate love of liberty*, so essential to real republicanism? There may as to particular individuals, and at particular times, be occasional exceptions to these remarks, yet such is the general rule. The influx of foreigners must, therefore, tend to produce a heterogeneous compound; to change and corrupt the national spirit; to complicate and confound public opinion; to introduce foreign propensities. In the composition of society, the harmony of the ingredients is all important, and whatever tends to a discordant intermixture must have an injurious tendency.[31]

Drawing depicting the south and east sides of the Grange, the Federal-style home Hamilton had built in upper Manhattan. The building was completed in 1802.

Hamilton knew that his authority had been eclipsed, and one can detect a diminished vigor in his writing by this time. He had already begun to shift his focus to his new life with his family at the Grange, the country home he was building on thirty-two acres in northern Manhattan. In February, he wrote in a melancholy frame of mind to his good friend Gouverneur Morris.

To Gouverneur Morris:

[New York, February 29, 1802]

Mine is an odd destiny. Perhaps no man in the UStates has sacrificed or done more for the present Constitution than myself—and contrary to all my anticipations of its fate, as you know from the very begginning I am still labouring to prop the frail and worthless fabric. Yet I have the murmurs of its friends no less than the curses of its foes for my rewards. What can I do better than withdraw from the Scene? Every day proves to me more and more that this American world was not made for me.[32]

By the end of the year, Hamilton's spirits had lifted, and his tone was more philosophical in this letter to Charles Cotesworth Pinckney.

To Charles Cotesworth Pinckney:

[Grange, New York, December 29, 1802]

My Dear Sir

A garden, you know, is a very usual refuge of a disappointed politician. Accordingly, I have purchased a few acres about 9 Miles from Town, have built a house and am cultivating a Garden. The melons in your country are very fine. Will you have the goodness to send me some seed both of the Water & Muss Melons?

My daughter adds another request, which is for three or four of your peroquets. She is very fond of birds. If there be any thing in this quarter the sending of which can give you pleasure, you have only to name them. As Farmers a new source of sympathy has risen between us; and I am pleased with every thing in which our likings and tastes can be approximated.

His thoughts in the letter turn to Jefferson's government, and to an ongoing crisis in New Orleans, where American ships had been denied use of the port by the Spanish government, which was then in control of the territory. His distaste for democracy—in Hamilton's view, rule by the mob—is apparent. He is not opposed, however, to expansionism, and proposes annexing to the United States all territories east of the Mississippi River, the sooner the better.

Amidst the triumphant reign of Decomocracy, do you retain sufficient interest in public affairs to feel any curiosity about what is going on? In my opinion the follies and vices of the Administration have as yet made no material impression to their disadvantage. On the contrary, I think the malady is rather progressive than upon the decline in our Northern Quarter. The last *lullaby* message, instead of inspiring contempt, attracts praise. Mankind are forever destined to be the dupes of bold & cunning imposture.

But a difficult *knot* has been twisted by the incident of the cession of Louisian [ceded by Spain to France in a secret deal made in 1800] and the interruption of the Deposit [the right for American merchants to use the port] at New Orleans. You have seen the soft tun given to this in the message. Yet we are told the President in conversation is very stout. The great embarrassment must be how to carry on war without taxes. The pretty scheme of substituting economy to taxation will not do here; and a war would be a terrible comment upon the abandonment of the Internal Revenue. Yet how is popularity to be preserved with the Western partisans if their interests are tamely sacrificed? Will the artifice be for the Chief to hold a bold language and the subalters to act a public part? Time must explain.

You know my general theory as to our Western affairs. I have always held that the Unity of our empire and the best interests of our Nation require that we should annex to the UStates all the territory East of the Mississippia, New Orleans included. Of course I infer that in an emergency like the present, Energy is Wisdom.[33]

Within months, Jefferson's administration had negotiated the Louisiana Purchase, famously one of the most lopsided real estate deals in history. The Louisiana Territory, including New Orleans, was now American, ensuring control of the Mississippi River and its trade and opening up enormous swaths of inland wilderness to development. The US government had paid $11.25 million and canceled France's debts of $3.75 million, for a total cost of $15 million. Hamilton published a grudgingly favorable response to the purchase in the Post, *arguing that it was historical circumstances rather than "wise or vigorous measures" on Jefferson's part that had forced an overextended France to make the sale to the Americans. Hamilton, dubious of the value of the inland territory, reminds his readers that Jefferson's rationale for cutting internal revenues, given in his "Message" speech to Congress, may come back to haunt him—and them:*

[July 5, 1803]

Mr. Jefferson in that part of his famous electioneering message, where he took so much pains to present a flattering state of the Treasury in so few words that every man could carry it in his noddle and repeat it at the poll, tells us, that "experience too so far authorises us to believe, *if no extraordinary event supervenes, and the expences which will be actually incurred shall not be greater than was contemplated* by Congress at their last session, that we shall not be disappointed in the expectations formed" that the debt would soon be paid, &c. &c. But the first and only measure of the administration that has really been of any material service to the country (for they have hitherto gone on the strength of the provisions made by their predecessors) is really *"an extraordinary event,"* and calls for more money than they have got. According to Mr. Gallatin's report, they had about 40.000 to spare for contingencies, and now the first *"extraordinary event"* that *"supervenes"* calls upon them for several millions. What a poor starvling system of administering a government! *But how is the money to be had? Not by taxing luxury and wealth and whiskey, but by increasing the taxes on the necessaries of life.* Let this be remembered.

Hamilton's criticism is caustic, but the underlying tone is one of resignation. Still, he could not resist a swipe at James Monroe, the man whom he suspected had betrayed his oath of confidentiality in the Reynolds affair, in an addendum to the article.

If reliance can be placed on the history given of the negociation of *Louisiana* in private letters, from persons of respectability residing at Paris, and who speak with confidence, the merit of it, after making due allowance for the great events which have borne it along with them, is due to our ambassador, Chancellor

Livingston, and not to the Envoy Extraordinary. "The cession was voted in the Council of State on the 8th of April, and Mr. Munro did not even arrive till the 12th." Judging from Mr. Munro's former communications to the French Government on this subject, we really cannot but regard it as fortunate, that the thing was concluded before he reached St. Cloud.[34]

Hamilton remained extremely busy with his legal practice and kept a hand in the affairs of the Federalist Party and in state politics. At the beginning of 1804, he represented Harry Croswell, who had been convicted of libeling President Jefferson in a news article in 1803, before the New York Supreme Court. The court denied Croswell a new trial, but Hamilton used the case as a platform to revise libel laws to allow the truth of a statement to be a defense for libel. The state legislature passed the revised law in 1806, in what was to be Hamilton's final legislative achievement—achieved through his private practice.

Hamilton appeared to accept, and even embrace, his new status as a would-be gentleman farmer. Characteristically, he approached even this genteel enterprise with energy, thoroughness, and even affection, as can be seen in this letter to his wife, Elizabeth, who was also called Eliza or Betsey.

To Elizabeth Hamilton:

[New York, October 14, 1803]

I arrived here this day, in about as good health as I left home though somewhat fatigued.

There are some things necessary to be done which I omitted mentioning to you. I wish the Carpenters to make and insert two Chimnies for ventilating the Ice-House, each about two feet

Square & four feet long half above and half below the ground—to have a cap on the top sloping downwards so that the rain may not easily enter—the aperture for letting in and out the air to be about a foot and a half square in the side immediately below the cap (see *figure* on the other side).

Let a separate compost bed be formed near the present one; to consist of 3 barrels full of the *clay* which I bought 6 barrels of *black mould* 2 waggon loads of the best clay on the Hill opposite the *Quakers place* this side of Mrs. Verplanks (the Gardener must go for it himself) and one waggon load of pure cow-dung. Let these be well and repeatedly mixed and pounded together to be made use of hereafter for the Vines.

I hope the apple trees will have been planted so as to profit by this moderate and wet weather. If not done—Let *Tough* be reminded that a temporary fence is to be put up along the declivity of the Hill from the Kings bridge road to the opposite wood so as to prevent the cattle injuring the young trees—the fence near the entrance to the *Helicon spring* ought for the same reason to be attended to. The materials of the fence taken down in making the Kitchen Garden & some rubbish which may be picked up will answer.

Remember that the piazzas are also to be caulked & that additional accommodations for the pidgeons are to be made.

You see I do not forget the Grange. No that I do not; nor any one that inhabits it. Accept yourself my tenderest affection.[35]

But this peaceful phase of Hamilton's life did not last long. When George Clinton announced that he would not run for reelection as governor of New York (he was to replace Aaron Burr as vice president on the Republican ticket under Jefferson), Burr saw an opportunity to salvage

Cornelia Schuyler Morton (1775–1808), Elizabeth Hamilton's youngest sister, shown in a detail from a miniature painting by John Trumbull, painted when she was about seventeen.

his political career by running to replace Clinton as the New York governor. Hamilton feared that Burr, as a nationally known Republican with significant Federalist support, had a good chance of succeeding. So he leapt into action, publicly and privately denouncing Burr during the campaign. Though Burr carried New York City, he lost the statewide election. He was not a happy man when he wrote to Hamilton on June 18, 1804, demanding an explanation for a published report of one of Hamilton's repeated personal attacks on his character.

A volley of letters went back and forth between the two men over the next three weeks, almost comically polite, yet filled with anger and petty vindictiveness. The letters culminated in the infamous "interview" in Weehawken on July 11, 1804. Burr, the sitting vice president of the United States, mortally wounded Hamilton that morning. Hamilton was rowed back across the Hudson to Manhattan, where he died the next day at the home of his friend William Bayard in Greenwich Village. On July 14, he was buried with military honors at Trinity Church in lower Manhattan. (See p. 239 for correspondence relating to the duel and for details of Hamilton's relationship with Burr.)

HAMILTON'S
CIRCLE

★ ★ ★

Hamilton, a self-made man, believed in meritocracy, and it shows in his selection of the people he made a part of his personal circle. There were two notable exceptions to this (Maria Reynolds and Aaron Burr), and true to the formula of tragedy, these were colossal blunders, fueled by hubris, which contributed to his downfall.

Taken as a whole, Hamilton's personal correspondence shows many of the same characteristics of his public life: intensely focused, breathtakingly capable and intelligent, controlling, charming, sensitive, and arrogant. It also shows a playful, tender, and charismatic side of the man—direct in his expression of affection, flirtatious, deeply caring, and funny.

GEORGE WASHINGTON

No individual was more important to the ascendancy of Alexander Hamilton than George Washington. Washington was Hamilton's sponsor and protector, a father figure in ways mostly positive and occasionally negative. Their abilities were so complementary—Hamilton was able to give voice and organization to Washington's masterful plans; Washington provided the gravitas and reputation that the outsider Hamilton otherwise lacked. Washington kept a steady hand on

George Washington (1732–1799), shown here in a portrait by Gilbert Stuart,
relied on Hamilton to give voice to his ideas and to implement his plans;
respectful but distant early in their relationship, the two men developed genuine
affection for one another over their years together.

the tiller; Hamilton's encyclopedic knowledge of political, economic,
and military history gave them the guidance and persuasive powers
that they needed to lead the army and the nation. Arguably, no duo
accomplished more than Washington and Hamilton in the effort to win
independence from Great Britain and establish the form of government
that we recognize today as American.

It would be inaccurate to characterize Hamilton's relationship
with Washington as a friendship for much of their entwined lives as
soldiers and statesmen—Washington was more of a paternal figure
for Hamilton. Yet a genuine affection grew between them over the

course of their long association. When Hamilton became Washington's aide-de-camp in March 1777, Washington had already become familiar with Hamilton's military acumen in battles ranging from White Plains to Trenton to Princeton. Hamilton clearly relished being at the center of operations, but his desire to be a field commander (see p. 38) and the differences in their temperaments sometimes caused him to lose patience with Washington. In February 1781, tensions reached a climax, and Hamilton resigned his commission, as he peevishly describes in this letter to his father-in-law. The letter contains an unusually high number of deletions and insertions, indicating that Hamilton was being extremely careful in relating the story to his influential father-in-law of just over a year, who was a friend of Washington's. The lines Hamilton attributes to himself in his confrontation with Washington ("I replied without petulancy, but with decision 'I am not conscious of it Sir, but since you have thought it necessary to tell me so we part'") read like those of a B-list actor, and ring as very un-Hamiltonian.

To George Washington:

[Head Quarters New Windsor, New York,
February 18, 1881]

My Dear Sir.

Since I had the pleasure of writing you last an unexpected change has taken place in my situation. I am no longer a member of the General's family. This information will surprise you, and the manner of the change will surprise you more. Two day ago The General and I passed each other on the stairs. He told me he wanted to speak to me. I answered that I would wait upon him immediately. I went below and delivered Mr. [Tench] Tilghman a letter to be sent to The Commissary containing an order of a pressing and interesting nature. Returning to The General I was stopped, in the way, by the Marquis De la Fayette, and we conversed together about a minute on a matter of business. He can testify how impatient I was to get back, and that I left him in a manner which but for our intimacy would have been more than abrupt. Instead of finding the General as usual in his room, I met him at the head of the stairs, where accosting me in a very angry tone, "Col Hamilton (said he), you have kept me waiting at the head of the stairs these ten minutes. I must tell you Sir you treat me with disrespect." I replied without petulancy, but with decision "I am not conscious of it Sir, but since you have thought it necessary to tell me so we part" "Very well Sir, said he) if it be your choice" or something to this effect and we separated.

I sincerely believe my absence which gave so much umbrage did not last two minutes.

Hamilton continues the story, recounting how he rebuffed an aide sent by Washington to ask Hamilton to engage in a "candid conversation" and patch things up. Hamilton refused, assuring the general (through the aide) that he would remain until Washington could find a replacement.

Thus we stand. . . .

I have given you so particular a detail of our difference from the desire I have to justify myself in your opinion.

Perhaps you may think I was precipitate in rejecting the overture made by the general to an accommodation. I assure you My Dr Sir it was not the effect of resentment, it was the deliberate result of maxims I had long formed for the government of my own conduct.

I always disliked the office of an Aide de Camp as having in it a kind of personal dependance. I refused to serve in this capacity with two Major General's at an early period of the war. Infected, however, with the enthusiasm of the times, an idea of the Generals character which experience soon taught me to be unfounded, overcame my scruples and induced me to *accept his invitation* to enter into his family. I believe you know the place I held in The Generals confidence and councils of which will make it the more extraordinary to you to learn that for three years past I have felt no friendship for him and have professed none. The truth is our own dispositions are the opposites of each other & the pride of my temper would not suffer me to profess what I did not feel. Indeed when advances of this kind [have been made] to me on his part, they were rec[eived in a manner] that showed at least I had no inclination [to court them, and that] I wished to stand rather upon a footing of m[ilitary confidence than] of private attachment. You are too good a judge of human nature not to be sensible how this conduct in me must have operated on a man to whom all the world is offering incense. With this key you will easily unlock the present mystery. At the end of the war I may say many things to you concerning which I shall impose upon myself 'till then an inviolable silence.

The General [is a very honest] man. His competitors [have slender]abilities, and less integ[rity]. His popularity] has often [been essential to the safety of America, and is still of great importance to it. These considerations have influenced my past conduct respecting him, and will influence my future. I think it is necessary he should be supported.

...I wish what I have said to make no other impression than to satisfy you I have not been in the wrong. It is also said in confidence, for as a public knowledge of the breach would in many ways have [an ill effect.] it will probably be [the policy of both sides] to conceal it and cover the [separation with] some plausible pretext. [I am importuned by such friends as are privy to the affair, to listen to a reconciliation: but my resolution is unalterable...

I have written to you on this subject with all the freedom and confidence to which you have a right and with an assurance of the interest you take in all that concerns me.[1]

Washington gave Hamilton the field command that he longed for within months of their "separation." The mutual dependence between the two men only increased when the war ended and the business of establishing a government began. By the time news of the Reynolds affair became public in 1797, Washington's expression of friendship and support for Hamilton, deeply needed and appreciated by the younger man, demonstrated how far their relationship had come. Washington sent this letter to Hamilton with the gift of a wine cooler.

To George Washington:

[Mount Vernon, August 21, 1797]

My dear Sir,

Not for any intrinsic value the thing possesses, but as a token of my sincere regard and friendship for you, and as a remembrancer of me; I pray you to accept a Wine cooler for four bottles, which Coll. Biddle is directed to forward from Philadelphia (where with other articles it was left) together with this letter, to your address.

It is one of four, which I imported in the early part of my late Administration of the Government; two only of which were ever used.

I pray you to present my best wishes, in which Mrs. Washington joins me, to Mrs. Hamilton & the family; and that you would be persuaded, that with every sentiment of the highest regard, I remain your sincere friend, and affectionate Hble Servant.[2]

When Washington died in 1799, Hamilton lost his mentor and protector as well as someone for whom he had come to have genuine feelings of affection (see his letter to Charles Coteworth Pinckney, p. 184). Hamilton's gracious sympathy letter to Martha Washington offers solace in the knowledge that they shared a precious private connection to a man whose public stature was unparalleled. The letter displays the deeply sensitive side of Hamilton's nature.

New York Jany. 12. 1800
To Martha Washington

Martha Washington, 1731–1802

I did not thing it proper, Madam, to intrude amidst the first effusions of your grief. But I can no longer restrain my sensibility from conveying to you an imperfect expression of my affectionate sympathy in the sorrows you experience. No one, better than myself, knows the greatness of your loss, or how much your excellent heart is formed to feel it in all its extent. Satisfied that you cannot receive consolation, I will attempt to offer none. Resignation to the will of Heaven, which the practice of your life ensures, can alone alleviate the sufferings of so heart-rending an affliction.

There can be few, who equally with me participate in the loss you deplore. In expressing this sentiment, I may without impropriety allude to the numerous and distinguished marks of confidence and friendship, of which you have yourself been a Witness; but I cannot say in how many ways the continuance of that confidence and friendship was necessary to me in future relations.

Vain, however, are regrets. From a calamity, which is common to a mourning nation, who can expect to be exempt? Perhaps it is even a privilege to have a claim to a larger portion of it than others.

I will only add, Madam, that I shall deem it a real and a great happiness, if any future occurrence shall enable me to give you proof of that respectful and cordial attachment.[3]

JOHN LAURENS

Perhaps no relationship in Hamilton's life has generated more speculation than the profound friendship he enjoyed with Laurens, a fellow officer on George Washington's staff during the Revolutionary War.

John Laurens (1754–1782), Hamilton's closest friend, served with him on George Washington's staff during the Revolutionary War. Laurens was killed in battle shortly before the war ended.

Were they or were they not lovers? There is no conclusive evidence one way or the other, no eyewitness accounts, no secret diaries, though there are plenty of indicators if one looks back at their personal histories with twenty-first-century eyes. On the other hand, their overt expressions of love for one another were not unusual for men of their station and education for the period, during which sensibility was prized as a quality of the ideal man.

Whether or not the two men had a physical relationship, there is no doubt that they had a deep affinity and a mutual love. Not only did Laurens share many of Hamilton's political views; he shared Hamilton's penetrating intellect and penchant for physical daring and courage *in battle, having won that reputation at the Battles of Monmouth and Brandywine. Deepening the connection between the two, Hamilton served as Laurens's second in a duel with General Charles Lee after Lee challenged George Washington's competency as a military strategist.*

Laurens, who was the son of a wealthy South Carolina planter and slave trader, and Hamilton also shared what for the time was an extraordinarily progressive view of African American men. The two collaborated to organize a battalion of enslaved men in South Carolina during the late stages of the war. (See p. 31 for details.)

Hamilton gives unbridled expression of his regard for Laurens in this letter from April 1779.

To John Laurens:

[Middlebrook, New Jersey, April 1779]

Cold in my professions, warm in [my] friendships, I wish, my Dear Laurens, it m[ight] be in my power, by action rather than words, [to] convince you that I love you. I shall only tell you that 'till you bade us Adieu, I hardly knew the value you had taught my heart to set upon you. Indeed, my friend, it was not well done. You know the opinion I entertain of mankind, and how much it is my desire to preserve myself free from particular attachments, and to keep my happiness independent on the caprice of others. You sh[ould] not have taken advantage of my sensibility to ste[al] into my affections without my consent. But as you have done it and as we are generally indulgent to those we love, I shall not scruple to pardon the fraud you have committed, on condition that for my sake, if not for your own, you will always continue to merit the partiality, which you have so artfully instilled into [me].

Hamilton playfully turns to a more personal matter—that of finding a wife.

And Now my Dear as we are upon the subject of wife, I empower and command you to get me one in Carolina. Such a wife as I want will, I know, be difficult to be found, but if you succeed, it will be the stronger proof of your zeal and dexterity. Take her description—She must be young, handsome (I lay most stress upon a good shape) sensible (a little learning will do), well bred (but she must have an aversion to the word *ton*) chaste and tender (I am an enthusiast in my notions of fidelity and fondness) of some good nature, a great deal of generosity (she must neither love money nor scolding, for I dislike equally a termagent and an economist). In politics, I am indifferent what side she may be of; I think I have arguments that will easily convert her to mine. As to religion a moderate stock will satisfy me. She must believe in god and hate a saint. But as to fortune, the larger stock of that the better. You know my temper and circumstances and will therefore pay special attention to this article in the treaty. Though I run no risk of going to Purgatory for my avarice; yet as money is an essential ingredient to happiness in this world—as I have not much of my own and as I am very little calculated to get more either by my address or industry; it must needs be, that my wife, if I get one, bring at least a sufficiency to administer to her own extravagancies. NB You will be pleased to recollect in your negotiations that I have no invincible antipathy to the *maidenly beauties* & that I am willing to take the *trouble* of them upon myself.

If you should not readily meet with a lady that you think answers my description you can only advertise in the public papers and doub[t]less you will hear of many competitors for most of the qualifications required, who will be glad to become candidates for such a prize as I am. To excite their emulation, it will be necessary for you to give an account of the lover—his *size*, make, quality of mind and *body*, achievements, expectations, fortune, &c. In drawing my picture, you will no doubt be civil to your friend; mind you do justice to the length of my nose and don't forget, that I [-----]. . . .

Here, tantalizingly, a phrase of Hamilton's letter was excised by his son James when he collected Hamilton's letter for publication in 1869.

After reviewing what I have written, I am ready to ask myself what could have put it into my head to hazard this Jeu *de follie*. Do I want a wife? No—I have plagues enough without desiring to add to the number that *greatest of all*; and if I were silly enough to do it, I should take care how I employ a proxy. Did I mean to show my wit? If I did, I am sure I have missed my aim. Did I only intend to [frisk]? In this I have succeeded, but I have done more. I have gratified my feelings, by lengthening out the only kind of intercourse now in my power with my friend. Adieu.[4]

Not long after Hamilton wrote that letter to Laurens, he met Eliza-beth Schuyler, a woman who met many, if not most, of the criteria he described. Interestingly, Hamilton withheld this news from Laurens for a period of a few months. Nearly two years later, as the war was winding down, he envisioned a happy and productive future for him-self and his friend as nation builders.
    To John Laurens:

[Albany, New York, August 15, 1782]

Peace made, My Dear friend, a new scene opens. The object then will be to make our independence a blessing. To do this we must secure our *union* on solid foundations; an herculean task and to effect which mountains of prejudice must be levelled!

It requires all the virtue and all the abilities of the Country. Quit your sword my friend, put on the *toga*, come to Congress. We know each others sentiments, our views are the same: we have fought side by side to make America free, let us hand in hand struggle to make her happy.[5]

Less than two weeks later, Laurens was killed in action by British troops near one of their two remaining strongholds near Charleston, South Carolina, on August 27. In all probability, he never received Hamilton's letter.

With reserve typical of his professional correspondence, Hamilton wrote to General Nathanael Greene of the news.

To General Nathanael Greene:

[Albany, October 12, 1782]

I feel the deepest affliction at the news we have just received of the loss of our dear and [inesti]mable friend Laurens. His career of virtue is at an end. How strangely are human affairs conducted, that so many excellent qualities could not ensure a more happy fate? The world will feel the loss of a man who has left few like him behind, and America of a citizen whose heart realized that patriotism of which others only talk. I feel the loss of a friend I truly and most tenderly loved, and one of a very small number.[6]

JAMES HAMILTON

Though Hamilton had little contact with his brother, James, after leaving St. Croix for the American colonies, he retained an obvious affection for him, and clearly, a sense of duty as the "successful" sibling in an otherwise-struggling family. Hamilton's dream of helping his brother settle in the United States never materialized. His inquiry regarding the health and whereabouts of their "dear father" is especially poignant.

To James Hamilton:

[New York, June 22, 1785]

My Dear Brother:

I have received your letter of the 31st of May last, which, and one other, are the only letters I have received from you in many years. I am a little surprised you did not receive one which I wrote to you about six months ago. The situation you describe yourself to be in gives me much pain, and nothing will make me happier than, as far as may be in my power, to contribute to your relief. I will cheerfully pay your draft upon me for fifty pounds sterling, whenever it shall appear. I wish it was in my power to desire you to enlarge the sum; but though my future prospects are of the most flattering kind my present engagements would render it inconvenient to me to advance you a larger sum. My affection for you, however, will not permit me to be inattentive to your welfare, and I hope time will prove to you that I feel all the sentiment of a brother. Let me only request of you to exert your industry for a year or two more where you are, and at the end of that time I promise myself to be able to comfortable settlement...

from him or of him, though I have written him several letters. Perhaps, alas! he is no more, and I shall not have the pleasing opportunity of contributing to render the close of his life more happy than the progress of it. My heart bleeds at the recollection of his misfortunes and embarrassments. Sometimes I flatter myself his brothers have extended their support to him, and that he now enjoys tranquillity and ease. At other times I fear he is suffering in indigence. I entreat you, if you can, to relieve me from my doubts, and let me know how or where he is, if alive, if dead, how and where he died....

I do not advise your coming to this country at present, for the war has also put things out of order here, and people in your business [carpentry] find a subsistence difficult enough. My object will be, by-and-by, to get you settled on a farm.[7]

THE HAMILTON CHILDREN

Hamilton and Elizabeth Schuyler Hamilton had eight children over the course of their nearly twenty-four years of marriage: Philip (January 22, 1782–November 23, 1801); Angelica (September 25, 1784– February 6, 1857); Alexander (May 16, 1786–August 2, 1875); James Alexander (April 14, 1788–September 24, 1878); John Church (August 22, 1792–July 25, 1882); William Stephen (August 4, 1797– October 9, 1850); and Eliza (November 26, 1799–October 17, 1859). After Philip, the eldest, was killed in a duel in 1801, the Hamiltons gave their eighth child, a son born on June 2, 1802, the same name.

For a man so driven by political and career concerns, Hamilton was a remarkably involved and loving father. The Hamilton household was a "joyous one to his children" according to James Alexander Hamilton, the third child and second-born son.[8] Hamilton's letters

to his son Philip—the only child with whom he corresponded in any
meaningful way—captured both an abiding paternal love and a will-
ingness to engage a child on his own terms. This letter was written
when Philip was nine and had recently begun attending an Episcopal
boarding school in Trenton, New Jersey.

To Philip Hamilton:

[Philadelphia, December 5, 1791]

I received with great pleasure My Dear Philip the letter which
you wrote me last week. Your Mama and myself were very happy
to learn that you are pleased with your situation and content to
stay as long as shall be thought for your good. We hope and
believe that nothing will happen to alter this disposition.

Your Master also informs me that you recited a lesson the
first day you began, very much to his satisfaction. I expect every
letter from him will give me a fresh proof of your progress. For
I know that you can do a great deal, if you please, and I am sure
you have too much spirit not to exert yourself, that you may make
us every day more and more proud of you....

You remember that I engaged to send for you next Saturday
and I will do it, unless you request me to put it off. For a promise
must never be broken; and I never will make you one, which I will
not fulfill as far as I am able. But it has occurred to me that the
Christmas holidays are near at hand, and I suppose your school
will then break up for some days and give you an opportunity of
coming to stay with us for a longer time than if you should come
on Saturday. Will it not be best for you, therefore, to put off your
journey till the holidays? But determine as you like best and let
me know what will be most pleasing to you.[9]

Philip graduated from Alexander's alma mater, Columbia College (formerly known as King's College and renamed after the Revolution) in 1800, the same year that his father set out this set of rules for him. In spite of the rather demanding schedule that Hamilton laid out for his son, one can detect a fond paternal wink in the tone of the letter.

[New York, 1800]

Rules for *Mr Philip Hamilton* from the first of April to the first of October he is to rise not later than Six Oclock—The rest of the year not later than Seven. If Earlier he will deserve commendation. Ten will be his hour of going to bed throughout the year.

From the time he is dressed in the morning till nine o clock (the time for breakfast Excepted) he is to read Law.

At nine he goes to the office & continues there till dinner time—he will be occupied partly in the writing and partly in reading law.

After Dinner he reads law at home till five O clock. From this hour till Seven he disposes of his time as he pleases. From Seven to ten he reads and Studies what ever he pleases.

From twelve on Saturday he is at Liberty to amuse himself.

On Sunday he will attend the morning Church. The rest of the day may be applied to innocent recreations.

He must not Depart from any of these rules without my permission.[10]

Hamilton's dreams for Philip were boundless. Philip was by all accounts handsome and charming, possessed of his father's keen intellect and quick wit. Unlike Hamilton, Philip was well born in the

United States, with none of the "outsider" stigmas of illegitimacy and foreignness that had caused the elder Hamilton such pain and embarrassment throughout his life. When Philip was killed, Hamilton was inconsolable; it took him four months to even acknowledge the condolence letters he had received. Characteristically, he is gracious in a letter to Dr. Benjamin Rush.

To Dr. Benjamin Rush:

[New York, March 29, 1802]

I felt all the weight of the obligation which I owed to you and to your amiable family, for the tender concern they manifested in an event, beyond comparison, the most afflicting of my life. But I was obliged to wait for a moment of greater calm, to express my sense of the kindness.

My loss is indeed great. The highest as well as the eldest hope of my family has been taken from me. You estimated him rightly—He was truly a fine youth. But why should I repine? It was the will of heaven; and he is now out of the reach of the seductions and calamities of a world, full of folly, full of vice, full of danger—of least value in proportion as it is best known. I firmly trust also that he has safely reached the haven of eternal repose and felicity.

You will easily imagine that every memorial of the goodness of his heart must be precious to me. You allude to one recorded in a letter to your son. If no special reasons forbid it, I should be very glad to have a copy of that letter.

Mrs. Hamilton, who has drank deeply of the cup of sorrow, joins me in affectionate thanks to Mrs. Rush and yourself. Our wishes for your happiness will be unceasing.[11]

MARIA REYNOLDS

If there was one mistake over the course of his life that Hamilton could have undone, it undoubtedly would have been allowing a twenty-three-year-old, uneducated, and (as it turned out) unscrupulous woman named Maria Reynolds into his intimate circle in August 1791. Hamilton's wife, Elizabeth, and their children were away visiting her family in Albany, leaving Hamilton in Philadelphia (which was then the nation's capital) to cope with the new Congress and the oppressive summer heat. That is precisely when Maria Reynolds entered the picture. Hamilton relates the story in a pamphlet he published in 1797 in response to the public exposure of the affair:

Some time in the summer of the year 1791 a woman called at my house in the city of Philadelphia and asked to speak with me in private. I attended her into a room apart from the family. With a seeming air of affliction she informed that she was a daughter of a Mr. Lewis, sister to a Mr. G. Livingston of the State of New-York, and wife to a Mr. Reynolds whose father was in the Commissary Department during the war with Great Britain, that her husband, who for a long time had treated her very cruelly, had lately left her, to live with another woman, and in so destitute a condition, that though desirous of returning to her friends she had not the means—that knowing I was a citizen of New-York, she had taken the liberty to apply to my humanity for assistance.

I replied, that her situation was a very interesting one—that I was disposed to afford her assistance to convey her to her friends, but this at the moment not being convenient to me (which was the fact) I must request the place of her residence, to which I should bring or send a small supply of money. She told me the street and the number of the house where she lodged. In the evening I put a bank-bill in my pocket and went to the house. I inquired for Mrs. Reynolds and was shown up stairs, at the head of which she met me and conducted me into a bed room. I took the bill out of my pocket and gave it to her. Some conversation ensued from which it was quickly apparent that other than pecuniary consolation would be acceptable.

After this, I had frequent meetings with her, most of them at my own house.

The affair had begun. Knowing Elizabeth and their son James to be ill, Hamilton offers to "sacrifice" his happiness to allow her more time away from him to get well in this letter from 1791.

To Elizabeth Hamilton:

[New Jersey, August 9, 1791]

...Since you left me I have received but one letter from you, which informed me of the indisposition of My Dear James and left me in no small anxiety on his account. I hope on my return to Philadelphia I shall find a letter from you & Heaven Grant that it may assure me of your being all well!

I am myself in good health but I cannot be happy without you. Yet I must not advise you to urge your return. The confirmation of your health is so essential to our happiness that I am willing to make as long a sacrifice as the season and your patience will permit. Adieu my precious. My best love to all the family.[12]

It was a low point in Hamilton's life. By the end of 1791, the affair had soured. Hamilton had long since stopped being charmed by Maria, and to make matters worse, he started to receive urgent requests for "loans" from her aggrieved husband, James Reynolds. It turned out that Hamilton had been set up. A letter from Maria to Hamilton in December 1791 begins to lay bare the teeth of the trap.

From Maria Reynolds:

[Philadelphia, December 15, 1791]

I have not time to tell you the cause of my present troubles only that Mr. has rote to you this morning and I know not whether you have got the letter or not and he has swore that If you do not answer It or If he dose not se or hear from you to day he will write Mrs. Hamilton he has just Gone oute and I am a Lone I think you had better come here one moment that you May know the Cause then you will the better know how to act Oh my God I feel more for you than myself and wish I had never been born to give you so mutch unhappisness do not rite to him no not a Line but come here soon do not send or leave any thing in his power.[13]

A letter for Hamilton from James Reynolds arrived on the same day.

From James Reynolds:

[Philadelphia, December 15, 1791]

I am very sorry to find out that I have been so Cruelly treated by a person that I took to be my best friend instead of that my greatest Enimy. You have deprived me of every thing thats near and dear to me, I discovred whenever I Came into the house.... Sir you have bin the Cause of Cooling her affections for me.... for you have made me an unhappy man for eve. put it to your own case and Reflect one Moment. that you should know shush a thing of your wife. would not you have satisfaction yes. and so will I before one day passes me more.

After another letter expressing hurt and outrage, Reynolds lowered the boom:

From James Reynolds:

[Philadelphia. December 19, 1791]

...Sir I have Considered on the matter Serously. I have This preposial to make to you. give me the Sum Of thousand dollars and I will leve the town and take my daughter with me and go where my Friends Shant here from me and leve her to Yourself to do for as you thin[k] proper. I hope you wont think my Request is in a vew of making Me Satisfaction for the injury done me. for there is nothing that you Can do will Compensate for it. your answer I shall expect This evening or in the morning early, as I am Determened to wate no longer till. I know my lot.[14]

The year did not end well for Hamilton. On December 15, 1792, he was visited by Representatives Frederick Muhlenberg and Abraham Venable together with Senator James Monroe, who questioned him about payments he had made to James Reynolds, which they suspected had been used to illicitly speculate in Treasury funds. It turned out that Reynolds had at least one friend who managed to temporarily land in a high place: Jacob Clingman, who had been an aide in Muhlenberg's office. Reynolds had contrived to have Clingman, an avowed anti-Federalist, witness Hamilton's comings and goings from his house while the affair with Maria was active. Now, Reynolds and Clingman had engaged in a fraudulent scheme to get

*government money that was owed to war veterans and were jailed
for it in November 1792. Reynolds tried to reach Hamilton for help
(he refused); Clingman went to Muhlenberg, his old boss. Hence the
inquiry.*

*Hamilton succeeded in convincing the three inquisitors that he had
engaged in adultery, not fraud. The affair ended, for the time being,
with gentlemanly assurances of mutual respect and confidentiality.*

*Hamilton must have lived on edge for a time, but eventually, he
likely settled into the belief that he had weathered a self-administered
storm of stupidity and shabby behavior. Whispers about the affair
in the Republican press never seemed to amount to anything more
than that.*

In June 1797 that all changed, when James Callender published
The History of the United States for 1796, *with its recycled false
allegations of financial chicanery and a true charge of adultery by
Hamilton—the latter claim now substantiated with documents from
the affair. (See p. 233.)*

*In one of the colossal misjudgments of his public life, Hamilton
sought to contain the damage by publishing his own version of the
story.* Observations on Certain Documents Contained in No. V
& VI of "The History of the United States for the Year 1796,"
In Which the Charge of Speculation Against Alexander Hamilton, Late Secretary of the Treasury, is Fully Refuted. Written
by Himself *was nearly 100 pages of venom against his enemies and
lawyerly defense of himself.*

I owe perhaps to my friends an apology for condescending to
give a public explanation....

The charge against me is a connection with one James Reynolds for purposes of improper pecuniary speculation. My real

crime is an amorous connection with his wife, for a considerable time with his privity and connivance, if not originally brought on by a combination between the husband and wife with the design to extort money from me.

This confession is not made without a blush. I cannot be the apologist of any vice because the ardour of passion may have made it mine. I can never cease to condemn myself for the pang, which it may inflict in a bosom eminently intitled to all my gratitude, fidelity and love. But that bosom will approve, that even at so great an expence, I should effectually wipe away a more serious stain from a name, which it cherishes with no less elevation than tenderness. The public too will I trust excuse the confession. The necessity of it to my defence against a more heinous charge could alone have extorted from me so painful an indecorum....

Thus has my desire to destroy this slander, completely, led me to a more copious and particular examination of it, than I am sure was necessary. The bare perusal of the letters from Reynolds and his wife is sufficient to convince my greatest enemy that there is nothing worse in the affair than an irregular and indelicate amour. For this, I bow to the just censure which it merits. I have paid pretty severely for the folly and can never recollect it without disgust and self condemnation. It might seem affectation to say more.[15]

Hamilton had proven his public integrity at the cost of inflicting humiliation and hurt on Elizabeth. He and Elizabeth weathered the difficult period, remained married, and appeared to resume a genuinely affectionate relationship. Maria and James Reynolds did not. Maria was represented by Aaron Burr at the divorce proceeding.

AARON BURR

Left to his own devices, Burr likely would have happily coexisted with Hamilton, his simple ambition to attain and hold a position of prestige and authority in public life. It was Hamilton who was offended by Burr's seeming lack of moral conviction, and who repeatedly criticized and confronted Burr. Perhaps he sensed that his own path in life could easily have led him to the same dark place, governed by ambition and the lust for worldly possessions, had he not hewed to a sense of moral rectitude and honor that had nothing to do with social class or wealth. Or perhaps he simply resented Burr's privileged upbringing.

Nonetheless, the two men mixed in the same social circles and were colleagues, working together frequently as attorneys before the bar. As late as 1800, Hamilton and Burr had worked closely together on the

Aaron Burr (1756–1836), Hamilton's contemporary, colleague, and adversary shown in a lithograph made around the time of his death.

Weeks murder case. Yet hard feelings between the two dated back to the Revolutionary War. Burr was known to have disparaged the military judgment of Hamilton's mentor, General Washington. When General Charles Lee was court-martialed for disobeying Washington's orders during the Battle of Monmouth in 1778, Burr publicly supported Lee, whereas Hamilton's friend John Laurens challenged Lee to a duel, and Hamilton served as Laurens's second.

The conflict became more personal for Hamilton when in 1791 Burr challenged and defeated the incumbent US Senator from New York, Hamilton's father-in-law, Philip Schuyler, for his Senate seat. Burr's victory cost Hamilton a key ally in the senate. Upon learning the next year that Burr was testing the waters for a possible run at the vice presidency, Hamilton, as was his wont, picked up his pen to derail Burr. Also running was George Clinton, the governor of New York, who was another Hamilton antagonist. Nevertheless, in this letter to an unidentified Federalist ally, Hamilton throws his support to his long-time foe Clinton, writing that Burr "is for or against nothing, but as it suits his interest or ambition."

Unknown recipient:

[Philadelphia, September 21, 1792]

Mr. Clinton's success I should think very unfortunate. I am not for trusting the Government too much in the hands of its enemies. But still Mr. C———is a man of property, and, in private life, as far as I know of probity. I fear the other Gentleman [Burr] is unprincipled both as a public and private man. When the constitution was in deliberation, his conduct was equivocal; but its enemies, who I believe best understood him considered him as with them. In fact, I take it, he is for or against nothing, but as it suits his interest or ambition. He is determined, as I conceive, to make his way to be the head of the popular party and to climb per *fas et nefas* to the highest honors of the state; and as much higher as circumstances may permit. Embarrassed, as I understand, in his circumstances, with an extravagant family—bold enterprising and intriguing, I am mistaken, if it be not his object to play the game of confusion, and I feel it a religious duty to oppose his career.[16]

Clinton received the Republican nomination, but to Hamilton's relief, George Washington and John Adams were reelected.

Hamilton had further reason to mistrust Burr. When in 1800 details of Hamilton's "private" pamphlet criticizing the qualifications of John Adams to be president were leaked to the Republican press (see p. 190), many, including Hamilton, suspected Burr of being the source.

But it can be said that Burr had even greater reason to mistrust Hamilton. Hamilton's "religious duty" to oppose Burr's career reached new heights later in 1800 and in early 1801, when Hamilton secretly torpedoed Burr's presidential aspirations in a letter-writing campaign to key Federalists in the House of Representatives, which would decide the deadlocked contest, urging them to withhold their votes for Burr in favor of the Republican Thomas Jefferson—this in spite of the fact that Jefferson had long been Hamilton's chief political antagonist (see p. 91). In Burr's eyes, Hamilton had become a hypocritical thorn in his side.

The hostilities became overt in the New York gubernatorial election of 1804. Burr, the sitting vice president, drew the support of a splinter group of the Federalist Party for the post, though Burr was a Democratic-Republican. Hamilton, as was his wont, engaged in a speaking tour in favor of another candidate, Morgan Lewis, and one can easily imagine Hamilton letting a tidbit or two about Burr fall from his lips during these speeches. A man who had attended one of these speeches, Dr. Charles Cooper, included remarks made by Hamilton after a dinner in Albany in a letter he had printed in an Albany newspaper. When the heat of the election had passed—Burr was defeated—the wounded Burr demanded that Hamilton acknowledge or deny his comments:

From Aaron Burr:

[New York, June 18, 1804]

I send for your perusal a letter signed Ch. D. Cooper which, though apparently published some time ago, has but very recently come to my knowledge. Mr Van Ness who does me the favor to deliver this, will point out to you that Clause of the letter to which I particularly request your attention.

You might perceive, Sir, the necessity of a prompt and unqualified acknowledgment or denial of the use of any expressions which could warrant the assertions of Dr Cooper.[17]

Hamilton's response, parsing the distinction between "despicable" and "more despicable," seems calculated to infuriate Burr:

To Aaron Burr:

[New York, June 20, 1804]

I have maturely reflected on the subject of your letter of the 18th instant; and the more I have reflected the more I have become convinced, that I could not, without manifest impropriety, make the avowal or disavowal which you seem to think necessary.

The clause pointed out by Mr. Van Ness is in these terms "I could detail to you a *still more despicable opinion*, which General

Hamilton has expressed of Mr. Burr." To endeavour to discover the meaning of this declaration, I was obliged to seek in the antecedent part of the letter, for the opinion to which it referred, as having been already disclosed. I found it in these words "General Hamilton and Judge Kent have declared, *in substance*, that they looked upon Mr. Burr to be *a dangerous man*, and one *who ought not to be trusted with the reins of Government*". The language of Doctor Cooper plainly implies, that he considered this opinion of you, which he attributes to me, as a *despicable* one; but he affirms that I have expressed some other *still more despicable;* without however mentioning to whom, when, or where. 'Tis evident, that the phrase "still more dispicable" admits of infinite shades, from very light to very dark. How am I to judge of the degree intended? Or how shall I annex any precise idea to language so indefinite?

Between Gentlemen, *despicable* and *more despicable* are not worth the pains of a distinction. When therefore you do not interrogate me, as to the opinion which is specifically ascribed to me, I must conclude, that you view it as within the limits, to which the animadversions of political opponents, upon each other, may justifiably extend; and consequently as not warranting the idea of it, which Doctor Cooper appears to entertain. If so, what precise inference could you draw as a guide for your future conduct, were I to acknowledge, that I had expressed an opinion of you, *still more despicable*, than the one which is particularised? How could you be sure, that even this opinion had exceeded the bounds which you would yourself deem admissible between political opponents?

But I forbear further comment on the embarrassment to which the requisition you have made naturally leads. The occasion forbids a more ample illustration, though nothing would be more easy than to pursue it.

Repeating, that I cannot reconcile it with propriety to make the acknowledgement, or denial, you desire—I will add, that I deem it inadmissible, on principle, to consent to be interrogated as to the justness of the *inferences*, which may be drawn by *others*, from whatever I may have said of a political opponent in the course of a fifteen years competition. If there were no other objection to it, this is sufficient, that it would tend to expose my sincerity and delicacy to injurious imputations from every person, who may at any time have conceived the import of my expressions differently from what I may then have intended, or may afterwards recollect.

I stand ready to avow or disavow promptly and explicitly any precise or definite opinion, which I may be charged with having declared of any Gentleman. More than this cannot fitly be expected from me; and especially it cannot reasonably be expected, that I shall enter into an explanation upon a basis so vague as that which you have adopted. I trust, on more reflection, you will see the matter in the same light with me. If not, I can only regret the circumstance, and must abide the consequences.

The publication of Doctor Cooper was never seen by me 'till after the receipt of your letter.[18]

If Hamilton viewed the matter with a degree of amusement, Burr certainly didn't. Anger and steely resolve glimmering through, he maintains a decorous tone in this response. He challenges Hamilton's adherence to the very qualities he knows Hamilton prizes the most and believes Burr to be deficient in: sincerity, delicacy, and honor. He could not have constructed a more precisely targeted challenge.

From Aaron Burr:

[New York, June 21, 1804]

Your letter of the 20th. inst. has been this day received. Having Considered it attentively I regret to find in it nothing of that sincerity and delicacy which you profess to Value.

Political opposition can never absolve Gentlemen from the necessity of a rigid adherence to the laws of honor and the rules of decorum: I neither claim such priviledge nor indulge it in others.

The Common sense of Mankind affixes to the epithet adopted by Dr Cooper the idea of dishonor: it has been publicly applied to me under the Sanction of your name. The question is not whether he has understood the meaning of the word or has used it according to Syntax and with grammatical accuracy, but whether you have authorised this application either directly or by uttering expressions or opinions derogatory to my honor. The time "when" is in your own knowledge, but no way material to me, as the calumny has now first been disclosed so as to become the Subject of my Notice, and as the effect is present and palpable.

Your letter has furnished me with new reasons for requiring a definite reply.[19]

Burr's arrow hit its mark. Choosing to forget that it was he who had provoked Burr in the first place, Hamilton now dug in his heels.

To Aaron Burr:

[New York, June 22, 1804]

Your first letter, in a style too peremptory, made a demand, in my opinion, unprecedented and unwarrantable. My answer, pointing out the embarrassment, gave you an opportunity to take a less exceptionable course. You have not chosen to do it, but by your last letter, received this day, containing expressions indecorous and improper, you have increased the difficulties to explanation, intrinsically incident to the nature of your application.

If by a "definite reply" you mean the direct avowal or disavowal required in your first letter, I have no other answer to give than that which has already been given. If you mean any thing different admitting of greater latitude, it is requisite you should explain.[20]

The die was cast. Further communication between the two principals was turned over to their seconds—William P. Van Ness for Burr, Nathaniel Pendleton for Hamilton. Unable to find an honorable solution to the dispute, a date for a duel was set. Hamilton pushed the date back into July to allow himself time to complete matters pending before the circuit court; he also turned to getting his affairs in order. Ever the pragmatist, he began with a statement regarding his financial situation, fascinating for its matter-of-fact assessment of his estate. "[M]y public labours have amounted to an absolute sacrifice of the interests of my family," he wrote, adding that his "chief apology" was due to friends who had endorsed his discounted paper at banks—while Elizabeth's financial future was left primarily to anticipated inheritances from her family.

[New York, July 1, 1804]

Herewith is a general statement of my pecuniary affairs; in which there can be no material error. The result is that calculating my property at what it stands me in, I am now worth about Ten thousand pounds, and that estimating according to what my lands are now selling for and are likely to fetch, the surplus beyond my debts may fairly be stated at nearly double that sum. Yet I am pained to be obliged to entertain doubts whether, if an accident should happen to me, by which the sales of my property should come to be forced, it would be even sufficient to pay my debts.

In a situation like this, it is perhaps due to my reputation to explain why I have made so considerable an establishment in the country. This explanation shall be submitted.

To men, who have been so much harassed in the busy world as myself, it is natural to look forward to a comfortable retirement, in the sequel of life, as a principal desideratum. This desire I have felt in the strongest manner; and to prepare for it has latterly been a favourite object. I thought that I might not only expect to accomplish the object, but might reasonably aim at it and pursue the preparatory measures, from the following considerations.

It has been for some time past pretty well ascertained to my mind, that the emoluments of my profession would prove equal to the maintenance of my family and the gradual discharge of my debts, within a period to the end of which my faculties, for business might be expected to extend, in full energy. I think myself warranted to estimate the annual product of those emoluments at Twelve [thousand] Dollars at the least. My expences while the first improvements of my country establishment were going on have been great; but they would this summer and fall reach the point, at which it is my intention they should stop, at least 'till I should be better able than at present to add to them; and after a fair examination founded upon an actual account of my expenditures, I am persuaded that a plan I have contemplated for the next and succeeding years would bring my expences of every kind within the compass of four thousand Dollars yearly, exclusive of the interest of my country establishment. To this limit, I have been resolved to reduce them, even though it should be necessary to lease that establishment for a few years.

In the mean time, my lands now in a course of sale & settlement would accelerate the extinguishment of my debt, and in the end leave me a handsome clear property. It was also allowable for me to take into view, collaterally, the expectations of my wife; which have been of late partly realised. She is now intitled to a property of between two and three thousand pounds (as I compute) by descent from her mother; and her father is understood to possess a large estate. I feel all the delicacy of this allusion; but the occasion I trust will plead my excuse. And that venerable father, I am sure, will pardon. He knows well all the nicety of my past conduct.

Viewing the matter in these different aspects, I trust the opinion of candid men will be, that there has been no impropriety in my conduct; especially when it is taken into the calculation that my Country establishment, though costly, promises, by the progressive rise of property on this Island, and the felicity of its situation to become more and more valuable.

My chief apology is due to those friends, who have from mere kindness, indorsed my paper discounted at the Banks. On mature reflection I have thought it jus[ti]fiable to secure them in preference to other Creditors, lest perchance there should be *a deficit*. Yet while this may save them from eventual loss, it will not exemp[t] them from some present inconvenience. As to this I can only throw myself upon their kindn[ess,] and entreat the indulgence of the Banks for them. Perhaps this request may be supposed entitled to some regard.

In the event, which would bring this paper to the public eye, one thing at least would be put beyond a doubt. This is, that my public labours have amounted to an absolute sacrifice of the interests of my family—and that in all pecuniary concerns the delicacy, no less than the probity of my conduct in public stations, has been such as to defy even the shadow of a question.

Indeed, I have not enjoyed the ordinary advantages incident to my military services. Being a member of Congress, while the question of the commutation of the half pay of the army in a sum in gross was in debate, delicacy and a desire to be useful to the army, by removing the idea of my having an interest in the question, induced me to write to the Secretary of War and relinquish my claim to half pay; which, or the equivalent, I have accordingly never received. Neither have I ever applied for the lands allowed by the United States to Officers of my rank. Nor did I ever obtain from this state the allowan[ce] of lands made to officers of similar rank. It is true that having served through the latter period of the War on the general staff of the UStates and not in the line of this State. I could not claim that allowance as a matter of course. But having before the War resided in this State and having entered the military career at the head of a company of Artillery raised for the particular defence of this State, I had better pretensions to the allowance than others to whom it was actually made—Yet has it not been extended to me.[21]

Hamilton prepared a collection of his important personal papers for his second (among them the document that allowed Elizabeth Hamilton to collect his unclaimed military pension in 1816), and let him know where to find others in his home. He gave his brother-in-law John Church power of attorney. He wrote a moving letter to his wife,

1. The parties will leave town tomorrow morning about five o'clock and meet at the place agreed on. The party arriving first shall wait for the other

2. The weapons shall be pistols not exceeding eleven inches in the barrel. The distance ten paces.

3. The choice of positions to be determined by lot.

4. The parties having taken their positions. one of the seconds to be determined by lot (after having ascertained that both parties are ready) shall loudly and distinctly give the word "present" —. If one of the parties fires, and the other hath not fired, the opposite shall say one, two, three, fire, and he shall then fire or lose his shot. a snap or flash is a fire

Monday.
11 July 1804.

Nathaniel Pendleton, Hamilton's second, specified the procedures for the duel.

Elizabeth, to be opened in the event that he fail to survive the duel (see p. 275). He wrote a brief will. Had there been any doubts as to whether Hamilton had illicitly enriched himself while in government, this document was intended to eliminate them. Uncertain of whether

there would be sufficient funds left for Elizabeth to live, he entreated his children to support her and suggested that perhaps her father's resources would be sufficient for that purpose. Philip Schuyler, who died a few months after Hamilton, was in financial straits at the time, though Hamilton may not have known it.

Though if it shall please God to spare my life I may look for a considerable surplus out of my present property—Yet if he should speedily call me to the eternal wor[l]d, a forced sale as is usual may possibly render it insufficient to satisfy my Debts. I pray God that something may remain for the maintenance and education of my dear Wife and Children. But should it on the contrary happen that there is not enough for the payment of my Debts, I entreat my Dear Children, if they or any of them shall ever be able, to make up the Deficiency. I without hesitation commit to their delicacy a wish which is dictated by my own. Though conscious that I have too far sacrificed the interests of my family to public avocations & on this account have the less claim to burthen my Children, yet I trust in their magnanimity to appreciate as they ought this my request. In so unfavourable an event of things, the support of their dear Mother with the most respectful and tender attention is a duty all the sacredness of which they will feel. Probably her own patrimonial resources will preserve her from Indigence. But in all situations they are charged to bear in mind that she has been to them the most devoted and best of mothers. In Testimony whereof I have hereunto subscribed my hand the Ninth day of July in the year of our lord One thousand Eight hundred & four.[22]

Amid his other preparations, he sat down to write an explanation of the thinking behind his decision to engage in the duel with

Burr—ostensibly for family and friends, but also seemingly aimed at posterity.

[New York, June 28–July 10, 1804]

On my expected interview with Col Burr, I think it proper to make some remarks explanatory of my conduct, motives and views.

I am certainly desirous of avoiding this interview, for the most cogent reasons.

1. My religious and moral principles are strongly opposed to the practice of Duelling, and it would even give me pain to be obliged to shed the blood of a fellow creature in a private combat forbidden by the laws.
2. My wife and Children are extremely dear to me, and my life is of the utmost importance to them, in various views.
3. I feel a sense of obligation towards my creditors; who in case of accident to me, by the forced sale of my property, may be in some degree sufferers. I did not think my self at liberty, as a man of probity, lightly to expose them to this hazard.
4. I am conscious of no *ill-will* to Col Burr, distinct from political opposition, which, as I trust, has proceeded from pure and upright motives.

Lastly, I shall hazard much, and can possibly gain nothing by the issue of the interview.

But it was, as I conceive, impossible for me to avoid it. There were *intrinsick* difficulties in the thing, and *artificial* embarrassments, from the manner of proceeding on the part of Col Burr.

Intrinsick—because it is not to be denied, that my animadversions on the political principles character and views of Col Burr have been extremely severe, and on different occasions, I, in common with many others, have made very unfavourable criticisms on particular instances of the private conduct of this Gentleman.

In proportion as these impressions were entertained with sincerity and uttered with motives and for purposes, which might appear to me commendable, would be the difficulty (until they could be removed by evidence of their being erroneous), of explanation or apology. The disavowal required of me by Col Burr, in a general and indefinite form, was out of my power, if it had really been proper for me to submit to be so questionned; but I was sincerely of opinion, that this could not be, and in this opinion, I was confirmed by that of a very moderate and judicious friend whom I consulted. Besides that Col Burr appeared to me to assume, in the first instance, a tone unnecessarily peremptory and menacing, and in the second, positively offensive. Yet I wished, as far as might be practicable, to leave a door open to accommodation. This, I think, will be inferred from the written communications made by me and by my direction, and would be confirmed by the conversations between Mr van Ness and myself, which arose out of the subject.

I am not sure, whether under all the circumstances I did not go further in the attempt to accommodate, than a pun[c]tilious delicacy will justify. If so, I hope the motives I have stated will excuse me.

It is not my design, by what I have said to affix any odium on the conduct of Col Burr, in this case. He doubtless has heared of animadversions of mine which bore very hard upon him; and it is probable that as usual they were accompanied with some falsehoods. He may have supposed himself under a necessity of acting as he has done. I hope the grounds of his proceeding have been such as ought to satisfy his own conscience.

I trust, at the same time, that the world will do me the Justice to believe, that I have not censured him on light grounds, or from unworthy inducements. I certainly have had strong reasons for what I may have said, though it is possible that in some particulars, I may have been influenced by misconstruction or misinformation. It is also my ardent wish that I may have been more mistaken than I think I have been, and that he by his future conduct may shew himself worthy of all confidence and esteem, and prove an ornament and blessing to his Country.

As well because it is possible that I may have injured Col Burr, however convinced myself that my opinions and declarations have been well founded, as from my general principles and temper in relation to similar affairs—I have resolved, if our interview is conducted in the usual manner, and it pleases God to give me the opportunity, to *reserve* and *throw away* my first fire, and I *have thoughts* even of *reserving* my second fire—and thus giving a double opportunity to Col Burr to pause and to reflect.

It is not however my intention to enter into any explanations on the ground. Apology, from principle I hope, rather than Pride, is out of the question.

To those, who with me abhorring the practice of Duelling may think that I ought on no account to have added to the number of bad examples—I answer that my *relative* situation, as well in public as private aspects, enforcing all the considerations which constitute what men of the world denominate honor, impressed on me (as I thought) a peculiar necessity not to decline the call.[23]

Lithograph depicting the "interview" between Hamilton and Burr conducted on a bluff in Weehawken, New Jersey, early in the morning of July 11, 1804.

Early in the morning of July 11, 1804, Hamilton and Burr were ferried separately across the Hudson River to the dueling grounds in Weehawken, New Jersey, directly opposite where Times Square is today. The two exchanged salutations in the presence of their seconds and chose their weapons—the same dueling pistols used by Philip Hamilton and George Eacker in 1801. Burr and Hamilton took their positions ten paces apart. Hamilton's second, Nathaniel Pendleton, gave the command to "Present." The question of whether Hamilton "threw away" his first shot is one that can never be categorically answered. Eyewitness accounts conflict on the point. Of the result of the duel, there could be no dispute. Pendleton and Van Ness, the seconds, issued joint and individual statements several days after the duel.

Joint Statement by William P. Van Ness and Nathaniel Pendleton

[New York, July 17, 1804]

Col: Burr arrived first on the ground as had been previously agreed. When Genl Hamilton arrived the parties exchanged salutations and the Seconds proceeded to make their arrangements. They measured the distance, ten full paces, and cast lots for the choice of positions as also to determine by whom the word should be given, both of which fell to the Second of Genl Hamilton. They then proceeded to load the pistols in each others presence, after which the parties took their stations. The Gentleman who was to give the word, then explained to the parties the rules which were to govern them in firing which were as follows: The parties being placed at their stations The Second who gives the word shall ask them whether they are ready—being answered in the affirmative, he shall say *"present"* after which the parties shall present & fire when they please. If one fires before the other the opposite second shall say one two, three, fire, and he shall fire or loose his fire. And asked if they were prepared, being answered in the affirmative he gave the word *present* as had been agreed on, and both of the parties took aim, & fired in succession, the Intervening time is not expressed as the seconds do not precisely agree on that point. The pistols were discharged within a few seconds of each other and the fire of Col: Burr took effect; Genl Hamilton almost instantly fell. Col: Burr then advanced toward Genl H——n with a manner and gesture that appeared to Genl Hamilton's friend to be expressive of regret, but without Speaking turned about & withdrew. Being urged from the field by his friend as has been subsequently stated, with a view to prevent his being recognised by the Surgeon and Bargemen who were then approaching. No farther communications took place between the principals and the Barge that carried Col: Burr immediately returned to the City. We conceive it proper to add that the conduct of the parties in that interview was perfectly proper as suited the occasion.[24]

Nathaniel Pendleton's Amendments to the Joint Statement Made by William P. Van Ness and Him on the Duel between Alexander Hamilton and Aaron Burr.

[New York, July 19, 1804]

The statement containing the facts that led to the interview between General Hamilton and Col. Burr, published in the Evening Post on Monday, studiously avoided mentioning any particulars of what past at the place of meeting. This was dictated by suitable considerations at the time, and with the intention, that whatever it might be deemed proper to lay before the public, should be made the subject of a future communication. The following is therefore now submitted.

In the interviews that have since taken place between the gentlemen that were present, they have not been able to agree in two important facts that passed there—for which reason nothing was said on those subjects in the paper lately published as to other particulars in which they were agreed.

Mr. P. expressed a confident opinion that General Hamilton did not fire first—and that he did not fire at all *at Col. Burr.* Mr. V. N.

seemed equally confident in the opinion that Gen. H. did fire first—and of course that it must have been *at* his antagonist.

General Hamilton's friend thinks it to be a sacred duty he owes to the memory of that exalted man, to his country, and his friends, to publish to the world such facts and circumstances as have produced a decisive conviction in his own mind, that he cannot have been mistaken in the belief he has formed on these points.

1st. Besides the testimonies of Bishop Moore, and the paper containing an express declaration, under General Hamilton's own hand, enclosed to his friend in a packet, not to be delivered but in the event of his death, and which have already been published, General Hamilton informed Mr. P. at least ten days previous to the affair, that he had doubts whether he would not receive and not return Mr. Burr's first fire. Mr. P. remonstrated against this determination, and urged many considerations against it, as dangerous to himself and not necessary in the particular case, when every ground of accommodation, not humiliating, had been proposed and rejected. He said he would not decide lightly, but take time to deliberate fully. It was incidentally mentioned again at their occasional subsequent conversations, and on the evening preceding the time of the appointed interview, he informed Mr. P. he had made up his mind *not to fire at Col. Burr the first time, but to receive his fire, and fire in the air.* Mr. P. again urged him upon this subject, and repeated his former arguments. His final answer was in terms that made an impression on Mr. P's mind which can never be effaced. "My friend, it is the effect of A RELIGIOUS SCRUPLE, and does not admit of reasoning, it is useless to say more on the subject, as my purpose is definitely fixed."

2d. His last words before he was wounded afford a proof that this purpose had not changed. When he received his pistol, after having taken his position, he was asked if he would have the hair spring set? His answer was, *"Not this time."*

3d. After he was wounded, and laid in the boat, the first words he uttered after recovering the power of speech, were, (addressing himself to a gentleman present, who perfectly well remembers it) *"Pendleton knows I did not mean to fire at Col. Burr the first time."*

4th. This determination had been communicated by Mr. P. to that gentleman that morning, before they left the city.

5th. The pistol that had been used by General Hamilton, lying loose over the other apparatus in the case which was open; after having been some time in the boat, one of the boatmen took hold of it to put it into the case. General Hamilton observing this, said *"Take care of that pistol—it is cocked. It may go off and do mischief."* This is also remembered by the gentleman alluded to.

This shews he was not sensible of having fired at all. If he had fired *previous* to receiving the wound, he would have remembered it, and therefore have known that the pistol could not go off; but if *afterwards* it must have been the effect of an involuntary exertion of the muscles produced by a mortal wound, in which case, he could not have been conscious of having fired.

6. Mr. P. having so strong a conviction that if General Hamilton had fired first, it could not have escaped his attention (all his anxiety being alive for the effect of the first fire, and having no reason to believe the friend of Col. Burr was not sincere in the contrary opinion) he determined to go to the spot where the affair took place, to see if he could not discover some traces of the course of the ball from Gen. Hamilton's pistol.

He took a friend with him the day after General Hamilton died, and after some examination they fortunately found what they were in search of. They ascertained that the ball passed through the limb of a cedar tree, at an elevation of about twelve feet and a half, perpendicularly from the ground, between thirteen and fourteen feet from the mark on which General Hamilton stood, and about four feet wide of the direct line between him and Colonel Burr, on the right side; he having fallen on the left. The part of the limb through which the ball passed was cut off and brought to this city, and is now in Mr. Church's possession.

No inferences are pointed out as resulting from these facts, nor will any comments be made. They are left to the candid judgment and feelings of the public.[25]

William P. Van Ness's Amendments to the Joint Statement Made by Nathaniel Pendleton and Him on the Duel between Alexander Hamilton and Aaron Burr.

[New York July 21, 1804]

The second of G H having considered it proper to subjoin an explanatory note to the statement mutually furnished, it becomes proper for the gentleman who attended Col Burr to state also his impressions with respect to those points on which their exists a variance of opinion. In doing this he pointedly disclaims any idea disrespectful to the memory of G H, or an intention to ascribe any conduct to him that is not in his opinion perfectly honorable & correct.

The parties met as has been above related & took their respective stations as directed: the pistols were then handed to them by the seconds. Gen Hamilton elevated his, as if to try the light, & lowering it said I beg pardon for delaying you but the direction of the light renders it necessary, at the same time feeling his pockets with his left hand, & drawing forth his spectacles put them on. The second then asked if they were prepared which was replied to in the affirmative. The word *present* was then given, on which both parties took aim. The pistol of General Hamilton was first discharged, and Col Burr fired immediately after, only five or six seconds of time intervening. On this point the second of Col Burr has full & perfect reccollection. He noticed particularly the discharge of G H's pistol, & looked to his principal to ascertain whether he was hurt, he then clearly saw Col Bs pistol discharged. At this moment of looking at Col B on the discharge of G H's pistol he perceived a slight motion in his person, which induced the idea of his being struck. On this point he conversed with his principal on their return, who ascribed that circumstance to a small stone under his foot, & observed that the smoke of G Hs pistol obscured him for a moment in the interval of their firing.

When G H fell Col B advanced toward him as stated & was checked by his second who urged the importance of his immediately repairing to the barge, conceiving that G H was mortally wounded, & being desirous to secure his principal from the sight of the surgeon & bargemen who might be called in evidence. Col B complied with his request.

He shortly followed him to the boat, and Col B again expressed a wish to return, saying with an expression of much concern, I must go & speak to him. I again urged the obvious impropriety stating that the G was surrounded by the Surgeon & Bargemen by whom he must not be seen & insisted on immediate departure.[26]

The duel effectively ended Burr's political career. A warrant was issued for his arrest in August, and he fled New York and New Jersey for

South Carolina. The charges were later reduced and Burr never stood trial for the murder of Hamilton. Nonetheless, many of Hamilton's friends and colleagues referred to Burr as an "assassin." In November, he returned to preside over the Senate briefly (he was still vice president and under indictment), but when he stepped down, he never held another position in the government.

In the years that followed his duel with Burr, his life took a great many bizarre turns, many of which took place in the frontier territories, west of the Appalachians. There, Burr conspired to liberate Mexico from Spanish rule—whether on behalf of the United States or in order to establish his own private fiefdom remains the subject of debate. Jefferson charged him with treason, another charge of which Burr was acquitted.

Burr died in 1836 after suffering the second of two strokes. He never expressed remorse for having killed Hamilton.

ANGELICA SCHUYLER CHURCH

Elizabeth Schuyler's sister Angelica was already married to John Church, a British-born businessman, at the time that she and Hamilton met. Urbane, witty, and worldly, Angelica charmed nearly everyone she met, and Hamilton was no exception. His sparkle in a social setting seemed to match hers perfectly, and people took note of their powerful connection.

"Amiable Angelica!" Hamilton wrote in a letter written years later, "how much you are formed to endear yourself to every good heart!"[27] Rumors of a romantic connection between the two in-laws abounded throughout their lives, but there is no conclusive evidence of this. The utter lack of rancor within the Schuyler family and from John Church suggest otherwise.

An engraving of Angelica Schuyler Church (1757–1815), Hamilton's sister-in-law and soulmate.

In 1783, John Church needed to attend to some business matters in Europe, and he and Angelica left the United States for the Continent, theoretically for a short period. In fact, they remained in Europe until 1797 (though Angelica visited the United States in 1789), and she quickly established herself as a presence in Paris, befriending both Thomas Jefferson and Benjamin Franklin. After a couple of years had passed, Hamilton was doubtful of her return and bereft.

To Angelica Schuyler Church:

[New York, August 3, 1785]

But now my Dear Sister let us talk a little of something else that interests us all much more nearly. You have I fear taken a final leave of America and of those that love you here. I saw you depart from Philadelphia with peculiar uneasiness, as if foreboding you were not to return. My apprehensions are confirmed and unless I see you in Europe I expect not to see you again.

This is the impression we all have; judge the bitterness it gives to those who love you with the *love of nature* and to me who feel an attachment for you not less lively.

I confess for my own part I see one great source of happiness snatched away. My affection for Church and yourself made me anticipate much enjoyment in your friendship and neighbourhood. But an ocean is now to separate us.

Let me entreat you both not precipitately to wed yourselves to a soil less propitious to you than will be that of America: You will not indeed want friends wherever you are on two accounts: One is You will have no need of them: another is that You have both too many qualities to engage friend ship. But go where you will you will find no *such* friends as those you have left behind.[28]

In 1791, Hamilton added the following postscript to a letter that Elizabeth had written to Angelica that reveals the depth of his feelings for his sister-in-law. This letter coincided with Hamilton's affair with Maria Reynolds.

To Angelica Schuyler Church:

[Philadelphia, October 2, 1791]

You hurt my republican nerves by your intimacy with 'amiable' princes. I cannot endure that you should be giving such folks dinners, while I at the distance of 3000 miles can only console myself by thinking of you. You are not however to conclude from what I have said that I am in a violent fit of dudgeon with you. If

it will give you pleasure, assure yourself that you are as much in
my good graces as ever and that you must be a very naughty girl
indeed before you can lose the place you have in my affection.[29]

*Angelica had visited the United States briefly, in 1789, but returned
to Europe when her children became ill. Hamilton chastised her for
the lack of correspondence from her, and she responded with this reassurance, gently tweaking him for his ambition.*

From Angelica Schuyler Church:

[August 15, 1793]

Are you too happy to think of us? Ah *petit Fripon* you do not
believe it:—no I am not too happy, can I be so on this side of the
Atlantic? ask your heart, and read my answer there.

My silence is caused by dispair; for do not years, days and
moments pass and still find me separated from those I love! yet
were I in America, would ambition give an hour to *Betsey* and
to me. Can a mind engaged by Glory taste of peace and ease?[30]

*Acknowledging his quixotic streak, Hamilton boasts of his return to
soldiering in this correspondence written at the time of the Whiskey
Rebellion (see p. 129). John Jay and Thomas Pinckney were in London
at the time negotiating the controversial treaty that became known as
the Jay Treaty (see p. 147).*

To Angelica Schuyler Church:

[Philadelphia, October 23, 1794]

I am thus far my dear Angelica on my way to attack and subdue
the wicked insurgents of the West. But you are not to promise

yourself that I shall have any trophies to lay at your feet. A large army has cooled the courage of those madmen & the only question seems now to be how to guard best aganst the return of the phrenzy.

You must not take my being here for a proof that I continue a quixot. In popular governments 'tis useful that those who propose measures should partake in whatever dangers they may involve. Twas very important there should be no mistake in the management of the affair—and I *might* contribute to prevent one. I wish to have every thing well settled for Mr. Church & you, that when you come, you may tread on safe ground. Assure him that the insurrection will do us a great deal of good and add to the solidity of every thing in this country. Say the same to Mr Jay to whom I have not time to write & to Mr Pinkney.[31]

Six weeks later, Hamilton proudly announced to Angelica his plan to resign from public office in order to devote himself to his law practice and his family.

To Angelica Schuyler Church:

[Philadelphia, December 8, 1794]

You say I am a politician, and good for nothing. What will you say when you learn that after January next, I shall cease to be a politician at all? So is the fact. I have formally and definitely announced my intention to resign at that period, and have ordered a house to be taken for me at New York.

My dear Eliza has been lately very ill. Thank God, she is now quite recovered, except that she continues somewhat weak. My absence on a certain expedition was the cause (with army to suppress the whisky insurrection in Pennsylvania). You will see, notwithstanding your disparagement of me, I am still of consequence to her....

...Don't let Mr. Church be alarmed at my retreat—all is well with the public. Our insurrection is most happily terminated. Government has gained by it reputation and strength, and our finances are in a most flourishing condition. *Having contributed to place those of the Nation on a good footing, I go to take a little care of my own; which need my care not a little.*

Love to Mr. Church. Betsy will add a line or two. Adieu.[32]

Clearly in a more relaxed frame of mind after leaving office, Hamilton looked to the future, and confirmed to Angelica that for him the rewards of public service were other than pecuniary.

To Angelica Schuyler Church:

[March 6, 1795]

Eliza & our Children are with me here at your fathers house who is himself at New York attending the Legislature. We remain till June, when we become stationary at New York, where I resume the practice of law. For My Dear Sister, I tell you without regret what I hope you anticipate, that I am poorer than when I went into office. I allot myself full five or six years of more work than will be pleasant though much less than I have had for the last five years.[33]

In the last extant letter from Hamilton to Angelica, he tells her delightedly of a recent visit to her parents' home in Albany. Her father, who had been ill, appeared to be fully recovered, and Hamilton enjoyed a dinner in their home in the presence of an intriguing "lady": a painting of Angelica herself by the well-known portraitist John Trumbull.

To Angelica Schuyler Church:

[January 22, 1800]

The pleasure of this was heightened by that of dining in the presence of a lady for whom I have a particular friendship. I was placed directly in front of her and was much occupied with her during the whole Dinner. She did not appear to her usual advantage, and yet she was very interesting. The eloquence of silence is not a common attribute of hers; but on this occasion she employed it *par force* and it was not considered as a fault. Though I am fond of hearing her speak, her silence was so well placed that I did not attempt to make her break it. You will conjecture that I must have been myself dumb with admiration. Perhaps so, and yet this was not the reason of my forbearing to invite a conversation with her. If you cannot find yourself a solution for this enigma, you must call in the aid of Mr. Church—and if he should fail to give you the needful assistance write to your friend Mr. Trumbull for an explanation.[34]

Angelica, herself devastated, consoled and comforted Elizabeth after Hamilton's death in 1804. She remained a presence in the New York social scene (she and Church had returned from Europe in 1797) until she died in 1814. She was buried near Hamilton in Trinity Churchyard.

ELIZABETH SCHUYLER HAMILTON

If Angelica Schuyler Church spoke to Hamilton's worldly side, her sister Elizabeth connected with the earnest and upstanding part of his character. From the moment he met Elizabeth, or Eliza (most often

*Elizabeth Schuyler Hamilton (1757–1854), the second daughter of an
influential upstate New York family, married Alexander Hamilton on
December 14, 1780 and outlived him by fifty years.*

*called "Betsey" by Hamilton), in 1780 at a gathering in the home of
her aunt near the Continental Army encampment at Morristown,
New Jersey, Hamilton was enchanted not just by her beauty, but also
by her evident lack of vanity. Elizabeth was twenty-two, Hamilton
twenty-five. Their courtship was rapid.*

*Elizabeth instructed Hamilton to introduce himself to her younger
sister, Margarita (known as Peggy), who had remained in Albany, by letter. Hamilton obediently did so, attributing his attraction to Elizabeth as
much to her lack of affectation as to her beauty, good nature, and vivacity.*

To Margarita Schuyler:

[New Jersey, February, 1780]

I venture to tell you in confidence, that by some odd contrivance or other, your sister has found out the secret of interesting me in every thing that concerns her...yet notwithstanding this, I have some things of a very serious and heinous nature to lay to her charge. She is most unmercifully handsome and so perverse that she has none of those pretty affectations which are the prerogatives of beauty. Her good sense is destitute of that happy mixture of vanity and ostentation which would make it conspicuous to the whole tribe of fools and foplings as well as to men of understanding so that as the matter now stands it is [very] little known beyond the circle of these. She has good nature affability and vivacity unembellished with that charming frivolousness which is justly deemed one of the principal accomplishments of a *belle*. In short she is so strange a creature that she possesses all the beauties virtues and graces of her sex without any of those amiable defects, which from their general prevalence are esteemed by connoisseurs necessary shades in the character of a fine woman.[35]

Hamilton set about wooing Elizabeth immediately. His wit and courtliness are on display in this letter to her in which he regrets that he is unavailable to transport her (and her friend Kitty Livingston) to a nearby social gathering.

To Elizabeth Schuyler:

[New Jersey, January–February 1780]

Col Hamiltons compliments to Miss Livingston and Miss Schuyler. He is sorry to inform them that his zeal for their service make him forget that he is so bad a Charioteer as hardly to dare to trust himself with so precious a charge; though if he were only to consult his own wishes like Phaeton he would assemble the chariot of the sun, if he were sure of experiencing the same fate. Col Tilghman offers himself a volunteer. Col Hamilton is unwilling to lose the pleasure of the party; but one or the other will have the honor to attend the ladies.[36]

Writing to her from the army's encampment at Amboy, New Jersey. Hamilton had begun a letter to her, more reserved in tone, when a letter from Elizabeth was delivered to him. Her correspondence now in hand, Hamilton is over the moon as he resumes writing.
    To Elizabeth Schuyler:

[New Jersey, March 17, 1780]

I had written so far when the express arrived with your dear billet under cover of one from your guardian. I cannot tell you what extacy I felt in casting my eye over the sweet effusions of tenderness it contains. My Betseys soul speaks in every line and bids me be the happiest of mortals. I am so and will be so. You give me too many proofs of your love to allow me to doubt it and in the conviction that I possess that, I possess every thing the world can give.... But notwithstanding all I have to thank you and to love you for, I have a little quarrel with you. I will not permit you to say you do not deserve the preference I give you, you deserve all I think of you and more and let me tell you your diffidence with so many charms is an unpardonable amiableness. I am pleased with it however on one account which is that it will induce you to call your good qualities into full activity, and there is nothing I shall always delight in more than to assist you in unfolding them in their highest perfection.... Adieu my charmer; take care of your self and love your Hamilton as well as he does you.[37]

Elizabeth Schuyler and Alexander Hamilton were married at the Schuyler mansion in Albany on December 14, 1780. Just eight months after their wedding, a group of Tories surrounded Philip Schuyler's home in Albany and attempted to kidnap him. Elizabeth, pregnant with their first child, was visiting at the time, so she witnessed the mayhem, which ended when the quick-thinking Schuyler was able to summon help using a prearranged signal to neighbors. No one was hurt, but the attack was terrifying. Elizabeth wrote about it to Hamilton in a letter, to which Hamilton responds here.

To Elizabeth Schuyler Hamilton:

[New York, August 16, 1781]

I have received my beloved Betsey your letter informing me of the happy escape of your father. He showed an admirable presence of mind, and has given his friends a double pleasure arising from the manner of saving himself and his safety. Upon the whole I am glad this unsuccessful attempt has been made. It will prevent his hazarding himself hereafter as he has been accustomed to do. He is a character too valuable to be trifled with, and owes it to his country and to his family to be upon his guard.

My heart in spite of myself would realize your situation at the time. It has felt all the horror and anguish attached to the idea of your being yourself and seeing your father in the power of ruffians as unfeeling as unprincipled; for such I dare say composed the band. I am inexpressably happy to learn that my [love] has suffered nothing in this disagreeable adventure, and equally so to find that you seem at presen[t] to be confirmed in your hopes.[38]

Hamilton soon traveled south with the Continental Army, facing the likelier prospect of combat there. He reassures Elizabeth, making a promise that in all likelihood she knew to be preposterous even at the time.

To Elizabeth Schuyler Hamilton:

[Maryland, September 6, 1781]

Early in November, as I promised you, we shall certainly meet. Cheer yourself with this idea, and with the assurance of never more being separated. Every day confirms me in the intention of renouncing public life, and devoting myself wholly to you. Let others waste their time and their tranquillity in a vain pursuit of power and glory; be it my object to be happy in a quiet retreat with my better angel.[39]

As the Continental troops prepared to surround the British army's troops in Yorktown, Virginia, which proved to be the decisive battle of the war, Hamilton sent this brief, philosophical note to Elizabeth.

To Elizabeth Schuyler Hamilton:

[Maryland, September 15–18, 1781]

How chequered is human life! How precarious is happiness! How easily do we often part with it for a shadow! These are the reflections that frequently intrude themselves upon me, with a painful application. I am going to do my duty. Our operations will be so conducted, as to economize the lives of men. Exert your fortitude and rely upon heaven.[40]

The next year, Hamilton learned that his half-brother, Peter Lavien, had passed away, leaving Hamilton only a small bequest. Believing that he had been cheated of a fair portion of the estate that Lavien had inherited on their mother's death, Hamilton is nevertheless dispassionate in this letter to his wife.

To Elizabeth Schuyler Hamilton:

[1782]

Engrossed by our own immediate concerns, I omitted telling you of a disagreeable piece of intelligence I have received from a gentleman of Georgia. He tells me of the death of my brother Levine [Lavien]. You know the circumstances that abate my distress, yet my heart acknowledges the rights of a brother. He dies rich, but has disposed of the bulk of his fortune to strangers. I am told he has left me a legacy. I did not inquire how much. When you have occasion for money you can draw upon Messrs. Stewart & [Totten], Philadelphia. They owe me upwards of an hundred pounds.[41]

Hamilton remained committed to his family, even after his affair with Maria Reynolds had begun and ended. His relationship with Elizabeth suffered before it eventually recovered, but his love for her and for their children was genuine. Their third son, James (who lived to be ninety), suffered frequent and severe illnesses as a child. As might be expected, Hamilton was assiduous in the administration of his care, even from afar.
To Elizabeth Schuyler Hamilton:

[Philadelphia, August 12, 1794]

If my darling child is better when this reaches you persevere in the plan which has made him so. If he is worse—abandon the laudanum & try the cold bath—that is abandon the laudanum by degrees giving it over night but not in the morning—& then leaving it off altogether. Let the water be put in the Kitchen over night & in the morning let the child be dipped in it head foremost wrapping up his head well & taking him again immediately out, put in flannel & rubbed dry with towels. Immediately upon his being taken out let him have two tea spoons full of brandy mixed with just enough water to prevent its taking away his breath.

Observe well his lips. If a glow succeeds continue the bath. If a chill takes place forbear it. If a glow succeeds the quantity of brandy may be lessened after the first experiment.

Try the bark at the same time in tincture about mid day, but if this disagrees discontinue it.

When you exercise him, if he can bear it, give him eight or ten Miles at a time.

Shew this letter to your father & tell the Doctor of the advice I have given. But if the child be certainly worse do not easily be persuaded from the course I advise.

Over the course of their marriage, Hamilton's correspondence with Elizabeth predictably assumes a routine quality, though never less than attentive and affectionate. In a letter from 1798, he gave voice to a sentiment that was almost certainly understood between them throughout the latter part of their lives together, "I am much more in debt to you than I can ever pay; but my future life will be more than ever devoted to your happiness."

His most poignant written communication with her came in the form of a letter that he wrote to her in preparation for his duel with Aaron Burr, in July 1804.

To Elizabeth Schuyler Hamilton:

[New York, July 4, 1804]

This letter, my very dear Eliza, will not be delivered to you, unless I shall first have terminated my earthly career; to begin, as I humbly hope from redeeming grace and divine mercy, a happy immortality.

If it had been possible for me to have avoided the interview, my love for you and my precious children would have been alone a decisive motive. But it was not possible, without sacrifices which would have rendered me unworthy of your esteem. I need not tell you of the pangs I feel, from the idea of quitting you and exposing you to the anguish which I know you would feel. Nor could I dwell on the topic lest it should unman me.

The consolations of Religion, my beloved, can alone support you; and these you have a right to enjoy. Fly to the bosom of your God and be comforted. With my last idea; I shall cherish the sweet hope of meeting you in a better world.

Adieu best of wives and best of Women. Embrace all my darling Children for me.[42]

Elizabeth Hamilton was left widowed and deeply in debt, but unbroken. In the span of three years, she had endured more hardship than most people contend with in a lifetime: the death of her eldest son and her beloved husband in duels; the death of her sister Peggy; and the mental dissolution of her eldest daughter, Angelica. Yet as Hamilton had urged her, Elizabeth remained steadfast and found comfort in her Christian faith.

She lived for another fifty years after Hamilton was killed, looking after her family and the Grange. She grew closer to her sister Angelica, who died in 1814. She burnished Hamilton's legacy, ensuring that his papers were preserved until she could prevail on her son James to write his biography, which was finally published in 1869.

In 1806, Elizabeth, the widow of an orphan, founded the New York Orphan Asylum Society, which continues to aid destitute orphan children today under the name Graham Windham.

NOTES

★ ★ ★

Introduction

1. From Alexander Hamilton to Edward Stevens, 11 November 1769, Founders Online, National Archives (http://founders .archives.gov/documents/Hamilton/01-01-02-0002 [last update: 2016-03-28]). Source: *The Papers of Alexander Hamilton*, vol. 1, *1768–1778*, ed. Harold C. Syrett. New York: Columbia University Press, 1961, pp. 4–5.
2. Ron Chernow, *Alexander Hamilton* (New York: Penguin Press, 2004), p. 4.
3. "James Madison's Version, [18 June 1787]," *Founders Online*, National Archives, last modified June 29, 2016, http://founders .archives.gov/documents/Hamilton/01-04-02-0098-0003. [Original source: *The Papers of Alexander Hamilton*, vol. 4, *January 1787–May 1788*, ed. Harold C. Syrett. New York: Columbia University Press, 1962, no pagination.]
4. "From Alexander Hamilton to George Washington, 25 March 1783," *Founders Online*, National Archives, last modified June 29, 2016, http://founders.archives.gov/documents/Hamilton/01-03-02-0194. [Original source: *The Papers of Alexander Hamilton*, vol. 3, *1782–1786*, ed. Harold C. Syrett. New York: Columbia University Press, 1962, no pagination.]

5. From Alexander Hamilton to Charles Cotesworth Pinckney, 29 December 1802, Founders Online, National Archives (http://founders.archives.gov/documents/Hamilton/01-26-02-0001-0056 [last update: 2016-03-28]). Source: *The Papers of Alexander Hamilton*, vol. 26, *1 May 1802–23 October 1804, Additional Documents 1774–1799, Addenda and Errata*, ed. Harold C. Syrett. New York: Columbia University Press, 1979, pp. 71–73.

Chapter 1: "Bastard Brat of a Scottish Pedlar"

1. Probate Court Transaction on Estate of Rachel Lavien, [19 February 1768], Founders Online, National Archives (http://founders.archives.gov/documents/Hamilton/01-01-02-0001 [last update: 2016-03-28]). Source: *The Papers of Alexander Hamilton*, vol. 1, ed. Syrett, pp. 1–3.
2. From Alexander Hamilton to William Jackson, 26 August 1800, Founders Online, National Archives (http://founders.archives.gov/documents/Hamilton/01-25-02-0068 [last update: 2016-03-28]). Source: *The Papers of Alexander Hamilton*, vol. 25, *July 1800–April 1802*, ed. Harold C. Syrett. New York: Columbia University Press, 1977, pp. 88–91.
3. From Alexander Hamilton to Edward Stevens, 11 November 1769, Founders Online, National Archives (http://founders.archives.gov/documents/Hamilton/01-01-02-0002 [last update: 2016-03-28]). Source: *The Papers of Alexander Hamilton*, vol. 1, *1768–1778*, ed. Syrett, pp. 4–5.
4. From Alexander Hamilton to the *Royal Danish American Gazette*, [6 April 1771], Founders Online, National Archives (http://founders.archives.gov/documents/Hamilton/

01-01-02-0003 [last update: 2016-03-28]). Source: *The Papers of Alexander Hamilton*, vol. 1, *1768–1778*, ed. Syrett, pp. 6–7.

5. From Alexander Hamilton to Nicholas Cruger, 24 February 1772, Founders Online, National Archives (http://founders.archives.gov/documents/Hamilton/01-01-02-0026 [last update: 2016-03-28]). Source: *The Papers of Alexander Hamilton*, vol. 1, *1768–1778*, ed. Syrett, pp. 27–29.

6. From Alexander Hamilton to the *Royal Danish American Gazette*, 6 September 1772, Founders Online, National Archives (http://founders.archives.gov/documents/Hamilton/01-01-02-0042 [last update: 2016-03-28]). Source: *The Papers of Alexander Hamilton*, vol. 1, *1768–1778*, ed. Syrett, pp. 34–38.

Chapter 2: The Student Turns Revolutionary

1. Alexander Hamilton, *A Full Vindication of the Measures of the Congress, &c.*, [15 December] 1774, Founders Online, National Archives (http://founders.archives.gov/documents/Hamilton/01-01-02-0054 [last update: 2016-03-28]). Source: *The Papers of Alexander Hamilton*, vol. 1, *1768–1778*, ed. Syrett, pp. 45–78.

2. Alexander Hamilton, *The Farmer Refuted, &c.*, [23 February] 1775, Founders Online, National Archives (http://founders.archives.gov/documents/Hamilton/01-01-02-0057 [last update: 2016-03-28]). Source: *The Papers of Alexander Hamilton*, vol. 1, *1768–1778*, ed. Syrett, pp. 81–165.

3. From Alexander Hamilton to John Jay, 26 November 1775, Founders Online, National Archives (http://founders

.archives.gov/documents/Hamilton/01-01-02-0060 [last update: 2016-03-28]). Source: *The Papers of Alexander Hamilton*, vol. 1, *1768–1778*, ed. Syrett, pp. 176–178.

Chapter 3: Soldier and Statesman

1. From Alexander Hamilton to the Provincial Congress of the Colony of New York, [26 May 1776], Founders Online, National Archives (http://founders.archives.gov/documents/ Hamilton/01-01-02-0067 [last update: 2016-03-28]). Source: *The Papers of Alexander Hamilton*, vol. 1, *1768–1778*, ed. Syrett, pp. 183–185.

2. From Alexander Hamilton to George Washington, [before 29 January 1778], Founders Online, National Archives (http:// founders.archives.gov/documents/Hamilton/01-01-02-0353 [last update: 2016-03-28]). Source: *The Papers of Alexander Hamilton*, vol. 1, *1768–1778*, ed. Syrett, pp. 414–421.

3. From Alexander Hamilton to John Jay, [14 March 1779], Founders Online, National Archives (http://founders .archives.gov/documents/Hamilton/01-02-02-0051 [last update: 2016-03-28]). Source: *The Papers of Alexander Hamilton*, vol. 2, *1779–1781*, ed. Harold C. Syrett. New York: Columbia University Press, 1961, pp. 17–19.

4. From Alexander Hamilton to James Duane, [3 September 1780], Founders Online, National Archives (http://founders .archives.gov/documents/Hamilton/01-02-02-0838 [last update: 2016-03-28]). Source: *The Papers of Alexander Hamilton*, vol. 2, *1779–1781*, ed. Syrett, pp. 400–418.

5. From Alexander Hamilton to Joshua Mersereau, [24 October 1780], Founders Online, National Archives (http://founders .archives.gov/documents/Hamilton/01-02-02-0934 [last

update: 2016-03-28]). Source: *The Papers of Alexander Hamilton*, vol. 2, *1779–1781*, ed. Syrett, p. 488.

6. From Alexander Hamilton to George Washington, [22 November 1780], Founders Online, National Archives (http://founders.archives.gov/documents/Hamilton/01-02-02-0981 [last update: 2016-03-28]). Source: *The Papers of Alexander Hamilton*, vol. 2, *1779–1781*, ed. Syrett, pp. 509–510.

7. "Continental Congress Report on a Letter from the Speaker of the Rhode Island Assembly, 16 December 1782," Founders Online, National Archives (http://founders.archives.gov/documents/Hamilton/01-03-02-0123 [last update: 2016-03-28]). Source: *The Papers of Alexander Hamilton*, vol. 3, *1782–1786*, ed. Harold C. Syrett. New York: Columbia University Press, 1962, pp. 213–223.

8. From Alexander Hamilton to George Washington, 13 February 1783, Founders Online, National Archives (http://founders.archives.gov/documents/Hamilton/01-03-02-0155 [last update: 2016-03-28]). Source: *The Papers of Alexander Hamilton*, vol. 3, *1782–1786*, ed. Harold C. Syrett. New York: Columbia University Press, 1962, pp. 253–255.

9. From Alexander Hamilton to George Washington, 25 March 1783, Founders Online, National Archives (http://founders.archives.gov/documents/Washington/99-01-02-10919 [last update: 2016-03-28]). Source: Papers of George Washington (not an authoritative final version).

Chapter 4: Nation Builder

1. Alexander Hamilton, First Speech on the Address of the Legislature to Governor George Clinton's Message, New

York Assembly, [19 January 1787], Founders Online, National Archives (http://founders.archives.gov/documents/ Hamilton/01-04-02-0004 [last update: 2016-03-28]). Source: *The Papers of Alexander Hamilton*, vol. 4, *January 1787–May 1788*, ed. Harold C. Syrett. New York: Columbia University Press, 1962, pp. 3–12.

2. Alexander Hamilton, "Remarks on an Act Granting to Congress Certain Imposts and Duties," [15 February 1787] Founders Online, National Archives (http://founders .archives.gov/documents/Hamilton/01-04-02-0030 [last update: 2016-03-28]). Source: *The Papers of Alexander Hamilton*, vol. 4, *January 1787–May 1788*, ed. Syrett, pp. 71–92.

3. From Alexander Hamilton to George Washington, [3 July 1787], Founders Online, National Archives (http://founders .archives.gov/documents/Hamilton/01-04-02-0110 [last update: 2016-03-28]). Source: *The Papers of Alexander Hamilton*, vol. 4, *January 1787–May 1788*, ed. Syrett, pp. 223–225.

4. [Alexander Hamilton], Federalist No. 1, [27 October 1787], Founders Online, National Archives (http://founders .archives.gov/documents/Hamilton/01-04-02-0152 [last update: 2016-03-28]). Source: *The Papers of Alexander Hamilton*, vol. 4, *January 1787–May 1788*, ed. Syrett, pp. 301–306.

5. [Alexander Hamilton], Federalist No. 15, [1 December 1787], Founders Online, National Archives (http://founders .archives.gov/documents/Hamilton/01-04-02-0168 [last update: 2016-03-28]). Source: *The Papers of Alexander Hamilton*, vol. 4, *January 1787–May 1788*, ed. Syrett, pp. 356–364.

6. [Alexander Hamilton], Federalist No. 67, [11 March 1788], Founders Online, National Archives (http://founders .archives.gov/documents/Hamilton/01-04-02-0217 [last

update: 2016-03-28]). Source: *The Papers of Alexander Hamilton*, vol. 4, *January 1787–May 1788*, ed. Syrett, pp. 581–586.

7. [Alexander Hamilton], Federalist No. 68, [12 March 1788], Founders Online, National Archives (http://founders.archives.gov/documents/Hamilton/01-04-02-0218 [last update: 2016-03-28]). Source: *The Papers of Alexander Hamilton*, vol. 4, *January 1787–May 1788*, ed. Syrett, pp. 586–590.

8. [Alexander Hamilton], Federalist No. 78, [28 May 1788], Founders Online, National Archives (http://founders.archives.gov/documents/Hamilton/01-04-02-0241 [last update: 2016-03-28]). Source: *The Papers of Alexander Hamilton*, vol. 4, *January 1787–May 1788*, ed. Syrett, pp. 655–663.

9. [Alexander Hamilton], Federalist No. 84, [28 May 1788], Founders Online, National Archives (http://founders.archives.gov/documents/Hamilton/01-04-02-0247 [last update: 2016-03-28]). Source: *The Papers of Alexander Hamilton*, vol. 4, *January 1787–May 1788*, ed. Syrett, pp. 702–714.

10. [Alexander Hamilton], Federalist No. 85, [28 May 1788], Founders Online, National Archives (http://founders.archives.gov/documents/Hamilton/01-04-02-0248 [last update: 2016-03-28]). Source: *The Papers of Alexander Hamilton*, vol. 4, *January 1787–May 1788*, ed. Syrett, pp. 714–721.

Chapter 5: The Secretary

1. From Alexander Hamilton to George Washington, September 1788, Founders Online, National Archives (http://founders.archives.gov/documents/Hamilton/01-05-02-0037 [last update: 2016-03-28]). Source: *The Papers of Alexander Hamilton*, vol. 5, *June 1788–November 1789*, ed. Harold C. Syrett. New York: Columbia University Press, 1962, pp. 220–222.

2. From Alexander Hamilton to James Wilson, [25 January 1789], Founders Online, National Archives (http://founders .archives.gov/documents/Hamilton/01-05-02-0075 [last update: 2016-03-28]). Source: *The Papers of Alexander Hamilton*, vol. 5, *June 1788–November 1789*, ed. Syrett, pp. 247–249.

3. [Alexander Hamilton], H. G. Letter I, 20 February 1789, Founders Online, National Archives (http://founders .archives.gov/documents/Hamilton/01-05-02-0087 [last update: 2016-03-28]). Source: *The Papers of Alexander Hamilton*, vol. 5, *June 1788–November 1789*, ed. Syrett, pp . 263–264.

4. [Alexander Hamilton], H. G. Letter II, 21 February 1789, Founders Online, National Archives (http://founders .archives.gov/documents/Hamilton/01-05-02-0088 [last update: 2016-03-28]). Source: *The Papers of Alexander Hamilton*, vol. 5, *June 1788–November 1789*, ed. Syrett, pp. 265–266.

5. From Alexander Hamilton to George Washington, [5 May 1789], Founders Online, National Archives (http://founders .archives.gov/documents/Hamilton/01-05-02-0128 [last update: 2016-03-28]). Source: *The Papers of Alexander Hamilton*, vol. 5, *June 1788–November 1789*, ed. Syrett, pp. 335–337.

6. Alexander Hamilton, Treasury Department Circular to the Collectors of the Customs, 14 September 1789, Founders Online, National Archives (http://founders.archives .gov/documents/Hamilton/01-05-02-0155 [last update: 2016-03-28]). Source: *The Papers of Alexander Hamilton*, vol. 5, *June 1788–November 1789*, ed. Syrett, p. 373.

7. Alexander Hamilton, Treasury Department Circular to the Collectors of the Customs, 2 October 1789, Founders Online, National Archives (http://founders.archives

.gov/documents/Hamilton/01-05-02-0193 [last update: 2016-03-28]). Source: *The Papers of Alexander Hamilton*, vol. 5, *June 1788–November 1789*, ed. Syrett, pp. 419–421.

8. Alexander Hamilton, "Report Relative to a Provision for the Support of Public Credit," [9 January 1790], Founders Online, National Archives (http://founders.archives .gov/documents/Hamilton/01-06-02-0076-0002-0001 [last update: 2016-03-28]). Source: *The Papers of Alexander Hamilton*, vol. 6, *December 1789–August 1790*, ed. Harold C. Syrett. New York: Columbia University Press, 1962, pp. 65–110.

9. Alexander Hamilton, "Report Relative to a Provision for the Support of Public Credit," [9 January 1790], Founders Online, National Archives (http://founders.archives.gov/ documents/Hamilton/01-06-02-0076-0002-0001 [last update: 2016-03-28]). Source: *The Papers of Alexander Hamilton*, vol. 6, *December 1789–August 1790*, ed. Syrett, pp. 65–110.

10. Alexander Hamilton, Final Version of the Second "Report on the Further Provision Necessary for Establishing Public Credit (Report on a National Bank), 13 December 1790," Founders Online, National Archives (http://founders.archives .gov/documents/Hamilton/01-07-02-0229-0003 [last update: 2016-03-28]). Source: *The Papers of Alexander Hamilton*, vol. 7, *September 1790–January 1791*, ed. Harold C. Syrett. New York: Columbia University Press, 1963, pp. 305–342.

11. Alexander Hamilton, Final Version of "An Opinion on the Constitutionality of an Act to Establish a Bank," [23 February 1791], Founders Online, National Archives (http://founders .archives.gov/documents/Hamilton/01-08-02-0060-0003 [last update: 2016-03-28]). Source: *The Papers of Alexander*

Hamilton, vol. 8, *February 1791–July 1791*, ed. Harold C. Syrett. New York: Columbia University Press, 1965, pp. 97–134.

12. Alexander Hamilton, Final Version of "Report on the Subject of Manufactures," [5 December 1791], Founders Online, National Archives (http://founders.archives.gov/documents/ Hamilton/01-10-02-0001-0007 [last update: 2016-03-28]). Source: *The Papers of Alexander Hamilton*, vol. 10, *December 1791–January 1792*, ed. Harold C. Syrett. New York: Columbia University Press, 1966, pp. 230–340.

13. From Alexander Hamilton to George Washington, 30 July[–August 3], 1792, Founders Online, National Archives (http://founders.archives.gov/documents/Hamilton/ 01-12-02-0109 [last update: 2016-03-28]). Source: *The Papers of Alexander Hamilton*, vol. 12, *July 1792–October 1792*, ed. Harold C. Syrett. New York: Columbia University Press, 1967, pp. 137–139.

14. [Alexander Hamilton], An American No. 1, [4 August 1792], Founders Online, National Archives (http://founders.archives .gov/documents/Hamilton/01-12-02-0126 [last update: 2016-03-28]). Source: *The Papers of Alexander Hamilton*, vol. 12, *July 1792–October 1792*, ed. Syrett, pp. 157–164.

15. From Alexander Hamilton to George Washington, 9 September 1792, Founders Online, National Archives (http://founders .archives.gov/documents/Hamilton/01-12-02-0267 [last update: 2016-03-28]). Source: *The Papers of Alexander Hamilton*, vol. 12, *July 1792–October 1792*, ed. Syrett, pp. 347–350.

16. From Alexander Hamilton to Edward Carrington, 26 May 1792, Founders Online, National Archives (http://founders .archives.gov/documents/Hamilton/01-11-02-0349 [last

update: 2016-03-28]). Source: *The Papers of Alexander Hamilton*, vol. 11, *February 1792–June 1792*, ed. Harold C. Syrett. New York: Columbia University Press, 1966, pp. 426–445.

Chapter 6: Foreign Affairs, and a Foolish One

1. From Alexander Hamilton to John Jay, 9 April 1793, Founders Online, National Archives (http://founders.archives .gov/documents/Hamilton/01-14-02-0190 [last update: 2016-03-28]). Source: *The Papers of Alexander Hamilton*, vol. 14, *February 1793–June 1793*, ed. Harold C. Syrett. New York: Columbia University Press, 1969, pp. 297–299.

2. Alexander Hamilton, "Defense of the President's Neutrality Proclamation," [May 1793], Founders Online, National Archives (http://founders.archives.gov/documents/ Hamilton/01-14-02-0340 [last update: 2016-03-28]). Source: *The Papers of Alexander Hamilton*, vol. 14, *February 1793–June 1793*, ed. Syrett, 1969, pp. 502–507.

3. [Alexander Hamilton],"Pacificus No. I," [29 June 1793], Founders Online, National Archives (http://founders .archives.gov/documents/Hamilton/01-15-02-0038 [last update: 2016-03-28]). Source: *The Papers of Alexander Hamilton*, vol. 15, *June 1793–January 1794*, ed. Harold C. Syrett. New York: Columbia University Press, 1969, pp. 33–43.

4. From Alexander Hamilton to John Jay, 6 May 1794, Founders Online, National Archives (http://founders.archives.gov/ documents/Hamilton/01-16-02-0324 [last update: 2016-03-28]). Source: *The Papers of Alexander Hamilton*, vol. 16, *February 1794–July 1794*, ed. Harold C. Syrett. New York: Columbia University Press, 1972, pp. 381–385.

5. From Alexander Hamilton to George Washington, [5 August] 1794, Founders Online, National Archives (http://founders .archives.gov/documents/Hamilton/01-17-02-0017 [last update: 2016-03-28]). Source: *The Papers of Alexander Hamilton*, vol. 17, *August 1794–December 1794*, ed. Harold C. Syrett. New York: Columbia University Press, 1972, pp. 24–58.

6. From Alexander Hamilton to George Washington, 19 September 1794, Founders Online, National Archives (http:// founders.archives.gov/documents/Hamilton/01-17-02-0217 [last update: 2016-03-28]). Source: *The Papers of Alexander Hamilton*, vol. 17, *August 1794–December 1794*, ed. Syrett, pp. 254–255.

7. From Alexander Hamilton to Henry Lee, 20 October 1794, Founders Online, National Archives (http://founders .archives.gov/documents/Hamilton/01-17-02-0317 [last update: 2016-03-28]). Source: *The Papers of Alexander Hamilton*, vol. 17, *August 1794–December 1794*, ed. Syrett, pp. 331–336.

8. Alexander Hamilton, "The French Revolution," [1794], Founders Online, National Archives (http://founders .archives.gov/documents/Hamilton/01-17-02-0496 [last update: 2016-03-28]). Source: *The Papers of Alexander Hamilton*, vol. 17, *August 1794–December 1794*, ed. Syrett, pp. 586–588.

9. From George Washington to Alexander Hamilton, 2 February 1795, Founders Online, National Archives (http://founders.archives.gov/documents/Hamilton/01-18-02-0148 [last update: 2016-03-28]). Source: *The Papers of Alexander Hamilton*, vol. 18, *January 1795–July 1795*, ed. Harold C. Syrett. New York: Columbia University Press, 1973, pp. 247–248.

10. From Alexander Hamilton to George Washington, 3 February 1795, Founders Online, National Archives (http://founders.archives.gov/documents/Hamilton/01-18-02-0150 [last update: 2016-03-28]). Source: *The Papers of Alexander Hamilton*, vol. 18, *January 1795–July 1795*, ed. Syrett, p. 253.

11. Alexander Hamilton, "Report on a Plan for the Further Support of Public Credit," [16 January 1795], Founders Online, National Archives (http://founders.archives.gov/documents/Hamilton/01-18-02-0052-0002 [last update: 2016-03-28]). Source: *The Papers of Alexander Hamilton*, vol. 18, *January 1795–July 1795*, ed. Syrett, pp. 56–129.

Chapter 7: Private Citizen, Public Power

1. Alexander Hamilton, "Remarks on the Treaty of Amity Commerce and Navigation lately made between the United States and Great Britain," [9–11 July 1795], Founders Online, National Archives (http://founders.archives.gov/documents/Hamilton/01-18-02-0281 [last update: 2016-03-28]). Source: *The Papers of Alexander Hamilton*, vol. 18, *January 1795–July 1795*, ed. Syrett, pp. 404–454.

2. [Alexander Hamilton], "Horatius No. II, [July 1795]," Founders Online, National Archives (http://founders.archives.gov/documents/Hamilton/01-19-02-0002 [last update: 2016-03-28]). Source: *The Papers of Alexander Hamilton*, vol. 19, *July 1795–December 1795*, ed. Harold C. Syrett. New York: Columbia University Press, 1973, pp. 74–77.

3. [Alexander Hamilton], "The Defence No. I," [22 July 1795], Founders Online, National Archives (http://founders.archives.gov/documents/Hamilton/01-18-02-0305-0002 [last update: 2016-03-28]). Source: *The Papers of Alexander*

Hamilton, vol. 18, *January 1795–July 1795*, ed. Syrett, pp. 479–489.

4. From Alexander Hamilton to George Washington, [7 March 1796], Founders Online, National Archives (http://founders .archives.gov/documents/Hamilton/01-20-02-0038-0002 [last update: 2016-03-28]). Source: *The Papers of Alexander Hamilton*, vol. 20, *January 1796–March 1797*, ed. Harold C. Syrett. New York: Columbia University Press, 1974, pp. 68–69.

5. From Alexander Hamilton to George Washington, Enclosure: Draft of Washington's Farewell Address, [30 July 1796], Founders Online, National Archives (http://founders .archives.gov/documents/Hamilton/01-20-02-0181-0002 [last update: 2016-03-28]). Source: *The Papers of Alexander Hamilton*, vol. 20, *January 1796–March 1797*, ed. Syrett, pp. 265–288.

6. "The Warning No. I, [27 January 1797]," Founders Online, National Archives, last modified June 29, 2016, http://found-ers.archives.gov/documents/Hamilton/01-20-02-0315. Source: *The Papers of Alexander Hamilton*, vol. 20, *January 1796–March 1797*, ed. Harold C. Syrett.

7. "Enclosure: Answer to Questions Proposed by the President of the U States, [29 April 1797]," Founders Online, National Archives, last modified June 29, 2016, http://founders .archives.gov/documents/Hamilton/01-21-02-0033-0002. Source: *The Papers of Alexander Hamilton*, vol. 21, *April 1797–July 1798*, ed. Harold C. Syrett.

8. "The Stand No. I, [30 March 1798]," Founders Online, National Archives, last modified June 29, 2016, http:// founders.archives.gov/documents/Hamilton/01-21-02-0225. Source: *The Papers of Alexander Hamilton*, vol. 21, *April 1797–July 1798*, ed. Harold C. Syrett.

9. Alexander Hamilton, "The Stand No. VI," [19 April 1798], Founders Online, National Archives (http://founders .archives.gov/documents/Hamilton/01-21-02-0240 [last update: 2016-03-28]). Source: *The Papers of Alexander Hamilton*, vol. 21, *April 1797–July 1798*, ed. Harold C. Syrett. New York: Columbia University Press, 1974, pp. 434–440.

10. From Alexander Hamilton to the Marquis de Lafayette, 28 April 1798, Founders Online, National Archives (http://founders .archives.gov/documents/Hamilton/01-21-02-0247 [last update: 2016-03-28]). Source: *The Papers of Alexander Hamilton*, vol. 21, *April 1797–July 1798*, ed. Syrett, 1974, pp. 450–452.

11. From Alexander Hamilton to George Washington, 19 May 1798, Founders Online, National Archives (http://founders .archives.gov/documents/Hamilton/01-21-02-0258 [last update: 2016-03-28]). Source: *The Papers of Alexander Hamilton*, vol. 21, *April 1797–July 1798*, ed. Syrett, pp. 466–468.

12. From Alexander Hamilton to George Washington, [8 July 1798], Founders Online, National Archives (http://founders .archives.gov/documents/Hamilton/01-21-02-0305 [last update: 2016-03-28]). Source: *The Papers of Alexander Hamilton*, vol. 21, *April 1797–July 1798*, ed. Syrett, pp. 534–536.

13. Alexander Hamilton, Aaron Burr, and Ebenezer Stevens to James McHenry, [14 June 1798], Founders Online, National Archives (http://founders.archives.gov/documents/Hamilton/ 01-21-02-0285 [last update: 2016-03-28]). Source: *The Papers of Alexander Hamilton*, vol. 21, *April 1797–July 1798*, ed. Syrett, pp. 515–517.

14. From Alexander Hamilton to Theodore Sedgwick, 2 February 1799, Founders Online, National Archives (http://founders.archives.gov/documents/Hamilton/01-22-02-0267 [last update: 2016-03-28]). Source: *The Papers of Alexander Hamilton*, vol. 22, *July 1798–March 1799*, ed. Harold C. Syrett. New York: Columbia University Press, 1975, pp. 452–454.

15. From Alexander Hamilton to James McHenry, 18 March 1799, Founders Online, National Archives (http://founders.archives.gov/documents/Hamilton/01-22-02-0344 [last update: 2016-03-28]). Source: *The Papers of Alexander Hamilton*, vol. 22, *July 1798–March 1799*, ed. Syrett, pp. 552–553.

16. From Alexander Hamilton to James McHenry, Enclosure: Plan for the Providing and Issuing of Military Supplies, [8 April 1799], Founders Online, National Archives (http://founders.archives.gov/documents/Hamilton/01-23-02-0013-0002 [last update: 2016-03-28]). Source: *The Papers of Alexander Hamilton*, vol. 23, *April 1799–October 1799*, ed. Harold C. Syrett. New York: Columbia University Press, 1976, pp. 16–19.

17. From Alexander Hamilton to Charles Cotesworth Pinckney, [22] December 1799, Founders Online, National Archives (http://founders.archives.gov/documents/Hamilton/01-24-02-0103 [last update: 2016-03-28]). Source: *The Papers of Alexander Hamilton*, vol. 24, *November 1799–June 1800*, ed. Harold C. Syrett. New York: Columbia University Press, 1976, pp. 116–117.

18. From Alexander Hamilton to Theodore Sedgwick, [4 May 1800], Founders Online, National Archives (http://founders.archives.gov/documents/Hamilton/01-24-02-0365-0002

[last update: 2016-03-28]). Source: *The Papers of Alexander Hamilton*, vol. 24, *November 1799–June 1800*, ed. Syrett, pp. 444–453.

19. From Alexander Hamilton to John Jay, 7 May 1800, Founders Online, National Archives (http://founders.archives.gov/documents/Hamilton/01-24-02-0378 [last update: 2016-03-28]). Source: *The Papers of Alexander Hamilton*, vol. 24, *November 1799–June 1800*, ed. Syrett, pp. 464–467.

20. From Alexander Hamilton to Theodore Sedgwick, 10 May 1800, Founders Online, National Archives (http://founders.archives.gov/documents/Hamilton/01-24-02-0387 [last update: 2016-03-28]). Source: *The Papers of Alexander Hamilton*, vol. 24, *November 1799–June 1800*, ed. Syrett, pp. 474–475.

21. From Alexander Hamilton to John Adams, 1 August 1800, Founders Online, National Archives (http://founders.archives.gov/documents/Hamilton/01-25-02-0036 [last update: 2016-03-28]). Source: *The Papers of Alexander Hamilton*, vol. 25, *July 1800–April 1802*, ed. Syrett, 1977, pp. 51–52.

22. From Alexander Hamilton to Oliver Wolcott Jr., 3 August 1800, Founders Online, National Archives (http://founders.archives.gov/documents/Hamilton/01-25-02-0039 [last update: 2016-03-28]). Source: *The Papers of Alexander Hamilton*, vol. 25, *July 1800–April 1802*, ed. Syrett, pp. 54–56.

23. Alexander Hamilton, *Letter from Alexander Hamilton, Concerning the Public Conduct and Character of John Adams, Esq. President of the United States*, [24 October 1800], Founders Online, National Archives (http://founders.archives.gov/documents/Hamilton/01-25-02-0110-0002 [last update:

2016-03-28]). Source: *The Papers of Alexander Hamilton*, vol. 25, *July 1800–April 1802*, ed. Syrett, pp. 186–234.

24. From Alexander Hamilton to Gouverneur Morris, 26 December 1800, Founders Online, National Archives (http://founders.archives.gov/documents/Hamilton/01-25-02-0145 [last update: 2016-03-28]). Source: *The Papers of Alexander Hamilton*, vol. 25, *July 1800–April 1802*, ed. Syrett, p. 275.

25. From Alexander Hamilton to John Rutledge, Enclosure: Opinions on Aaron Burr, [4 January 1801], Founders Online, National Archives (http://founders.archives.gov/documents/Hamilton/01-25-02-0156-0002 [last update: 2016-03-28]). Source: *The Papers of Alexander Hamilton*, vol. 25, *July 1800–April 1802*, ed. Syrett, pp. 295–298.

26. "From Alexander Hamilton to James A. Bayard, 16 January 1801," Founders Online, National Archives, last modified June 29, 2016, http://founders.archives.gov/documents/Hamilton/01-25-02-0169. Source: *The Papers of Alexander Hamilton*, vol. 25, *July 1800–April 1802*, ed. Harold C. Syrett.

27. PBS, "The Duel," *The American Experience*, http://www.pbs.org/wgbh/amex/duel/peopleevents/pande16.html.

28. [Alexander Hamilton], "The Examination Number II," [21 December 1801], Founders Online, National Archives (http://founders.archives.gov/documents/Hamilton/01-25-02-0266 [last update: 2016-03-28]). Source: *The Papers of Alexander Hamilton*, vol. 25, *July 1800–April 1802*, ed. Syrett, pp. 458–464.

29. [Alexander Hamilton], "The Examination Number III," [24 December 1801], Founders Online, National Archives (http://founders.archives.gov/documents/Hamilton/01-25-02-0267 [last update: 2016-03-28]). Source: *The*

Papers of Alexander Hamilton, vol. 25, *July 1800–April 1802*, ed. Syrett, pp. 464–468.

30. [Alexander Hamilton], "The Examination Number VI," [2 January 1802], Founders Online, National Archives (http://founders.archives.gov/documents/Hamilton/01-25-02-0277 [last update: 2016-03-28]). Source: *The Papers of Alexander Hamilton*, vol. 25, *July 1800–April 1802*, ed. Syrett, pp. 484–489.

31. [Alexander Hamilton], "The Examination Number VIII," [12 January 1802], Founders Online, National Archives (http://founders.archives.gov/documents/Hamilton/01-25-02-0282 [last update: 2016-03-28]). Source: *The Papers of Alexander Hamilton*, vol. 25, *July 1800–April 1802*, ed. Syrett, pp. 495–497.

32. From Alexander Hamilton to Gouverneur Morris, [29 February 1802], Founders Online, National Archives (http://founders.archives.gov/documents/Hamilton/01-25-02-0297 [last update: 2016-03-28]). Source: *The Papers of Alexander Hamilton*, vol. 25, *July 1800–April 1802*, ed. Syrett, pp. 544–546.

33. From Alexander Hamilton to Charles Cotesworth Pinckney, 29 December 1802.

34. Alexander Hamilton, "Purchase of Louisiana," [5 July 1803], Founders Online, National Archives (http://founders.archives.gov/documents/Hamilton/01-26-02-0001-0101 [last update: 2016-03-28]). Source: *The Papers of Alexander Hamilton*, vol. 26, *1 May 1802–23 October 1804*, ed. Syrett, pp. 129–136.

35. From Alexander Hamilton to Elizabeth Hamilton, 14 October 1803, Founders Online, National Archives (http://founders.archives.gov/documents/Hamilton/01-26-02-0001-0125 [last

update: 2016-03-28]). Source: *The Papers of Alexander Hamilton*, vol. 26, *1 May 1802–23 October 1804*, ed. Syrett, pp. 159–160.

Chapter 8: Hamilton's Circle

1. From Alexander Hamilton to Philip Schuyler, 18 February 1781, Founders Online, National Archives (http://founders .archives.gov/documents/Hamilton/01-02-02-1089 [last update: 2016-03-28]). Source: *The Papers of Alexander Hamilton*, vol. 2, *1779–1781*, ed. Syrett, pp. 563–569.

2. To Alexander Hamilton from George Washington, 21 August 1797, Founders Online, National Archives (http:// founders.archives.gov/documents/Hamilton/01-21-02-0137 [last update: 2016-03-28]). Source: *The Papers of Alexander Hamilton*, vol. 21, *April 1797–July 1798*, ed. Syrett, pp. 214–215.

3. From Alexander Hamilton to Martha Washington, 12 January 1800, Founders Online, National Archives (http://founders.archives.gov/documents/Hamilton/01-24-02-0140 [last update: 2016-03-28]). Source: *The Papers of Alexander Hamilton*, vol. 24, *November 1799–June 1800*, ed. Syrett, pp. 184–185.

4. From Alexander Hamilton to Lieutenant Colonel John Laurens, [April 1779], Founders Online, National Archives (http://founders.archives.gov/documents/Hamilton/ 01-02-02-0100 [last update: 2016-03-28]). Source: *The Papers of Alexander Hamilton*, vol. 2, *1779–1781*, ed. Syrett, pp. 34–38.

5. From Alexander Hamilton to Lieutenant Colonel John Laurens, [15 August 1782], Founders Online, National Archives (http://founders.archives.gov/documents/Hamilton/ 01-03-02-0058 [last update: 2016-03-28]). Source: *The*

Papers of Alexander Hamilton, vol. 3, *1782–1786*, ed. Syrett, pp. 144–146.

6. From Alexander Hamilton to Major General Nathanael Greene, [12 October 1782], Founders Online, National Archives (http://founders.archives.gov/documents/Hamilton/01-03-02-0090 [last update: 2016-03-28]). Source: *The Papers of Alexander Hamilton*, vol. 3, *1782–1786*, ed. Syrett, pp. 183–184.

7. From Alexander Hamilton to James Hamilton, 22 June 1785, Founders Online, National Archives (http://founders .archives.gov/documents/Hamilton/01-03-02-0444 [last update: 2016-03-28]). Source: *The Papers of Alexander Hamilton*, vol. 3, *1782–1786*, ed. Syrett, pp. 617–618.

8. James Alexander Hamilton, *Reminiscences of James A. Hamilton; or, Men and events, at home and abroad, during three quarters of a century* New York: C. Scribner & Co., 1869.

9. From Alexander Hamilton to Philip A. Hamilton, 5 December 1791, Founders Online, National Archives (http://founders .archives.gov/documents/Hamilton/01-09-02-0419 [last update: 2016-03-28]). Source: *The Papers of Alexander Hamilton*, vol. 9, *August 1791–December 1791*, ed. Harold C. Syrett. New York: Columbia University Press, 1965, pp. 560–561.

10. Alexander Hamilton, "Rules for Philip Hamilton," [1800], Founders Online, National Archives (http://founders .archives.gov/documents/Hamilton/01-25-02-0152 [last update: 2016-03-28]). Source: *The Papers of Alexander Hamilton*, vol. 25, *July 1800–April 1802*, ed. Syrett, pp. 288–289.

11. From Alexander Hamilton to Benjamin Rush, 29 March 1802, Founders Online, National Archives (http://founders .archives.gov/documents/Hamilton/01-25-02-0312 [last

update: 2016-03-28]). Source: *The Papers of Alexander Hamilton*, vol. 25, *July 1800–April 1802*, ed. Syrett, pp. 583–584.

12. From Alexander Hamilton to Elizabeth Hamilton, 9 August 1791, Founders Online, National Archives (http://founders .archives.gov/documents/Hamilton/01-09-02-0021 [last update: 2016-03-28]). Source: *The Papers of Alexander Hamilton*, vol. 9, *August 1791–December 1791*, ed. Syrett, p. 24.

13. From Maria Reynolds to Alexander Hamilton, [15 December 1791], Founders Online, National Archives (http://founders .archives.gov/documents/Hamilton/01-10-02-0031 [last update: 2016-03-28]). Source: *The Papers of Alexander Hamilton*, vol. 10, *December 1791–January 1792*, ed. Syrett, pp. 378–379.

14. From James Reynolds to Alexander Hamilton, 19 December 1791, Founders Online, National Archives (http://founders .archives.gov/documents/Hamilton/01-10-02-0045 [last update: 2016-03-28]). Source: *The Papers of Alexander Hamilton*, vol. 10, *December 1791–January 1792*, ed. Syrett, p. 396.

15. Alexander Hamilton, *Observations on Certain Documents Contained in No. V & VI of "The History of the United States for the Year 1796," In Which the Charge of Speculation Against Alexander Hamilton, Late Secretary of the Treasury, is Fully Refuted. Written by Himself,* Available as "Printed Version of the 'Reynolds Pamphlet,' 1797," Founders Online, National Archives (http://founders.archives.gov/documents/Hamilton/ 01-21-02-0138-0002 [last update: 2016-03-28]). Source: *The Papers of Alexander Hamilton*, vol. 21, *April 1797–July 1798*, ed. Syrett, pp. 238–267.

16. From Alexander Hamilton to——, 21 September 1792, Founders Online, National Archives (http://founders .archives.gov/documents/Hamilton/01-12-02-0309 [last

update: 2016-03-28]). Source: *The Papers of Alexander Hamilton*, vol. 12, *July 1792–October 1792*, ed. Syrett, p. 408.

17. From Aaron Burr to Alexander Hamilton, 18 June 1804, Founders Online, National Archives (http://founders.archives.gov/documents/Hamilton/01-26-02-0001-0203-0001 [last update: 2016-03-28]). Source: *The Papers of Alexander Hamilton*, vol. 26, *1 May 1802–23 October 1804*, ed. Syrett, pp. 242–243.

18. From Alexander Hamilton to Aaron Burr, 20 June 1804, Founders Online, National Archives (http://founders.archives.gov/documents/Hamilton/01-26-02-0001-0205 [last update: 2016-03-28]). Source: *The Papers of Alexander Hamilton*, vol. 26, *1 May 1802–23 October 1804*, ed. Syrett, pp. 247–249.

19. From Aaron Burr to Alexander Hamilton, 21 June 1804, Founders Online, National Archives (http://founders.archives.gov/documents/Hamilton/01-26-02-0001-0207 [last update: 2016-03-28]). Source: *The Papers of Alexander Hamilton*, vol. 26, *1 May 1802–23 October 1804*, ed. Syrett, pp. 249–251.

20. From Alexander Hamilton to Aaron Burr, 22 June 1804, Founders Online, National Archives (http://founders.archives.gov/documents/Hamilton/01-26-02-0001-0210 [last update: 2016-03-28]). Source: *The Papers of Alexander Hamilton*, vol. 26, *1 May 1802–23 October 1804*, ed. Syrett, pp. 253–254.

21. Alexander Hamilton, "Alexander Hamilton's Explanation of His Financial Situation," [1 July 1804], Founders Online, National Archives (http://founders.archives.gov/documents/Hamilton/01-26-02-0001-0244 [last update: 2016-03-28]).

Source: *The Papers of Alexander Hamilton*, vol. 26, *1 May 1802–23 October 1804*, ed. Syrett, pp. 287–291.

22. Alexander Hamilton, "Last Will and Testament of Alexander Hamilton," [9 July 1804], Founders Online, National Archives (http://founders.archives.gov/documents/Hamilton/ 01-26-02-0001-0259 [last update: 2016-03-28]). Source: *The Papers of Alexander Hamilton*, vol. 26, *1 May 1802–23 October 1804*, ed. Syrett, pp. 305–306.

23. Alexander Hamilton, "Statement on Impending Duel with Aaron Burr," [28 June–10 July 1804], Founders Online, National Archives (http://founders.archives.gov/documents/ Hamilton/01-26-02-0001-0241 [last update: 2016-03-28]). Source: *The Papers of Alexander Hamilton*, vol. 26, *1 May 1802–23 October 1804*, ed. Syrett, pp. 278–281.

24. William P. Van Ness and Nathaniel Pendleton, "Joint Statement by William P. Van Ness and Nathaniel Pendleton on the Duel between Alexander Hamilton and Aaron Burr," [17 July 1804], Founders Online, National Archives (http://founders .archives.gov/documents/Hamilton/01-26-02-0001-0275 [last update: 2016-03-28]). Source: *The Papers of Alexander Hamilton*, vol. 26, *1 May 1802–23 October 1804*, ed. Syrett, pp. 333–336.

25. Nathaniel Pendleton, "Nathaniel Pendleton's Amendments to the Joint Statement Made by William P. Van Ness and Him on the Duel between Alexander Hamilton and Aaron Burr," [19 July 1804], Founders Online, National Archives (http://founders.archives.gov/documents/Hamilton/ 01-26-02-0001-0277 [last update: 2016-03-28]). Source: *The Papers of Alexander Hamilton*, vol. 26, *1 May 1802–23 October 1804*, ed. Syrett, pp. 337–339.

26. William P. Van Ness, "William P. Van Ness's Amendments to the Joint Statement Made by Nathaniel Pendleton and Him on the Duel between Alexander Hamilton and Aaron Burr," [21 July 1804], Founders Online, National Archives (http://founders.archives.gov/documents/Hamilton/01-26-02-0001-0278 [last update: 2016-03-28]). Source: *The Papers of Alexander Hamilton*, vol. 26, *1 May 1802–23 October 1804*, ed. Syrett, pp. 340–341.

27. From Alexander Hamilton to Angelica Schuyler Church, [8 November 1789], Founders Online, National Archives (http://founders.archives.gov/documents/Hamilton/01-05-02-0297-0001 [last update: 2016-03-28]). Source: *The Papers of Alexander Hamilton*, vol. 5, *June 1788–November 1789*, ed. Syrett, pp. 501–502.

28. From Alexander Hamilton to Angelica Schuyler Church, [3 August 1785], Founders Online, National Archives (http://founders.archives.gov/documents/Hamilton/01-03-02-0448 [last update: 2016-03-28]). Source: *The Papers of Alexander Hamilton*, vol. 3, *1782–1786*, ed. Syrett, pp. 619–620.

29. From Alexander Hamilton to Angelica Schuyler Church, [2 October 1791], Founders Online, National Archives (http://founders.archives.gov/documents/Hamilton/01-09-02-0219 [last update: 2016-03-28]). Source: *The Papers of Alexander Hamilton*, vol. 9, *August 1791–December 1791*, ed. Syrett, pp. 266–267.

30. From Angelica Schuyler Church to Alexander Hamilton [15 August 1793], Founders Online, National Archives (http://founders.archives.gov/documents/Hamilton/01-15-02-0178 [last update: 2016-03-28]). Source:

The Papers of Alexander Hamilton, vol. 15, *June 1793–January 1794*, ed. Syrett, p. 247.

31. From Alexander Hamilton to Angelica Schuyler Church, 23 October 1794, Founders Online, National Archives (http://founders.archives.gov/documents/Hamilton/01-17-02-0324 [last update: 2016-03-28]). Source: *The Papers of Alexander Hamilton*, vol. 17, *August 1794–December 1794*, ed. Syrett, p. 340.

32. From Alexander Hamilton to Angelica Schuyler Church, 8 December 1794, Founders Online, National Archives (http://founders.archives.gov/documents/Hamilton/01-17-02-0407 [last update: 2016-03-28]). Source: *The Papers of Alexander Hamilton*, vol. 17, *August 1794–December 1794*, ed. Syrett, pp. 428–429.

33. From Alexander Hamilton to Angelica Schuyler Church, [6 March 1795], Founders Online, National Archives (http://founders.archives.gov/documents/Hamilton/01-18-02-0181 [last update: 2016-03-28]). Source: *The Papers of Alexander Hamilton*, vol. 18, *January 1795–July 1795*, ed. Syrett, pp. 287–288.

34. From Alexander Hamilton to Angelica Schuyler Church, 22 January [1800], Founders Online, National Archives (http://founders.archives.gov/documents/Hamilton/01-24-02-0156 [last update: 2016-03-28]). Source: *The Papers of Alexander Hamilton*, vol. 24, *November 1799–June 1800*, ed. Syrett, pp. 211–212.

35. From Alexander Hamilton to Margarita Schuyler, [February 1780], Founders Online, National Archives (http://founders.archives.gov/documents/Hamilton/01-02-02-0613 [last update: 2016-03-28]). Source: *The Papers of Alexander Hamilton*, vol. 2, *1779–1781*, ed. Syrett, pp. 269–271.

36. From Alexander Hamilton to Catharine Livingston and Elizabeth Schuyler, [January–February 1780], Founders Online, National Archives (http://founders.archives.gov/documents/Hamilton/01-02-02-0587 [last update: 2016-03-28]). Source: *The Papers of Alexander Hamilton*, vol. 2, *1779–1781*, ed. Syrett, p. 262.

37. From Alexander Hamilton to Elizabeth Schuyler, [17 March 1780], Founders Online, National Archives (http://founders.archives.gov/documents/Hamilton/01-02-02-0622 [last update: 2016-03-28]). Source: *The Papers of Alexander Hamilton*, vol. 2, *1779–1781*, ed. Syrett, pp. 285–287.

38. From Alexander Hamilton to Elizabeth Hamilton, 16 August 1781, Founders Online, National Archives (http://founders.archives.gov/documents/Hamilton/01-02-02-1188 [last update: 2016-03-28]). Source: *The Papers of Alexander Hamilton*, vol. 2, *1779–1781*, ed. Syrett, pp. 666–667.

39. From Alexander Hamilton to Elizabeth Hamilton, 6 September 1781, Founders Online, National Archives (http://founders.archives.gov/documents/Hamilton/01-02-02-1195 [last update: 2016-03-28]). Source: *The Papers of Alexander Hamilton*, vol. 2, *1779–1781*, ed. Syrett, p. 675.

40. From Alexander Hamilton to Elizabeth Hamilton, [15–18 September 1781], Founders Online, National Archives (http://founders.archives.gov/documents/Hamilton/01-02-02-1196 [last update: 2016-03-28]). Source: *The Papers of Alexander Hamilton*, vol. 2, *1779–1781*, ed. Syrett, pp. 675–676.

41. From Alexander Hamilton to Elizabeth Hamilton, [1782], Founders Online, National Archives (http://founders

.archives.gov/documents/Hamilton/01-03-02-0137 [last update: 2016-03-28]). Source: *The Papers of Alexander Hamilton*, vol. 3, *1782–1786*, ed. Syrett, p. 235.

42. From Alexander Hamilton to Elizabeth Hamilton, [4 July 1804], Founders Online, National Archives (http://founders .archives.gov/documents/Hamilton/01-26-02-0001-0248 [last update: 2016-03-28]). Source: *The Papers of Alexander Hamilton*, vol. 26, *1 May 1802–23 October 1804*, ed. Syrett, p. 293.

SUGGESTED
READING

★ ★ ★

Compilations of Hamilton's Writings

Freeman, Joanne B., ed. *Alexander Hamilton, Writings* (Library of America, 2001).

Hamilton, Alexander. *The Works of Alexander Hamilton*, edited by Henry Cabot Lodge (Federal edition, Putnam, 1904).

Hamilton, John C., ed. *The Works of Alexander Hamilton; Comprising His Correspondence. And His Political and Official Writings*, (7 vols., J. F. Trow Printing, 1850). Available as digital scans through https.babel.hathitrust.org.

Syrett, Harold C. et al., eds. *The Papers of Alexander Hamilton* (27 vols., Columbia University Press, 1961–1987).

Hamilton Biographies

Chernow, Ron. *Alexander Hamilton* (Penguin Press, 2004).

Hamilton, John C. *The Life of Alexander Hamilton* (Scribners, 1840).

Knott, Stephen F. *Alexander Hamilton and the Persistence of Myth* (University Press of Kansas, 2002).

McDonald, Forrest. *Alexander Hamilton: A Biography* (W. W. Norton & Company, 1982).

Newton, Michael E. *Alexander Hamilton: The Formative Years* (Eleftheria Publishing, 2015).

Randall, Willard Sterne. *Alexander Hamilton: A Life* (Harper-Collins, 2003).

Hamilton and Politics/Finance

Ellis, Joseph. *Founding Brothers: The Revolutionary Generation* (Alfred A. Knopf, 2000).

———. *The Quartet: Orchestrating the Second American Revolution, 1783–1789* (Alfred A. Knopf, 2015).

Federici, Michael. *The Political Philosophy of Alexander Hamilton* (Johns Hopkins University Press, 2012).

Ferling, John. *Jefferson and Hamilton: The Rivalry That Forged a Nation* (Reprint, Bloomsbury Press, 2014).

Fleming, Thomas. *Perils of Peace: America's Struggle for Existence After Yorktown* (Reprint, Harper Perennial, 2008).

Holloway, Carson. *Hamilton Versus Jefferson in the Washington Administration: Completing the Founding or Betraying the Founding?* (Cambridge University Press, 2016).

Knott, Stephen F. *Washington and Hamilton: The Alliance That Forged America* (Sourcebooks, 2016).

Wright, Robert E. *One Nation Under Debt: Hamilton, Jefferson, and the History of What We Owe* (McGraw-Hill Education, 2008).

Wright, Robert E., and David J. Cowen. *Financial Founding Fathers: The Men Who Made America Rich* (University of Chicago Press, 2006).

The Burr–Hamilton Duel

Fleming, Thomas. *Duel: Alexander Hamilton, Aaron Burr, and the Future of America* (Basic Books, 2000).

Freeman, Joanne B. *Affairs of Honor: National Politics in the New Republic* (Yale University Press, 2002).

Sedgwick, John. *War of Two: Alexander Hamilton, Aaron Burr, and the Duel That Stunned the Nation* (Berkley, 2015).

Books for Kids

Fritz, Jean. *Alexander Hamilton: The Outsider* (Putnam, 2011. Paperback reprint Puffin Books, 2012).

St. George, Judith. *The Duel: The Parallel Lives of Alexander Hamilton and Aaron Burr* (Viking Books, 2009).

ACKNOWLEDGMENTS

★ ★ ★

Thanks to J.P. Leventhal and Lisa Tenaglia of Black Dog & Leventhal for giving me the opportunity to indulge an abiding interest; to Kathryn Williams Renna for finding the pictures; and to Dr. Greg Brooking for keeping my facts on the straight and narrow and my biases on the level. Undying love and gratitude to Megan, for giving me the time and space to research and write this book; and to Stella, best of daughters and best of girls.

INDEX

★ ★ ★

Page numbers in italics refer to images, photographs and illustrations in the text

PHOTO CREDITS

★ ★ ★

the generous support of an anonymous donor. Conserved with funds from the Smithsonian Women's Committee, 223

Courtesy of the New-York Historical Society, Nathaniel Pendleton Papers, 250

From The New York Public Library, 160

Yale University Art Gallery: 92, 108, 181, 212